Dreamers & Schemers Series, Volume II

CAPITAL CHARACTERS
OF OLD CHEYENNE

Dreamers & Schemers Series, Volume II

CAPITAL CHARACTERS OF OLD CHEYENNE

Lori Van Pelt

HIGH PLAINS PRESS

FIRST PRINTING

10 9 8 7 6 5 4 3 2 1

Library of Congress Cataloging-in-Publication Data

Van Pelt, Lori, 1961-
Capital characters of old Cheyenne / Lori Van Pelt.
p. cm. -- (Dreamers & schemers ; v. 2)
Includes bibliographical references and index.
ISBN 0-931271-74-6 (limited ed. : alk. paper) --
ISBN 0-931271-75-4 (trade pbk. : alk. paper)
1. Cheyenne Region (Wyo.)--Biography.
2. Cheyenne Region (Wyo.)--History.
I. Title.
F769.C5V36 2004
978.7'19--dc22
2003025497

HIGH PLAINS PRESS

539 CASSA ROAD

GLENDO, WYOMING 82213

CATALOG AVAILABLE
WWW.HIGHPLAINSPRESS.COM

In memory of two remarkable women—Sarah Jane Van Pelt Johnston, my great-great aunt, and Jeannette Underhill, my aunt.

Sarah Jane, known to my family as "Aunt Sally," purchased land in Banner County, Nebraska, in the 1880s. Believing that security came from owning land, she worked as a domestic for a short time in Cheyenne, Wyoming Territory, so she could purchase more property and thus lay the foundation for herself, her brothers, and future generations of the Van Pelt family to live in Banner County.

Jeannette, my beloved "Aunt Jane," shared her memories of her special great-aunt Sarah Jane's story with me and gave me the courage to follow my dreams.

The chapter profiling Nathaniel Robertson appeared in slightly different format in Persimmon Hill *magazine.*

The Estelle Reel chapter appeared in slightly different format in True West *magazine and was a 2000 award-winner in the Publications Category from the Wyoming State Historical Society. Information from this profile was also presented by the author in a speech at the American Heritage Center's "Schoolmarms and Scholars" symposium.*

Contents

Foreword

Lori Van Pelt has created a unique collaboration of mini biographies of interesting persons who have each in their own different ways been a part of the city of Cheyenne. The material is most interesting and represents a multitude of hours of research.

Some of the individuals, such as Joseph M. Carey and Charles Irwin, spent most of their adult lives in Cheyenne—one contributing to the political necessities and the other to the world of rodeo, the very thing that put Cheyenne on the map and keeps it there. Another, Elwood Mead, went on to great accomplishments in the world of water rights, and Willis Van Devanter became the only person from Wyoming to serve as a justice for the Supreme Court of the United States.

Estelle Reel, the first woman to serve as a State Superintendent of Public Instruction, would marry and move from the state. Hiram Kelly was the first to ship cattle out of Wyoming from the Cheyenne depot but eventually spent his last years in Denver. Barney Ford came only briefly to Cheyenne to run the finest hostelry in the West at the time, the InterOcean Hotel.

M.P. Keefe left a lasting legacy in Cheyenne with his many buildings, and Daze Bristol added to the Cheyenne Frontier Days parades in a permanent way.

One nice feature of the book is that each chapter is unique in itself, so one does not need to read the entire book at one sitting to maintain its continuity. The thread of Cheyenne is woven into each biography with great skill and an obvious knowledge of each subject.

This book is a must for anyone interested in Cheyenne or Wyoming history. It will provide excellent source material for many years to come.

•• WILLIAM R. DUBOIS III, CHEYENNE

Introduction

RESEARCHING A BOOK of historical profiles is like peering into a dark attic with only a small flashlight for illumination. By shining my beam on one person's life, I obtain glimpses of early events, customs, and traditions. These intriguing glimpses lead me to research additional subjects, and then to focus the light on another person and repeat the process once again. Just as the flashlight's beam can eventually reveal the contents of the entire attic, a picture of the historical period and the accomplishments and disappointments of the people living in that period emerges from the shadows of archival materials, books, and newspapers. This piques my curiosity even more. I don't believe the emerging picture can ever be complete because I did not live during those bygone days. But looking into the documents left behind, reading about the era, and talking to contemporary people who remember stories about previous times does help enhance the image.

In researching this book, I wondered if the territorial settlers of Wyoming and the politicians they elected to lay foundations for a government felt the reverse of what I feel. Were they gazing into the future, following only a tiny circle of light? These people built the future for us just as we aspire to create a better future for those generations who will follow us. Their dreams—whether they were to create a new photographic paper, to ensure the good health of citizens, or to create a state from the fledgling Wyoming Territory—affect us still. Their schemes—ranging from delusions of riches to plotting to outwit political opponents—continue to haunt us.

Wyoming Territory was carved from Dakota Territory on January 9, 1867, and stretched from the borders of present-day Colorado to Montana. Laramie County was the easternmost county in the new territory. In the same year, the city of Cheyenne burst onto the landscape as an end-of-the-tracks town on the Union Pacific Railroad's construction route. The town grew so quickly that it was dubbed "Magic City of the Plains." The city's name is said to have been derived from the Sioux word "Shai-ena" meaning "people of an alien speech."

In this book—the second volume in the Dreamers and Schemers series—I've shined my flashlight on twenty-one people who somehow left their marks on Laramie County, from territorial days through the early twentieth century—roughly 1867 through 1917. I have attempted to include a cross section of races, genders, and careers. In this effort, I've been constricted somewhat by the time period I chose, by limitations on the number of pages a book may contain, and, of course, by the amount of information available. Some people remain lost in the shadows.

Each person I selected to profile is representative of many others who I could not write about. Only a few women and other minorities are represented such as Estelle Reel, the first woman to become National Superintendent of Indian Schools, and William J. Hardin, Wyoming's first African-American legislator.

Professions included here are lawmaker, saloon owner, writer, builder, engineer, judge, and carriage maker, physician, minister, cowgirl, and architect. Obviously, many others were important, including the early railroad crews and soldiers.

Politicians have always been a prominent group in Cheyenne, the state capital; however, I could not include every important politician. Readers familiar with Wyoming history will notice that I've left out two of Wyoming's best-known political figures—Francis E. Warren, first governor of the state and long-time U.S. senator, and Nellie Tayloe Ross, the first and only (as of this writing) woman governor of the state and the first woman to be inaugurated as a governor in the United States. Warren's name appears frequently throughout this book. His influence on Cheyenne is unparalleled and remains visible today in names like Warren Avenue and F. E. Warren Air Force Base (formerly Fort D. A. Russell). Instead of featuring these two important politicians—both of whom deserve complete books of their own—I've focused here on Joseph M. Carey, who eloquently brought Wyoming Territory's appeal for statehood before the U.S. Congress and who later served as governor and U.S. senator.

The chapters in this book barely scratch the surface of the history of Cheyenne and Laramie County. Another book could be written featuring numerous other persons. I found the stories of these people inspiring, sometimes odd, and always fascinating. I hope you will, too.

Nathan Baker

The young newspaperman wiped his brow in the mid-September heat as he spurred his oxteam toward the motley collection of tents and hastily built cabins dotting the prairie. He heard the ringing sounds of metal against metal and the thudding of hammers into wood as he approached the end-of-the-tracks town. Freighters called to one another. Businessmen, eager to begin new ventures, tipped their hats and prayed for profits. Cheyenne, the "Magic City of the Plains," had burst onto the prairie seemingly overnight. Soon locomotives would thunder along the tracks and connect this tiny western town to the opportunities present in the East. Frenzied residents worked hard day and night, including Sundays, to prepare for the coming of the Union Pacific Railroad.

Probably Nathan Baker had his mind on profits, too. Undoubtedly the thought of publishing a newspaper here, with the anticipation of the railroad moving west and the courage of people settling in a new place, excited him. News stories would surely be abundant here. Cheyenne and Wyoming Territory appeared promising. Baker chose that location for his new start.

Nathan Addison Baker was born August 3, 1843, near Lockport, Niagara County, New York. His family lived in Racine, Wisconsin, and Omaha, Nebraska, during his childhood. They moved to Denver, Colorado, in 1860 with hopes of finding gold. Unfortunately, Baker's father fell ill. To help his parents make ends meet, young Nathan worked in agriculture then lumbering, helping construct some of Denver's earliest buildings by hauling and selling lumber for twelve dollars per thousand feet. At the age of nineteen, he began teaching at the Ferry Street School, which he operated until the first public school was established. He served in the Governor's Guard in 1863 and enlisted in the Third Regiment, Colorado Cavalry, U.S. Volunteers, but it appears he remained in Denver during the Civil War years.

Events during Baker's late teens and early twenties forged his character and may have led to his future career choice in the newspaper business. In 1863, most of Denver's business district was destroyed by fire. The flames nearly reached the Baker family home. Baker had fought another fire that threatened the city a year earlier by taking charge of a bucket brigade. In 1864, Cherry Creek flooded, leaving destruction in its wake. Perhaps the young man's interest in journalism was piqued by this early exposure to newsworthy events.

In the early 1860s, Baker worked in the business department of the *Daily Rocky Mountain Herald,* serving as bookkeeper and collector. In 1864, he worked as a bookkeeper for the *Rocky Mountain News.* The Cherry Creek flood destroyed the newspaper's plant and equipment, but Baker saved valuable records from the office. He climbed to safety on a rope stretched between two buildings. That same year, at age twenty-one, Baker became the first business manager of the newspaper. In 1865, he married Clarissa Moyn. The couple had two children, Addison and Lily.

On July 6, 1867, Baker published the first issue of the *Colorado Leader,* but business was not as good as he had hoped. So he decided to search for success to the north, where the Union Pacific Railroad was being built across the Great Plains. Fortified with a newsman's nose for discovering a story and a strong courageous streak, Baker left Denver for Cheyenne. James E. Gates, who had worked with Baker on the failed newspaper, and four assistants headed to the new town with him, arriving in early September.

The stories Baker found in this new place were fresh and invigorating—the hopes of settlers building new lives, the plans of businessmen determined to earn profits, the excitement of unfolding events which would, of course, eventually include the arrival of the railroad. On July 4, 1867, at Crow Creek, General Grenville M. Dodge had established the first Union Pacific site. He named the spot

Nathan A. Baker published the first newspaper in Cheyenne, the Cheyenne Leader *in 1867.* (Courtesy Colorado Historical Society)

Cheyenne for the Great Plains Indian tribe. Fort D.A. Russell, just west of Cheyenne, was established in August to protect the progressing railroad from Indian hostilities. According to Wyoming historian Velma Linford, Dodge and his men had already protected a Mormon wagon train. Two of the wagon train's men had been killed in the conflict with the Indians, but Dodge's men saved most of the travelers' livestock. The two men were buried, and their graves marked the start of the first cemetery in the town. Because Fort Russell was located at the junction of military trails, the federal government decided to make the fort a permanent one. Camp Carlin, set up halfway between the fort and the new town, would serve as a military depot. But it was the railroad that would make the town. As Linford explains, "Again and again [Cheyenne's] newspapers carried the statement, 'Cheyenne is a creation of the Union Pacific Railroad.'" The survey of the railroad line was completed on July 19, 1867, and the Union Pacific Land Company sold lots.

The first issue of the town's first newspaper, the *Cheyenne Leader*, rolled off the press exactly two months later, on Thursday, September 19, 1867, weeks before the Union Pacific Railroad had reached the tent town destined to grow into Wyoming's capital. Baker used a hand press to print the newspaper in a store-front log building owned by E. A. Allen, near the intersection of Sixteenth and Eddy Streets (now Lincolnway and Pioneer Avenue). It was said to be the only building of its type in town that had a floor. Cheyenne soon boasted more than one newspaper. The *Argus* began publication in October 1867, and the *Rocky Mountain Star* began publication in December. Although later papers were short-lived, according to Linford, all the Cheyenne newspapers pushed the Union Pacific to "recognize its responsibility to Cheyenne, the city it created. All joined in the crusade for lawful government, and all were united in agreement that Cheyenne was permanent, was the natural seat of government, and the future capital of industry and transportation."

Baker liked to boast that his newspaper was the first in Wyoming. But researcher Elizabeth Keen identifies the earliest newspaper as an 1863 news sheet, *The Daily Telegraph,* published by telegraph operator Hiram Brundage at Fort Bridger to keep up with Civil War events. Historian Pat Hall states that Baker disliked the suggestion that the fort's *Daily Telegraph* preceded his *Leader* because he believed that the publications of the western forts, which relied on Army presses, required no financial investment from their editors.

In his first *Leader* issue, Baker told readers of the progress of the railroad, at that time still located about fifty-five miles from Cheyenne. Business proved brisk for the enterprising newspaperman. The first edition sold for twenty-five cents. Three hundred people waited in front of the newspaper office on Eddy Street to purchase a copy. Printed one page at a time on a quarter-medium Gordon press, the newspaper consisted of four pages containing four columns each. The community's hunger for news helped pay Baker's debts. He'd risked all his money in his journey to Cheyenne. The profits from that first issue paid for his assistants' labor as well as for his (and presumably his family's) board at the Bell House. Advertising generated revenue for the small newspaper as well. Notes in Baker's job book at the Wyoming State Archives state that a weekly ad for the *Leader* cost $2.50 for one year. Daily ads were run at a cost of $5.00 per quarter and $2.00 per month.

The arrival of the railroad in the town was slated for mid-October. During the two months it took track layers to reach Cheyenne, Baker published progress reports. On November 16, 1867, he reported on the celebration held just two days earlier when the first passenger train from Omaha, Nebraska, chugged into Cheyenne. "A vast assemblage of citizens and railroad men convened.... Eddy Street and the City Hall were splendidly illuminated. The large transparency near the speakers' stand bore the mottoes: 'The magic town greets the continental railway.'" The newspaper did not have enough space "to name the distinguished speakers that addressed the jolly, uproarious and jubilant crowd."

Baker's was one of just three newspapers in publication in Southeast Wyoming Territory when the railroad arrived. One of the others was the itinerant *Frontier Index*. Historian Keen suggests that when the *Index* located in Laramie City, both newspapers reflected the rivalry between the two towns. Each town wanted to boast of a brighter future and to secure the larger population, and each hoped the Union Pacific would construct important buildings within its limits. Keen explains further: "If a territorial editor had prejudices, he aired them in the columns of his newspaper, unrestrained by nonexistent laws of libel, undeterred by threats of tarring and feathering, gunshot wounds, or bruises and broken bones."

In their efforts to encourage people to come to Wyoming Territory, newspaper editors waxed enthusiastic, often sacrificing objectivity in the process. Baker, Keen writes, "was one of many who printed gushing tributes to the newly-opened frontier." In mid-October 1867, Baker extolled the virtues of his new city, Cheyenne, while stinging his former home of Denver, writing, "...Denver, look well to your laurels. Cheyenne and adjacent sections are outstripping you in all the material developments of material wealth. We will here incidentally mention that we can finish that burg with a neat and substantial tombstone upon its approaching demise, and we will make out of it a fine quality of marble, recently discovered in the Black Hills [now called the Laramie Range], specimens of which may be seen here on application."

Business boomed in Cheyenne during those early days, and the young newspaperman found his niche. The tri-weekly newspaper progressed to publishing daily editions in December 1867. Cheyenne had grown to a population of four thousand people. Real estate lots that had previously cost $250 sold for $3,500. Linford estimates that between three and four hundred businesses opened during the first summer, running the gamut from saloons and gambling houses to dry goods stores, law offices, and boarding houses. During the construction of the railroad, the population increased to more than ten thousand people.

Early in 1868, Baker ran a series of editorials to assure people of Cheyenne's importance, even as the railroad tracks passed beyond the town. "We have faith in the place," he stated in the January 17, 1868, issue, "and shall contribute all we can to make it a permanent and prosperous settlement. We follow no railway nor other excitements but came to Cheyenne knowing it to be a favored location, and with Cheyenne we are content to remain." Even so, Baker's news instinct had already guided him to fresh stories elsewhere in the territory. In January, he "began trying to open the eyes of his [*Leader*] readers to the possibility of a lucrative trade with the new town [of South Pass] and the surrounding Sweetwater mining country," Keen writes. On January 16, 1868, he had explained that readers should examine the issue in "dollars and cents" terms. Baker wrote, "If, next fall and winter, a few hundred thousand dollars worth of the precious metal finds its way into this place, there will be no indifference in trying to get hold of the shining stuff."

South Pass was the site of the first organized mining district in Wyoming Territory. Gold discoveries had been reported by eastern newspapers in mid-July 1867, though an employee of the American Fur Company had reported finding gold there in 1842. The town of South Pass City was platted in the summer of 1867, about fifteen miles southwest of the route of the Oregon Trail and a half mile from the famed Carissa mine. Another strike made news in September

1867, prompting the *Chicago Tribune* to send correspondent James Chisolm to the area in early 1868. On April 1, 1868, Baker announced in the *Cheyenne Leader* that the first shipment of gold from the Sweetwater country—ten ounces carried in a buckskin bag—had arrived in Cheyenne. The news was contained in a letter to the editor extolling the virtues of South Pass.

On April 8, 1868, Baker's *Leader* reported that the railroad tracks had reached the peak of Sherman Hill between Cheyenne and Laramie City, explaining, "the outside world was informed by telegraph that the highest eminence on the roadbed between the Missouri and the Pacific Ocean had been conquered...."

As exciting as that achievement was, the railroad's continual progress west meant that activity in Cheyenne would decline. In the April 24, 1868, issue, just a couple of weeks prior to the railroad's arrival in Laramie City, Baker voiced concern about Cheyenne's shrinking population, which had dropped to about fifteen hundred citizens. From a business standpoint, Baker realized that fewer people meant fewer papers sold and less advertising revenue generated. So the savvy newshound followed the railroad's tracks and expanded his enterprises. He published the *Laramie Sentinel* and the *South Pass News* in 1869. According to the Coutant Notes, "These three newspapers were owned and carried on simultaneously for about one year, and were each profitable ventures, despite the fact that the combined pay-rolls of these offices aggregated nearly one hundred dollars per day." Baker drew on his experience to achieve success. His previous work in the business department of the Denver newspapers helped him stay afloat while other newspapers failed. Linford writes of Baker that he "was once believed to own all the papers in the young territory." She calls him "the first publisher of note in Wyoming."

Remaining on the leading edge of the news, however, is sometimes dangerous, especially in a rowdy, end-of-the-tracks town like Cheyenne. "For a time the rougher elements of the city's population were turbulent and sometimes aggressive," according to the Coutant Notes. "Criticisms of the acts of evil-doers brought threats of violence to the editor. These threats were often accentuated by the display of a revolver." The Notes also reveal some of the stories that helped make the Cheyenne newspaper "a prominent and influential factor" in people's lives: "The first Territorial establishment of Wyoming, the official appointments, legislative work, woman suffrage and landgrabber lynching, an Indian massacre in the outskirts of Cheyenne, murders and vigilante work, municipal and Territorial politics, the simultaneous visit of Grant, Sherman, and Sheridan to the capital city, and finally in 1870, the great fire in Cheyenne constituted some of the topics faithfully recorded and fully discussed in Baker's paper."

Politics usually sparks controversy, and in 1869, Baker landed in the middle of a political fray. Newspapers during that time period often assumed political designations. For example, Baker's *Leader* was Republican, while the *Argus* was Democratic. Historian T.A. Larson reports that the 1869 campaign for Wyoming's territorial delegate to Congress was bitter. Baker began publishing the three Republican newspapers in the territory during that campaign. As a result, he was chosen chairman of the territorial Republican Central Committee, and he expected another political plum would come his way—the printing contract for the first session of the legislature. Instead, Territorial Secretary Edward M. Lee assigned the task to his own brother-in-law, S. Allen Bristol. This created a split within the Republican Party. Lee also helped Bristol begin a competing Republican newspaper, the *Wyoming Tribune.*

The fracture left Baker feeling distanced from the party and led to the demise of Lee's career. By early 1870, according to Larson, Lee was being accused of appearing drunk in public and of living openly with a prostitute. Such behavior was unseemly at best for a man holding high office. Larson writes of Baker's revenge, stating, "Baker of the *Leader* dispatched a long letter to President [U.S.] Grant elaborating on Lee's 'drunken revelries and licentious debaucheries.' Baker did not mention the printing business, but alleged that he was yielding reluctantly to the unanimous demand of the people."

Grant had also received information focusing on Lee's strong points, but he was not swayed. He named Major Herman Glafcke of Connecticut to replace Lee. Lee had been unable to travel to Washington to defend himself since he was serving as acting governor while Territorial Governor John Campbell was away. Campbell, who had been in Washington, presented favorable reports about

Lee to Grant. However, as Larson explains, "Governor Campbell, had he been so disposed, could probably have saved Lee's job for him. It appears that he made no fight for Lee." Larson believes that had Lee awarded the printing contract to Baker, Lee might have kept his job despite the accusations leveled against him. Lee's political adversaries probably exaggerated his misdeeds, though Larson states that "some of the allegations presumably were true...." He calls the "Lee affair...typical of Wyoming political behavior in the territorial period. Outrageously libelous statements, supported by long lists of signatures, were often dispatched to Washington." Baker supported Glafcke, but the territorial Republican Party remained divided until Campbell resigned in 1875. J.H. Hayford, who edited the *Sentinel,* had sided with the governor, U.S. Attorney Joseph M. Carey, and others. The Party's division, according to Larson, "may have helped [the Democrats] in winning most of the elective positions in the territory, although all federal positions remained in the hands of the Republicans."

Baker's editorial positions may have been swayed by personal predilections as well. Suffragists Anna Dickinson and Redelia Bates had visited Cheyenne in 1868 and 1869. Larson asserts that the twenty-seven-year-old Baker found both young women attractive and explains that the newspaper reports of Bates's visit focused more on her appearance and personality than on her message. (In contrast, in February 1870, Baker described forty-nine-year-old Susan B. Anthony, the leader of the suffrage movement, as "the old maid whom celibacy has dried, and blasted, and mildewed, until nothing is left but a half crazy virago.") Following Bates's visit, the *Leader* suddenly stopped discounting woman suffrage. The abrupt shift on the issue of women's rights was even more amazing because it occurred during the legislative session in which the bill for woman suffrage in Wyoming Territory was presented. Larson concludes, "[I]t was fortunate that Miss Dickinson and Miss Bates, and not Miss Anthony, came to Wyoming to promote woman suffrage in the autumn of 1869."

Only once did Baker fail to publish the *Leader* on time—on January 11, 1870, after a fire swept through Cheyenne. According to the Coutant Notes, Baker contracted for another building to replace his burned office, rented the presses from the defunct *Argus,* and traveled to Chicago the day after the fire to purchase new supplies and equipment. In thirty days, despite "severest winter weather," Baker began producing the *Leader* in a new building with its own equipment.

Baker eventually sold his profitable newspapers and returned to Denver in April 1872. He sold the *Sentinel* to Hayford and Gates, who had previously helped him with the *Leader.* Major Herman Glafcke, who became secretary of Wyoming Territory, purchased the *Leader.* The weekly *South Pass News* had ceased publication in December 1871, when a fire destroyed the building housing its offices. Back in Colorado, Baker served as president of the Pioneers Society of Denver, and in 1906 began working at the U.S. Mint. He is said to have planted the first row of shade trees near Cherry Creek, first hauling water to them, and later digging an irrigation ditch from springs near the Country Club district.

Baker was active in many fraternal organizations, including the Masons. He had been one of the earliest members of the Masonic lodge organized in Cheyenne. He is credited with being a twenty-five year member of Denver's Chamber of Commerce and one of the first members of the Young Men's Christian Association. Colorado Historian Wilbur Stone states that Baker "cooperated in every movement and measure for the benefit and upbuilding of the city along political, intellectual, material, social and moral lines." According to an article printed in the *Rocky Mountain News* on May 28, 1934, Baker was credited with beginning the first ice plant and the first mountain trout fish hatchery in the region. He was also the business manager of the Denver, Apex & Western Railroad.

Baker's *Leader* evolved into the *Cheyenne Daily Leader,* then became the *Cheyenne Daily Sun-Leader* when merged with the *Cheyenne Daily Sun.* In 1900, editor E.A. Slack changed the name back to the *Cheyenne Leader.* Nine years later, it became the *Cheyenne State Leader* owned by Omaha newspaperman W.S. Edmiston. Eventually this newspaper merged with William Deming's *Wyoming Tribune,* becoming the *Wyoming State Tribune and Cheyenne State Leader* in the early 1920s. In 1930, the newspaper became the *Wyoming State Tribune.* This paper eventually merged with the *Wyoming Eagle,* first with a morning and an evening edition, each with a different political slant, then became the daily *Wyoming Tri-bune-Eagle* in 1994, owned mostly by the McCraken family.

In 1932—two years before his death—Baker returned to Cheyenne. He was 90 years old. He told William C. Deming, who owned and published the *Tribune-Leader*, "I didn't dream when I dragged my little plant up from Denver by ox-team in 1867, and turned out a 300-copy edition of the *Leader* in a log cabin, that either Cheyenne or the newspaper would grow to what they have become today. I'm proud to have been the founder of an enterprise which has developed so marvelously." At the time of Baker's visit, the newspaper had grown to house eight typesetting machines and a printing press that could print 24,000 sixteen-page papers each hour. The interview was published on the front page of the June 17, 1932, issue of the *Wyoming State Tribune*. Baker died in Denver on May 27, 1934, after a long illness.

Hiram "Hi" Kelly

An Indian bride, a beautiful mansion, politics, a curious curse, and a tragic unsolved mystery are all woven into the tapestry of cattle baron Hiram "Hi" Kelly's life. Kelly, the man who shipped the first cattle out of Wyoming in 1870, earned and lost a fortune during his life. His story stands as one of the most colorful in the state's history. In *Cow Country Legacies*, historian Agnes Wright Spring calls Kelly "one of the most highly respected men among those who helped to develop the western cattle country." Kelly became best known as a cattle rancher and a builder of luxurious homes, but as a young man Kelly worked as a miner, freighter, bullwhacker, and stage driver before he began his ranching career.

According to Daze Bristol (whose sister-in-law was one of Kelly's daughters), Kelly was "a very handsome man throughout his life." He stood six feet, two inches tall, "as erect as a pine tree." He had thick curly black hair, a long black beard, and "piercing blue eyes that seemed to read your innermost thoughts."

Hiram Kelly was born in Sheridan County, Missouri, on October 14, 1834, one of ten children of Hiram and Mahala Kelly. Part of Kelly's childhood was spent in Kentucky. At age fifteen, Hiram persuaded his father to join one of the wagon trains headed to California during the Gold Rush. They left Independence, Missouri, on May 8, 1849. According to Bristol, the Kellys were among the thousand emigrants celebrating the Fourth of July at Independence Rock on the Sweetwater River that year. (Independence Rock was an important landmark for travelers along the Oregon Trail who painted and scratched their names on the huge rock formation.) The celebration that included the Kellys apparently took fireworks to an extreme. As Bristol explains, "The group blew up part of the rock destroying many of the listed names." (Although some sources list the date of the explosion as 1847, it seems likely it occurred in 1849 as gold-seekers and others traveled west.)

On that same trip, the Kelly party unexpectedly found itself in a tense situation with Indians. While one of the white men fried beans, Indians approached and asked if they could partake of the meal. Then one of the Indians kicked the frying pan over, and the cook hit him. The Indian fell beneath a pony and was kicked in the head. This insulted the other Indians, who gathered in anger. The travelers "placed chains around their cattle so they could not be run off," Bristol says. Throughout the night, the Indians threatened the group, demanding that the man who punched their colleague be turned over to them. The man hid in a wagon. Eventually, the whites offered the Indians some food and supplies. The white man escaped punishment at their hands.

Kelly worked in the California gold fields until 1852, returning "by way of the Isthmus to Independence, Missouri." In 1853, he drove six yoke of cattle to Santa Fe, New Mexico, and back in the fall with a "freight train [that] consisted of about 25 wagons and about 30 men." The next year, he drove ten mules along the same route, this time delivering goods for New Mexico merchants. He recalled that there were about thirty ten-mule teams in the train.

In 1855, Kelly worked for mail contractors Hockaday and Hall, transporting mail from Independence to Santa Fe. "The mail went each way every month," according to Kelly's reminiscences, published in the *Wyoming Tribune-Eagle*, "taking about 21 days to make the trip, allowing the balance of the time for lay-over for the teams to rest." The trip was treacherous and lonely, as few white people yet inhabited the country. Buffalo roamed the range in plentiful numbers, though, and great concern existed over the possibility of coming into contact with unfriendly Indians.

"We had many difficulties with the Indians at different times," Kelly recalled. In September 1856, he learned of a fracas involving the Indians and a Colonel Sumner. Kelly met Sumner at the Little Arkansas as he traveled to Fort Leavenworth. Sumner warned Kelly to be careful crossing the river because the Indians might be on the warpath. He went on to explain that he had killed eleven Cheyenne Indians during a fight in the Smoky Hill country. Kelly wisely asked for an escort for his party, but Sumner refused, blaming the poor condition of his mules.

Kelly forged ahead. About ten miles from the river crossing, according to his reminiscences, they "ran into a band of about 100 Cheyenne warriors, all painted up and on the war path. They jerked me off the seat of the coach and wanted to know if I was 'capital' meaning the man in charge." When he affirmed this, the Indians took wood from the top of the coach and built a fire. The Indians began smoking pipes and formed a ring around the mail carriers. "They told us that on account of the soldiers having killed some of their party, they wanted revenge, and proposed to take it out on us, but I outtalked them."

In Kelly's party, a man who could speak Spanish conversed with a Mexican captive of the Indians who, in turn, could translate to the Indians. Through the interpreters, Kelly told the Indians that his group was outnumbered and they should go ahead and kill them. But, he explained, "… [T]he Great White Father…will kill all of you if you kill us so there won't be any of you left." The Indians let the Kelly party go.

Kelly had to backtrack to catch the Russell, Majors, and Waddell freighters to replace the supplies the Indians had taken. The Indians agreed to leave the white party alone and "formed a line on both sides of the road as we turned around," Kelly recalls. Traveling day and night to make up lost time, Kelly finally reached Santa Fe. He learned later that the Indians had followed, planning to kill them, but they did not catch up.

Indians did not present the only challenge on the route. Nature brought another type of conflict with savage storms and bitter cold. Some sources state that Kelly froze his feet badly in 1857 and returned to Independence to recuperate. For the next couple of years, Kelly drove mule teams on long cross-country trips. In 1858, he left Atchison, Kansas, with a train of thirty-six eight-mule teams destined for Salt Lake City. The mule train carried merchandise and supplies for Livingstone and Kinckaid. The trip was a hard one; bad

(Hiram "Hi" Kelly, a prominent western cattleman, shipped the first cattle out of Wyoming in 1870. (Courtesy Colorado Historical Society)

weather wore the mules thin. The party was stopped at Fort Laramie by heavy snow. They wintered there. One source lists Kelly as traveling with his brother-in-law, Tom Maxwell, and wintering the mules in Goshen Hole near Torrington. In the spring, they delivered the goods to Salt Lake City and to Camp Floyd (about forty miles south of Salt Lake). The mules, originally brought to Utah to be sold to the government, were taken back to Independence. Kelly sold them at a Saint Louis auction.

Kelly worked as a miner in Leadville, Colorado, during the summer of 1860, then spent the winter in Denver in "a little old frame house" on Blake and Sixteenth Streets. City life was not his forte, however. Kelly enjoyed the outdoors. In the spring, he found government work, earning the hay contract at Fort Laramie. He earned twenty-nine dollars and put up one hundred ton, cutting the hay with scythes. That fall Kelly hitched his wagon again, this time serving as a messenger for Ben Holladay on the Overland Stage. He made several trips from Julesburg, Colorado, to South Pass. Kelly's affinity for livestock handling earned him command of the bull teams.

In 1862, Kelly established the Virginia Dale, Colorado, station on the stage line. That station later became the headquarters. He "got out the logs to build that station with" and built the stage station and the barns. The new route that allowed for this new station ran "the North Platte…across to Denver… from Denver to La Porte, Cache La Poudre and up Cherokee Trail to Bitter Creek, there intercepting the old road."

In 1863, Kelly returned to Fort Laramie. During the summer, he traded healthy stock for the lame animals of the influx of emigrants continuing to travel to California and Oregon. That fall, he worked with Elias W. Whitcomb, "putting up a lot of hay in Chugwater and cutting it with scythe, to feed our horses on that winter, right where the old station stands now." Kelly never did well with haying chores. He found them hard and tedious work. He told Whitcomb, "[I]f I could not make a living without cutting hay with that damn scythe, I would starve and so I quit my job." Even so, Kelly was good at this task. Charles Guernsey writes in *Wyoming Cowboy Days*, "I doubt if the mower or reaper has yet been invented that could cut as wide a swath and so great tonnage between sun-up and sundown as Hi could cut with his scythe. I never saw the implement, but he was in tune with it and according to his description of its capacity with him at the helm across a hayfield it must have been a wonder." Even though he found haying distasteful, Kelly worked hard. Undoubtedly, his growing family kindled his work ethic.

Kelly married Elizabeth Reshaw (sometimes listed as Richards), the daughter of French trapper John (Pete) Reshaw and his full-blooded Sioux wife, in 1864. Elizabeth, just fifteen years old, had been born in 1849 at Fort Laramie and was educated at an exclusive girls' school in Saint Louis, where she could learn more of the white man's culture. The newlyweds homesteaded in Chugwater, living first in a log and sod cabin. Elizabeth had a green thumb; she is credited with having the first private vegetable garden in Wyoming. The Kellys eventually had eight children.

In 1865, Kelly went to Fort Halleck (near Elk Mountain) and then wintered in Fort Collins. He then purchased Tod Reynolds's store near Fort Laramie, bought six five-yoke bull teams and wagons in Nebraska City, Nebraska Territory, and brought provisions with him so he could live in Fort Laramie for the winter. In the early 1860s, he had contracted with Edward Creighton of Omaha to provide poles for the telegraph line Creighton was building from Omaha to Salt Lake City. Kelly recalls, "I sent my men up Horse Creek to Bear Mountain to get out the poles and hired two men with four-mule teams to haul them down to the store on the road." But, according to historian Daze Bristol, "a group of Indians who had been raiding the entire region came across Kelly's men, loaded with poles, and killed and scalped them, stole their mules, and then moved on. A party of despoiled ranchers from the Laramie Valley found the dead men scalped and frozen as it was winter and Kelly sent word to the rest of his men to pack their teams and all moved to the store." Eventually, Kelly abandoned the store building and moved closer to Fort Laramie. Indians burned the store.

In 1867 Kelly purchased more teams and earned a wood and hay contract from Fort Laramie. In the fall, he sold the teams to Jim Porter, who loaded them with grain and provisions and took them north to Fort Reno and Fort Phil Kearny. Then in 1868, Kelly contracted to help move the government posts of Fort Reno and Fort Phil Kearny south to Fort Fred Steele.

In 1869, Kelly took a contract with his father-in-law John Reshaw for wood and hay for Fort Fetterman, located near the point where the Bozeman Trail crossed the North Platte River. Reshaw planned to haul the hay with his mule teams and, not surprisingly, Kelly opted instead to gather wood. He still disliked working with hay. Reshaw got drunk that summer and shot and killed a soldier sitting in front of the sutler's store at Fort Fetterman. He then joined

Indians on the warpath and fought with Kelly's men who were cutting hay along Deer Creek. The men refused to work under these conditions and two days later returned to camp "as wet as rats," pointedly refusing to bale any more hay.

Lacking one hundred tons of the hay needed to meet the requirements of the contract, Kelly traveled to Omaha to cancel his obligation, but the government held firm. So he traveled to Cache la Poudre and bought hay, which he baled and hauled, at a cost of twenty dollars per ton, to Fort Fetterman two hundred miles away. The misadventure cost him more than five thousand dollars and likely deepened his dislike of hayfield chores. But when Kelly gave his word, he kept it. As Bristol writes, "Thus he fulfilled his contract as he was to fulfill every contract he made during his 40 years on the frontier...."

In July 1870, Kelly sold his cattle to a man named Pritchard. "We loaded them right where the Cheyenne depot now stands [in the 1920s] into the [railroad] cars in one of those little short chutes that they loaded and unloaded horses in," Kelly recalled. "They were the first cattle loaded and shipped out of Wyoming and went to Paris for beef, as it was the time for the Franco-German war." He was paid $70 per head for them. Pritchard doubled that, selling them at $150 per head. "That sweltering day in 1870 portended the future of Wyoming," writes Bristol, "and began its...career as a leading livestock state in America." Wyoming Territory's assessment rolls for 1870 list 8,143 head in the territory, and, according to historian T.A. Larson, "the cattle business was soon recognized as the territory's most promising economic activity." By the mid-1880s, more than a million cattle grazed in Wyoming Territory.

In the fall of 1870, Kelly tried his hand at the range cattle business, buying two hundred head of two-year-old heifers and ten Durham bulls. The country "was all open then and I had a good success," Kelly writes. The only other cattle—a small herd—belonged to Bullock and Mills, which later became Bullock and Hunton. Kelly earned the government beef contract at Fort Fetterman for the winters of 1871 and 1872. Also in the early 1870s, Kelly became a charter member of the Laramie County Stockmen's Association, which became known in 1879 as the Wyoming Stock

Growers Association. He recalls, "The association was composed of the few stockmen in the country who had a number of herds in Western [*sic*] Nebraska, northern Colorado and at that time, southeastern Wyoming. The purpose of this association was to further the interests of the range cattle business, the principal work of which was to get a record of the brands and to formulate a system of roundups." The men met in Judge William Kuykendall's courtroom and often had heated discussions on the best way to achieve their goals. Kelly believed the association was successful because "we had an exceptionally good class of men in with us."

Not surprisingly for a progressive young stockman, Kelly increased his land holdings during the 1870s. In addition to his Chugwater homestead, he purchased the Y Ranch near La Grange, the D Ranch thirty-three miles north of Cheyenne, and the nearby LC Ranch, the Hamilton Place, and the North Chug Ranch. In 1879 he purchased Donald McPhee's 160 acres.

The Kellys started small, living first in a sod house, but soon they expanded their living quarters. In 1877, Kelly built a two-story, fourteen-room home of locally made brick on Chugwater Creek. The home "with its fine furniture from the East…became the showplace of the area. The main rooms all opened from a large central hallway. A wide staircase went to the second floor. It was one of the nicest stopping places on the Cheyenne Deadwood Stage Line," writes Bristol. A newspaper reporter visiting the Kelly ranch described it as having "the appearance of the home of a wealthy farmer. There are more trees about Kelly's ranch than there are in all Cheyenne," he commented. The Kelly ranch also became the site of one of Wyoming's first jails, holding notorious road agents so they could not terrorize the stage coaches transporting passengers and valuables along the recently established road to the Black Hills. Kelly built a hotel in 1876 on his brother-in-law Tom Maxwell's ranch nearby. Known as "The White House," the hotel and Maxwell's ranch in 1883 became the headquarters of the Swan Land and Cattle Company.

John "Portugee" Phillips owned a ranch about a mile upstream from Kelly. Phillips is best known for his breakneck ride from Fort Phil Kearny south to Fort Laramie on Christmas Eve 1866, to report the tragic Fetterman massacre. He later served as a postmaster in Chugwater. He built a two-story hotel in an open meadow across the creek from Kelly's hotel. A bridge allowed stage coaches and wagons to let passengers off in front of either place.

Kelly's luck with horses was about as good as his affinity for hay. In 1876 Sioux Indians ventured south to Kelly's station at Chugwater and "ran off twenty horses," according to historian Spring. Years earlier, in 1868, when he had returned from moving items from Fort Phil Kearny and Fort Reno to Fort Fred Steele, he arrived at his place on Horse Creek twenty-five miles north of Cheyenne to discover that Indians had dispersed his herd of more than twenty horses. This time, they left him one. He managed to do better with cattle, which afforded him a living and gained him entry into prestigious circles. By the mid-1870s, Kelly's herd numbered fifteen hundred head, including five valuable shorthorn bulls. He later purchased purebred Hereford bulls from the Swan brothers.

Kelly became a charter member and founder of the elite Cheyenne Club, organized in 1880. Members could enjoy the elegant clubhouse, which included a restaurant, bar, billiard room, and reading room, but they were expected to behave in a gentlemanly manner and could be expelled for drunkenness, cursing, cheating at games, or criminal acts. He also joined the Masons and became one of the first Masons in Wyoming.

In the early 1880s, cattlemen began stretching barbed-wire fences, sometimes including government-owned land within their sharp-spiked boundaries. Some who had purchased land along the Union Pacific Railroad, where private and public ownership of alternate square-mile sections of land formed a checkerboard pattern, fenced in the government land rather than taking extra time and money to fence the alternate sections. This practice drew fire in 1883, when the U.S. government brought suit against the ranchers who illegally fenced government property. M. C. Brown, the U.S. attorney for Wyoming Territory, filed suit in January against Alexander H. Swan and won. In December, Brown brought suit against John Hunton and Hiram B. Kelly. A Cheyenne attorney and cattleman, W. W. Corlett, blocked the reappointment of the judge who decided the Swan case, but the government did not falter in its efforts to regulate the illegal fencing. By

1886, many of the fences were taken down, and, as ordered by the court, Swan, Hunton, and Kelly removed theirs.

Kelly had already changed his mind about ranching by the time the fencing issue was raging. On April 28, 1884, he traveled to Scotland to sell his 3,200 acres to the Swan Land and Cattle Company, then headed by John Clay, for one-quarter of a million dollars. During his trip, Kelly visited several European countries. Kelly recalls, "After selling out, I handled some stock down on Bear Creek at the Y Cross Ranch. I didn't consider I was in the stock business after I sold out on Chugwater in 1884."

Kelly moved to Cheyenne and asked local contractor M. P. Keefe to build a magnificent home on Ferguson Street (now Carey Avenue). According to *Early Cheyenne Homes*, the Kelly home stood at 2408 Ferguson. Along with a carriage house and a stable, the house took up a quarter block. The lots were estimated to have cost three thousand dollars with the house's construction running about thirty thousand dollars. The new state capitol was located across the street from the Kelly home. Kelly's mansion stood on "Millionaire's Row." The street earned its nickname because about forty mansions, each costing in the range of thirty to fifty thousand dollars, were built there in the early 1880s. Kelly's home was located just a block away from the house of his old friend Elias Whitcomb, who had also taken an Indian bride.

In keeping with her love of gardening, Elizabeth Kelly planted a horse chestnut tree and white lilac bushes. The wrought-iron fence surrounding the property contained two crossed tomahawks and a snake, emblems of her tribe, in the gate. The interior of the house was magnificent, according to the description in *Early Cheyenne Homes*. Six fireplaces—one in every room except the kitchen—were topped with carved cherrywood mantels and framed in imported tiles depicting characters and events in Shakespearean plays. The front hall, entered through double hand-carved doors with brass fittings, had parquetry floors and a winding black walnut staircase. The six-arm parlor chandelier featured two unusual blue globes. The stairs sported hand-carved leaves and cherry clusters. The home also had inside shutters. There were six rooms on the second floor and a finished third floor. A unique feature of the home was concealed heating with cast-iron steam radiators located beneath the floors. The Kellys lived there for eighteen years, eventually selling to Edgar Boice. After the sale was made, Elizabeth regretted not taking her precious white lilacs. She asked the new owner if she could keep them, but he refused. Enraged, Elizabeth placed a curse on the lilacs, promising that they would never bloom again. They didn't.

According to Bristol, Kelly was devoted to his family, "providing his children with the very best that money could buy." The Kellys hired tutors from the East to help educate their children when they lived on the Chugwater ranch. But some of their cultured ways were undoubtedly learned from their mother, of whom Spring writes, "Mrs. Kelly was handsome and was said to perform her domestic duties in a manner that 'would reflect credit upon a New England housewife.'" The children—Kate, Cora, Clara, Chug, Will, Charles, Ben, and Jack—brought their parents the joy and heartaches common in all families, but Chug denounced the ranching life and disappeared under mysterious circumstances. Named for Chugwater Creek, he was educated at a Chicago boys' school and enjoyed the high life, belonging to exclusive clubs in Chicago, New York, and London. His parents gave him the Y Ranch for a wedding present when he married Ama Norton of Greeley, Colorado, but Chug soon sold it, using the money to tour Europe. He disappeared during a visit to Chicago. Because he supposedly had taken a substantial amount of cash along, foul play was suspected.

Will did better, attending the University of Michigan law school and clerking at the Colorado Supreme Court in Denver. Will also clerked at the Wyoming Supreme Court; Spring comments that she found him especially helpful when she served as the State Librarian for Wyoming. According to Bristol, Ben lived a life of leisure in San Francisco, and Charles died while serving in the military during the Spanish-American War. Clara married Bristol's brother, Robert McCabe, a superintendent of the Union Pacific Railroad. Kate married a man from Philadelphia associated with steel interests and lived in Fort Collins. Cora never married.

Following the sale of their Cheyenne mansion, the Kellys moved further west, spending the next several years in Seattle and then Portland before relocating to Denver. They spent their last years in Edgewater, a Denver suburb. Kelly tried his hand at real estate, mining, and investments after leaving Cheyenne. In 1898 and 1899, he mined at Central City, Colorado. He might have done better remaining a rancher because he did not "make hay" on these deals and lost most of his fortune through poor investments.

Elizabeth died July 8, 1922. Kelly passed away at age eighty-nine, on June 2, 1924. He and his wife are buried in adjoining graves in a Fort Collins cemetery.

Barney L. Ford

Cheyenne's InterOcean Hotel was considered the city's leading hostelry in the 1870s. Located at the corner of Sixteenth and Hill Streets (now Capitol Avenue), where the Hynds Building now stands, the InterOcean Hotel was three stories high, with a one-story veranda decorated with iron grillwork. The hotel's grandeur belied the life of the man who built it. Barney L. Ford overcame slavery to own the high-class hotel. His journey from slave to respected hotel owner included stops in such diverse places as Nicaragua, Georgia, Illinois, California, and Colorado. The variety of jobs Ford held and his experiences no doubt proved helpful in his later hotel career. Hotel work appears as one of the few constants in Ford's life. Ford, who contended with many peaks and valleys during his life, epitomizes the saying, "If at first you don't succeed, try, try again."

Barney Ford was born January 22, 1822, in Stafford Court House, Virginia. He was the son of a slave and a white plantation owner. Known only as Barney, he took the name "Launcelot Ford" from a steam engine after he later ran away from home. Raised on a plantation in South Carolina, Ford was entirely self-taught. His mother is said to have stolen books for him to use to educate himself and took him to a nearby plantation where another slave helped him learn to read.

Accounts of Ford's early years vary. According to historian Frank Hall, Ford drove hogs and mules from Kentucky to Columbus, Georgia, for four years; served as second steward on a cotton boat from Columbus to Apalachicola, Florida, for three years; and worked from 1846 to 1848 on a passenger steamer that traveled from Louisville to Saint Louis to New Orleans. In 1848, Ford traveled to Chicago, where he became a barber. There, he married Julia Lyoni. In 1851, he bought the United States Hotel at Greytown in Nicaragua, managing the facility until the U.S. Navy retaliated against a Nicaraguan attack on the U.S. warship *Prometheus*. According to author William Katz, the couple then moved to California, intending to search for gold, but decided instead to give the hotel business another try. They hosted many dignitaries and made a considerable amount of money—about five thousand dollars—in addition to many friends.

Ford then became steward for Commodore Cornelius Vanderbilt, working on vessels operating between Virgin Bay and Castillo Rapids along the San Juan River in Nicaragua. After eight months, Ford opened the California Hotel in Virgin Bay. According to Hall, he sold the hotel after the "filibustering expedition by the notorious General Walker, who came there from New Orleans with the purpose of conquering and appropriating that country, took place." Ford returned to Chicago. Until 1860, he managed a boarding stable.

Journalist Frances Melrose's account of Ford's early years differs a bit. She writes that as a slave Ford worked in the gold fields of Auraria, Georgia, when he was in his teens. When he was sent north on an errand, he escaped in Quincy, Illinois, traveling on to Chicago, where he met Henry O. Wagoner, a free African-American man who helped other slaves escape via the underground railroad. Julia Lyoni, Ford's wife, was Wagoner's sister-in-law. Melrose writes that Ford and Julia traveled through Nicaragua during the California gold rush. After a bout of illness Ford decided to stay in Nicaragua and open a hotel and restaurant there. When the couple returned to Chicago, he helped Wagoner operate the underground railroad there.

Katz's account also mentions that Ford's "good friend" Henry O. Wagoner was a correspondent for Frederick Douglass's newspaper. Wagoner, according to author Forbes Parkhill, taught Ford bookkeeping so he could open his first barber shop. As newlyweds, the Fords lived with the Wagoners, and Julia worked as a chambermaid at a downtown Chicago hotel. When Julia found that the hotel needed help in its barber shop, Ford spent two dollars for lessons and soon

Barney L. Ford, a former slave who became a respected hotel owner in both Cheyenne and Denver. (Courtesy Denver Public Library, Western History Collection)

realized this was a lucrative investment. He sometimes earned twenty-five cent tips because of his ability to quote the classics.

All accounts agree that Ford was bitten by the gold bug. He purchased mining claims in Gregory Gulch, near Central City, Colorado, in 1860. Katz locates these claims as near Breckenridge. Gold was not to be where Ford's fortunes were made, though. According to Melrose, Ford and several other African-American men struck gold in Summit County at a site known as "Nigger Hill." Because of the Dred Scott decision of the U.S. Supreme Court, African-Americans did not possess citizens' rights and could not file their claims. Ford apparently sought help from a white lawyer who filed the claim in Ford's name. When the attorney discovered that the property was potentially profitable, however, he turned coat and insisted it was his land all along. The sheriff removed the African-American men from the property. Other gold seekers soon swooped into the area to find their fortunes, but gold was never located. In 1964, the name "Nigger Hill"—"a less than fit tribute for a legendary Colorado figure"—was changed to "Barney Ford Hill."

While in Breckenridge, Ford devised an algebraic equation, which he called his "law of positivities," according to Parkhill. His formula convinced him that he would strike it rich gold mining. Julia did not much care for this lifestyle, and she brought their young son, Louis Napoleon, with her from Chicago to try to persuade Ford to return to the hotel business.

"After a brief, but rather unfortunate experience in mining," Hall reports, Ford went to Denver and worked in the "old Hemingway house." There he purchased a vacant lot adjacent to the hotel and built a barber shop. He then opened a miners' boarding house in French Gulch, hoping to capitalize on the huge numbers of people hunting for gold, but the severe winter weather closed the mines, and Ford returned to Denver to focus his efforts there.

He built an addition to the rear of his barber shop and opened a restaurant. The restaurant boomed from the beginning. Ford was "a superior caterer and cook," according to Hall. This venture finally began accumulating profits—as much as $250 each day in receipts—for the former slave.

According to Katz, Ford partnered with Wagoner in several businesses, including barber shops, restaurants, and hotels. "Ford's InterOcean Hotels in Denver and Cheyenne catered to Presidents and prospectors, and offered a wide variety of services from saloons to shaving," Katz writes. "The establishments had a reputation as far east as Chicago for 'the squarest meal between two oceans.' When fires three times gutted their premises, Ford and Wagoner each time were able to begin anew."

In April 1863, a fire hit Denver. Among the buildings destroyed was Ford's. He had no insurance, but Ford bounced back. He asked Luther Kountze of Kountze Brothers, bankers, for nine thousand dollars to rebuild. The money, lent to him at the astonishing rate of twenty-five percent interest per year, gave Ford a chance to build a larger building than he had before. He opened the People's Restaurant on the ground floor of his three-story building at 1514 Blake Street. Advertising, according to Melrose, "the most choice and delicate luxuries of Colorado and the East" with "oyster suppers to order," Ford also placed a bar on the top floor and a barber shop in the basement. Just three months after opening his restaurant, Ford paid the loan back in full. In two years, he sold his restaurant to John J. Reithman, leasing the building for $250 per month and earning $23,400 on the sale, according to Hall.

Parkhill suggests that Ford helped keep Andrew Johnson seated as president against opponent Samuel Tilden. Parkhill details Ford's political leanings, stating that Ford was "astounded and dismayed, scarcely able to believe that [Colorado Governor John] Evans, a Lincoln supporter and advocate of emancipation" had approved an 1864 amendment to the election laws which gave the vote to every male aged twenty-one or older "not being a Negro or mulatto." Ford began working to eliminate that discriminatory phrase from the constitution being drafted for Colorado statehood. Although the territory's constitutional convention did not endorse slavery, and even though Ford led the movement advocating the African-American vote, the amendment denying the vote to black men passed.

An embittered Ford then sold his restaurant to Reithman and left Colorado. With the encouragement of Wagoner, though, Ford continued to work for Negro suffrage. Governor Evans was in line for a Senate seat, along with Jerome Chaffee, when the territory became a state. As Republicans, they opposed President Johnson, who opposed statehood for Colorado. The president's career was in jeopardy; impeachment had been discussed. Johnson vetoed Colorado's statehood and, with it, Evans's and Chaffee's chances to become senators. A bill was passed in Congress that prohibited territories from denying votes to any adult males. The bill became law by constitutional limitation. Johnson was not impeached. Parkhill writes, "Had Barney not fought the statehood movement, perhaps Evans and Chaffee would have been seated in the Senate, Johnson would have been impeached, and the history of the United States would have been changed. Some Coloradans began to call Barney a president maker."

This logic seems a bit of a stretch, but Ford did work to promote African-American suffrage and undoubtedly was overjoyed at the congressional decision to allow all adult males to vote regardless of race. Melrose calls Ford's status as "president maker" doubtful but notes that "he did help keep Colorado from attaining statehood until its proposed constitution allowed African-Americans to vote. In this effort, Ford sold or leased his Denver properties and went to

Washington." According to Melrose, Ford was also instrumental in establishing adult education classes in reading and writing in Denver in 1866 to encourage an informed electorate.

At forty-three, Ford prepared to retire, planning to settle in Chicago. However, in another two years' time, Ford returned to Denver. Hall explains, "the agent with whom he had left his property and business affairs in Denver, proved treacherous and soon left him stranded again." In 1867, Ford decided to open a restaurant in Cheyenne where the Union Pacific Railroad was just passing through. Timing his operations to coincide with the arrival of the first train, Ford earned $1,150 in cash receipts during the first twenty-four hours. According to Hall, Ford later had a disagreement with his business partner and purchased his interest for $10,000 in May 1868. But even this exciting new venture would not last long.

Fire again claimed Ford's investment, and he returned to Denver in 1871, bought his old restaurant, then sold it in 1872. In that same year, Ford became the first African-American to serve on a federal grand jury in Colorado. According to Melrose, Ford also operated Denver's InterOcean Hotel at Sixteenth and Blake Streets, which was built in 1872 or 1873. Melrose writes that Ford built Denver's hotel for $53,000 and sold it two years later for $75,000—another illustration of how Ford's fortunes followed a roller coaster ride throughout his life. "At times," Melrose writes, "his assets were listed as greater than those of such Denver luminaries as A. B. Daniels of department store fame, real estate developer Walter Cheesman and railroad magnate David Moffatt."

Ford built Cheyenne's first InterOcean Hotel at the request of a committee of Cheyenne citizens but lost it during a financial panic. According to Parkhill, the Cheyenne Chamber of Commerce then offered to donate a building site if Ford would build a hotel as good or better as Denver's InterOcean, and Ford mortgaged some of his Denver property to raise capital for the new venture. Hall explains that Ford was "offered a considerable subsidy to go [to Cheyenne] and build a first-class hotel."

In 1875, the *Rocky Mountain News* proclaimed that the Cheyenne hotel "eclipses anything in the hotel line between Chicago and San Francisco, leaving out Denver, of course." According to the report, the four-story building was one hundred ten feet long and sixty-six feet wide, and cost forty thousand dollars to build. Cheyenne resident William G. Haas reports that the business was "prominent for its first-class reputation, was acceptable for its superior accommodations, especially for its dining room where the food specialty consisted of wild game, and its frequent 'rough house' management...." At the time of the InterOcean's construction in 1875, two other "larger-than-usual" hotels marked Cheyenne's skyline— the Metropolitan and the Dyer House. Haas recalls that Ford's new hotel was impressive because "along its entire front on 16th Street was a one-story veranda, ornamented by artistic iron grill work." At that time, the InterOcean was the city's "largest and finest structure."

In October 1875, President Ulysses S. Grant visited Cheyenne. The president was not expected to arrive until noon, and Ford had planned a luncheon of antelope steak, mountain trout, claret, and champagne. But when Grant arrived at breakfast time instead, Ford met the challenge. Soon after the president's unexpected arrival, Ford "served a sumptuous breakfast and by the time the reception was held in the hotel parlors members of the committee agreed that he had saved the day," writes Parkhill.

In spite of this triumph, writes Hall, the InterOcean "proved an unprofitable venture and in due course bankrupted [Ford]." According to Haas, the dearth of customers was due to Ford's being African-American. While Haas's assertion is not verifiable, African-Americans were scarce in Wyoming at that time. Historian T. A. Larson explains that only two African-American cowboys were listed in the 1880 census, and when two hundred African-American miners from Ohio were brought to work in the coal mines near Hanna in early 1890, most of them did not stay. Larson explains, "Newspaper references to them and to the few other Negroes who were in the state in the 1890s suggest that there were divided opinions with respect to their acceptance by whites."

The equally bleak picture of African-American life in the latter 1800s in Colorado makes Ford's achievements there even more impressive. According to Parkhill, Ford, through his interest in politics, had gained enough prestige to be invited into white people's homes, and some whites had even called on him from time to time.

After Ford's InterOcean Hotel failed, according to Melrose, he opened restaurants in Breckenridge, Colorado—Ford's Chop House and, later, the Saddle Rock. In the 1880s, Ford built a house on Capitol Hill in Denver; in 1898, his wife was included in the prestigious *Social Year Book*. Parkhill states that their white neighbors in the Capitol Hill section did not object to the Fords living there and further, "Everyone liked and respected Barney and the soft-spoken Julia." The Fords dressed well and he drove a fine carriage, according to Parkhill.

In later years, Ford enjoyed raising flowers and Belgian hares and telling stories to his grandchildren. Parkhill states that Ford continued to work on his algebra theory because he wanted to find the solution and disliked leaving anything undone. He always wanted to write an algebra book but never managed to do so.

Ford died on December 14, 1902, at Saint Joseph's Hospital of a stroke suffered while shoveling snow. He was buried in Riverside Cemetery beside his wife, Julia, who had died of pneumonia three years earlier. After Julia's death, Ford stayed with her niece, Marcelline Beatty, a nurse, and deeded some of his property to her in exchange for care. Many of his papers were destroyed by relatives after his death. Melrose lists many Colorado honors awarded to Ford since his death. His building at 1514 Blake Street is listed on the National Register of Historic Places, a chair was dedicated in his name at Central City's Opera House, and in 1981 the Colorado legislature honored Ford with a stained glass window in the Capitol. In 1968, a housing project was christened "Barney Ford Heights," and in 1975, Kathryne McKinney organized the Barney Ford Memorial Association. One oversight remains, however. According to Parkhill, although Ford's biographical sketch in Hall's *History of the State of Colorado* is longer than those of Governor John Evans and several other prominent Coloradans, it does not mention that Ford was African-American, and on the page where Ford's picture should have been, a white man is shown instead. Parkhill states that someone objected to printing a picture of an African-American man in the book and so a white man's photo was substituted.

Nathaniel Robertson

A SYMBOL OF ELEGANCE and luxury, horse-drawn carriages are sometimes used today for special occasions such as weddings. At one time however, carriages were nearly as prevalent as automobiles are now. In the late 1890s, the "golden years of the American carriage, cart and wagon industry," the United States boasted seven hundred major carriage manufacturers in addition to individual craftsmen working in many small towns and cities. Richard Davis, a volunteer at Cheyenne's Old West Museum, estimates that nearly half a dozen carriage makers were working in that city between 1870 and 1910.

Scotsman Nathaniel Robertson was one such carriage maker who plied his trade in Cheyenne and Denver. Robertson's story is that of a successful man and a hard worker who came from tough beginnings and endured.

Born in Aberdeen, Scotland, in 1841, Robertson was orphaned at the age of six after the family emigrated to Canada. His mother died en route, and his father died shortly after his arrival in the new country. Robertson lived with an uncle, attending school for only a short period during his eighth year. At age eighteen, he traveled to Montreal to learn the craft that would support him throughout his life. He then moved to New York with the grand sum of four dollars in his pocket and went to work as an apprentice.

In 1865, Robertson headed west, opening his own carriage-making shop in Denver, at the corner of Fifteenth and Wazee Streets. The Denver City Directory of 1866 lists him as a "Wagon Maker," with an address at Planters's House. Over the next several years, Robertson moved first to Cheyenne and then Salt Lake City. After marrying Alice Orr of Montreal in 1874, Robertson returned to Colorado to ranch near Greeley. But ranching was not to be his life's work, and soon Robertson returned to building carriages of all kinds.

He sold his ranch in 1875 and moved to Cheyenne where he established the Cheyenne Carriage Company. The firm billed itself a "manufactory of only first class work. Buggies, Carriages and Concord Wagons made to order. Repairing promptly attended to." The stockholders in his carriage business eventually included notable Wyomingites such as Francis E. Warren, territorial governor, first governor of the state, and U.S. senator; contractor M. P. Keefe, who built the Wyoming State Capitol; and Judge Charles N. Potter, who eventually presided over the Wyoming Supreme Court.

In 1882, Robertson sold a half-interest in his lot and shop to George A. Coffman, who became his superintendent. For three thousand dollars, Coffman received half of all stock and tools and a half-interest in the two-story brick building, brick warehouse, and wooden stable. His name was added to the business, and the firm became Robertson and Coffman.

In the 1880s, the business expanded into farming equipment. According to its 1883 statement to the Wyoming Secretary of State, the Cheyenne Carriage Company was formed to "manufacture, repair and sell Buggies, Carriages, Wagons and vehicles of all descriptions, and to buy and keep for sale all description of vehicles; also to manufacture, repair, buy, keep for sale and sell Agricultural Implements." The capital stock of twenty-five thousand dollars came from the sale of 250 shares. The Cheyenne City Directories for 1884–1885 list Robertson as general manager of the company, but Warren apparently subsidized the business, as evidenced by a mortgage deed for more than ten thousand dollars to Warren and Charles Hecht in 1894. This was the only encumbrance the business listed. In addition to his business, Robertson devoted time to community affairs in Cheyenne, serving as county commissioner and city councilman and urging the state's legislature to pass a bill to build a county hospital.

Among Robertson's best-known customers was the cattle baron Alexander H. Swan, owner of the Swan Land and Cattle Company. Robertson built a Stanhope trap—a light, one-horse carriage on springs—for Swan. (This vehicle was named for Fitzroy Stanhope, who created the design in 1815.) Swan's trap is one of the carriages on display at the Old West Museum in Cheyenne, along with a drop-front phaeton that Robertson manufactured for another customer.

The late 1800s, when Robertson was operating his business, were good times for carriage builders. But by the turn of the century, new-fangled vehicles such as bicycles and carriages that operated without animal power were developing, changing forever the modes of transportation throughout the nation.

In 1885, Robertson returned to Denver, perhaps hoping to serve a larger market of carriage customers. He had established the Robertson Carriage Company there in 1881, according to historian Frank Hall, and the firm later opted not to purchase the Cheyenne Carriage Company with its $9,800 of debt. The Denver City Directories of 1885 and 1886 list the Robertson Carriage Company located at 379 and 381 Arapahoe Street. Robertson is listed as president and general manager, with H.C. Doll named as secretary and treasurer. In late 1896, the Cheyenne firm was sold to Nicolaisen and Stuhr, one of the more prominent carriage manufacturers in the area at that time.

William Jefferson Hardin

WILLIAM JEFFERSON HARDIN served during the sixth and seventh Wyoming Territorial Legislative Assemblies — the only African-American elected to the assemblies. A slender man with "elfin whiskers" and a keen ability to make and keep friends, Hardin's public speaking skills enabled him to excel in politics. He supported interracial marriage, the expansion of the city of Cheyenne, and preservation of the public peace while remaining loyal to the wishes of his constituents.

Hardin was born in Kentucky in 1830 or 1831. Some sources say he was born to a white father and a mixed-blood mother, but historian Roger Hardaway traces Hardin's lineage to a free African-American mother and a white father. Hardin never was a slave because his mother was free. The *Cheyenne Daily Sun* of November 9, 1879, suggested Hardin was a nephew of Ben Hardin, "one of the most eminent barristers and the ablest and most eloquent criminal lawyer at the Kentucky bar." Raised and educated by Shakers — "an experience afforded few Blacks in the antebellum period" — Hardin taught "free children of color" in Bowling Green, Kentucky. He arrived in Denver in his early thirties, where he reportedly speculated in stock, managed a poolroom, and became a barber.

His teaching career had apparently perfected his speaking skills, and Hardin lectured in Denver and nearby towns. Soon, Hardin was known as the "Colored Orator of Denver," most often promoting African-American suffrage and the integration of public schools. Hardin is said to have been the first African-American to make a public political speech in Colorado. In 1867, when Congress granted

William Jefferson Hardin, a renowned orator, was the only African-American elected to the Wyoming Territorial Legislative Assembly. (Courtesy Wyoming State Archives)

African-American men suffrage in all the territories, Hardin helped the Republican Party win African-American votes. In 1872, he served as a delegate to the Republican National Convention. The following year, Republican Party officials rewarded Hardin's hard work by arranging a job for him at the U.S. Mint in Denver.

In 1873, the *Rocky Mountain News* praised Hardin profusely: his "accomplishments have completely eclipsed his fellows in this city who have hung spell-bound on the hooks of his eloquence and been led by his counselings." Historian Eugene H. Berwanger calls Hardin "an unquestioned voice of Denver's Black community," but notes there are several reasons for his [present day] obscurity. "In a sense he caused his own undoing," Berwanger argues. "His aggressiveness on behalf of Negro suffrage left a bitter taste among his white contemporaries; his lectures to Blacks on seemly conduct appeared a sham in light of his own lifestyle; his quest for personal recognition encouraged him to exaggerate his own contributions or to ignore those of other individuals. His domestic indiscretions, while amusing to gossip-mongers, were a breach of moral etiquette, and his marriage to a white woman surely stigmatized him within the white and Black communities alike."

Hardin's high status, along with his job at the mint, proved short-lived. Though Hardin had married Nellie Davidson, a white milliner in Denver, another woman claimed Hardin was already married to her. Caroline Hardin, an African-American woman, showed she had married Hardin in Kentucky in 1850 and that she had a daughter. She also accused Hardin of dodging the draft of the Union Army in 1863. Hardin agreed with all she said, except that he believed his marriage to her had been illegal because he had been a minor and she had been a slave at the time the vows were taken. Hardin was fired from his job at the mint, although he was never charged with a crime, and he remained with Nellie after the revelations came to light.

In 1873, Hardin moved to Cheyenne, opened a barber shop, and made his living as a barber for the next several years. In Cheyenne, Hardin seems to have put his past behind him. By the end of the 1870s, "Hardin was known and respected by most people in the territory's small capital city. The scandal that had forced him out of Denver apparently did not in any way limit his acceptance into Cheyenne social and political life," explains Hardaway. In his second public speech in Wyoming in March 1878, Hardin addressed the congregation of the Presbyterian church, advocating temperance. The *Cheyenne Daily Sun* reported that the speech was frequently interrupted by applause. As word of Hardin's skill at public speaking spread, he was invited to make more addresses throughout the city.

According to the *Wyoming Blue Book*, the Sixth Assembly convened November 4, 1879, and adjourned December 13, 1879. It was composed of two bodies—the Council and the House. The Council met in the McDaniels Building at 1615 Pioneer Avenue.

Hardin, who served in the House, met with fellow representatives in the N.J. O'Brien Building at 317 West Seventeenth. A Republican, Hardin was one of sixteen from that Party serving along with nine Democrats and two representatives from the People's Party that year. Other representatives from Laramie County were Thomas Conroy, J.E. Davis, B.F. Dietrick, J.S. Taylor, W.H. Hibbard, W.C. Irvine, E.W. Mann, and S.K. Sharpless. The abstract of votes showed that Hardin earned 988 votes for his first term. During his second campaign, he earned 1,277 votes, again serving as a Republican. The Seventh Legislative Assembly convened January 10, 1882, and adjourned March 10, 1882. Both the House and the Council met at the Opera House. Of the twenty-four House representatives in this group, ten were Republicans, thirteen were Democrats, and one was a Populist. Hardin served with J.D. Fraser, W.C. Lane, C.W. Riner, H. Oelrichs, I.S. Bartlett, H.E. Beuchner, and A. Gilchrist.

Although Hardin was re-elected to the legislature in November 1880, his term of office did not begin until January 1882. This was due, according to historian T.A. Larson, to "an unfortunate gap of fourteen months between the election of legislators and their session." In 1882, the legislature contained a Democratic majority in both houses. Strong racial bias among Wyomingites in the 1880s and 1890s makes Hardin's election to the legislature a great achievement.

Hardin was light skinned and, according to the *Cheyenne Daily Sun*, "of slim and slender build, five feet ten inches high. [He] has black curly hair with moustache and elfin whiskers of the same color and black eyes. Has sharp well cut features, thin lips and small mouth, long sharp nose and an orange complexion." The newspaper commented that Hardin bore "no resemblance…to the African race, he looks more like an Italian or Frenchman than a colored man." The newspaper also mentioned how "neat and tidy" Hardin was in his dress, calling him "modest and unassuming, polite and agreeable in his manners, treating every man as a gentleman and every woman as a lady, regardless of their dress, position or circumstance."

Hardin's popularity helped him earn election as a legislator. When the Republicans held their convention in Cheyenne in 1879, before the September 2 general election, they quickly elected two Council and four House nominees. But Cheyenne was allowed a fifth House nominee as well, and three people, including Hardin, who was a delegate to the convention, were considered for the spot, creating controversy. Democrats, who had already adjourned their convention in Cheyenne, attended the Republican convention to see what their opponents were doing. They campaigned openly for Hardin among the Republican delegates. After Hardin led two ballots, Francis E. Warren moved that he be declared the nominee. The *Cheyenne Daily Sun* endorsed the selection of Hardin as "one of the best nominations made," then continued, "Although classed with our colored brethren, he has broken down race prejudice…by pre-eminent manifestations of ability and upright conduct." The *Cheyenne Daily Leader* concurred, stating that Hardin's election was "a moral triumph for the people."

Forces beyond Hardin's control came into play in the general election, though, according to historian Hardaway. A fusion ticket made up of both Republicans and Democrats had been created prior to the conventions, allowing the delegates of the two conventions—instead of the voters—to choose the new Laramie County legislators. Some Cheyenne residents complained. Herman Glafcke, editor of the *Cheyenne Daily Leader,* who, ironically, had suggested the fusion idea in the first place, was among the group protesting. He had been out of town when the Party conventions were held. When he returned, he was disgusted to find his political enemy and rival editor, E. A. Slack of the *Cheyenne Daily Sun*, had been nominated as one of the candidates for the Council. (Slack had earlier supported having Glafcke removed from his position as Territorial Secretary.) A second, "Workingmen's convention" was held, and Glafcke was nominated for the Council seat against Slack and others.

Hardin's oratorical skills served him well in this situation. He "made a calculated political move that could have backfired, but ultimately proved to be beneficial to him," Hardaway writes. Hardin attended the Workingmen's convention as a spectator, then was urged by delegates to speak. Although his doing so might have upset those supporting the fusion idea, "it indirectly guaranteed his election because the day after the convention met, four of the nominees who had not attended the gathering declined to run." Hardin was offered one of the House positions, so he was nominated on both tickets. Quite a coup for any politician but most likely an especially sweet victory for the lone African-American politician of the day.

On election day, African-Americans in Cheyenne had a resolution published in the *Cheyenne Daily Sun*. The resolution stated in part, "We believe [Hardin] to be a good man, and one who is worthy of this position." They also shared their joy in the fact that "our white fellow-citizens were mindful enough of the colored race to give them one representative in Wyoming Territory."

Hardin served on the Indian and military affairs committee and was one of two members on a joint standing committee on printing, both of which were relatively minor positions. Hardin may have asked to be appointed to the committees on which he wanted to serve, or the House leaders may have been reluctant to assign an African-American to choice committee positions. Of the six bills that Hardin introduced, two proposals became law. One was "to protect dairymen," and the other was "to protect poultry," according to Hardaway. This last law required territorial counties to pay a twenty-five cent reward to anyone killing a hawk or an eagle. Hardin's original plan was to protect poultry by establishing a bounty for chicken hawks, and this idea gained unanimous House approval. The Council added the amendment to include eagles.

On December 23, 1879, Speaker of the House H.L. Myrick complimented Hardin in the *Daily Sun*, saying that the legislator "never attempted to gain a point through any abuse of parliamentary tactics, yet he was always faithful to the interests of his constituents; and from first to last acted like an honest man and a gentleman."

Though most members retired after completing their terms Hardin was the only House member of the Sixth Legislative Assembly to serve in the next session. Hardin was nominated for a seat on the Council at the 1880 Laramie County Republican convention but finished low in the ballot, and he declined the opportunity to run for the House. Even so, he received enough votes and became a nominee. Though he asked that his name be withdrawn, the delegates refused. Hardaway states that the Workingmen's votes helped Hardin win his second term in the Territorial House of Representatives, as did the popularity of Republicans in the county in that year. This time, he became the chair of the engrossment committee and introduced three bills. Two were enacted, including one that expanded Cheyenne's borders and another to preserve the public peace. The latter act, approved on March 4, 1882, made it a misdemeanor to "exhibit any kind of fire arms, bowie knife, dirk, dagger, slung shot [*sic*] or other deadly weapon in a rude, angry or threatening manner" except in self-defense. Hardin wanted a bill passed to require barber shops to close on Sundays, and he had another member introduce the bill to avoid conflict of interest accusations. Another barber knew that Hardin was responsible for the bill, however, and criticized him heavily. The bill passed the House but not the Council, so it was not enacted.

According to Hardaway, Hardin also supported the law allowing interracial marriage and spoke eloquently in behalf of it. The First Legislative Assembly in 1869 had enacted a law making it a crime for interracial couples to marry in Wyoming Territory, though the law had not been well enforced. Hardin had not violated the law because he had married his white wife outside of Wyoming Territory.

Hardin did not seek a third term. Though he was again considered as a candidate, he apparently managed to convince the Party leaders to withdraw his name.

Hardin and his wife sold their Cheyenne property in 1881 and 1882 and left town by 1884. A letter written by Hardin's grandson in 1956 reported that Hardin lived in both Utah and Colorado after leaving Wyoming, serving as mayor of Park City, Utah, and Leadville, Colorado, though both claims are doubtful. The date and place of his death cannot be verified, although it may have occurred in 1889 or 1890, according to Hardaway. Also suspect is a report in the *Cheyenne Daily Sun* on September 15, 1889, stating that Hardin committed suicide by shooting himself through the heart in Park City, Utah, on Friday the 13th. The report explained that Hardin had been beset by both financial and "domestic troubles" and that his wife had left him.

R.S. Van Tassell

A WIRY DUTCHMAN with an eye for the ladies and a way with livestock made his mark in Wyoming not only by acquiring vast landholdings, but also by giving his name to a tiny town in the state. Renesselaer Schuyler Van Tassell, listed in most sources simply as R.S. Van Tassell (or sometimes as "Good Old Van"), was, according to Cheyenne historian Shirley Flynn, "a 'man's man,' ramrod straight and steady in business. With a gleam in his eye, he loved life and lived it to the fullest." He rode with President Theodore Roosevelt, but not all of Van Tassell's life was easy riding. Broken romances punctuate his adventures. Through it all, Van Tassell remained a rugged, active man, known as someone who was a straight dealer with an appetite for money.

Van Tassell (spelled in some sources as Van Tassel), was born in 1845 in Comstock, New York. Not much is known about Van Tassell's early life, although he lived in Iowa as a teenager. Having come further west in the 1860s, Van Tassell planned to set out from Fort Kearny, Nebraska Territory, in 1865 with fifteen other men to follow the future route of the Union Pacific Railroad. The post commander, Major John Talbot, objected to the small party traveling west because of the dangers posed by Indians in the area. Talbot required Van Tassell to increase the party to fifty men before allowing them to proceed. Not much is known about Van Tassell's experiences with the Indians because he was close-mouthed about such things. One story tells of his shooting his own horse and using the animal's carcass for cover while Indians attacked.

In 1866, Van Tassell, along with John Sparks and Tom McGee, wintered on Sherman Hill, where they worked cutting ties for the railroad.

The tie camp was located at the point where Happy Jack Road now joins Telephone Road, near the base of Cheyenne Pass. The railroad builders caught up with the tie camp at Sherman Hill about eighteen months later. (Sparks moved west to Nevada, where he eventually became governor. The town of Sparks is named for him.) McGee settled in the area of the tie hack camp and became a rancher.

In 1867, at the age of twenty-two, Van Tassell settled in newly founded Cheyenne. He worked as a freighter and raised stock. He also contracted to carry mail between Cheyenne and Fort Collins, Colorado, before the railroad connected the towns. As "the youngest man in business in Cheyenne," he entered into a partnership with a man named Gline in a livery business. Cheyenne resident George L. Lemmon recalls that Van Tassell owned a black racehorse that threw Gline's son into the judge's stand during one race. Van Tassell enjoyed a lifelong love of horses.

In the early 1870s, Van Tassell made the acquaintance of Jim Moore, a former Pony Express rider. Moore was a partner in the Great Western Corral, a stabling establishment that housed 250 horses and 200 wagons and covered half a city block. According to Flynn, the Great Western Corral in Cheyenne "served as a teamster terminal, a market place for horses of all kinds, a rough hostel and stage line terminal," and it "easily outdistanced the Gline and Van Tassell operation." Van Tassell soon began freighting for Moore and considered himself a partner. Moore owned a mansion on Ferguson Street (now Carey Avenue) in Cheyenne, where he lived with his wife and two children.

In 1873, Moore suffered serious injuries in a hay wagon accident in Sidney, Nebraska. He died several months later. Van Tassell married Moore's widow, Mary, on November 26, 1875, and, as a result, came into the wealth Moore had accumulated. Moore's holdings included nine thousand head of cattle, the JM Ranch south of Lusk, the J Rolling M brand, and a large amount of property, including the Cheyenne mansion. In 1877, Van Tassell moved the cattle to Rawhide Creek. A small post office on Moore's holdings became known as Jay Em, named for his brand.

Five years earlier, Van Tassell's livery stable had been the setting for a meeting of five men gathered to form a vigilante committee to help

R.S. Van Tassell, a man who loved the ladies, parlayed his romances into live-stock and land holdings. (Courtesy Wyoming State Archives)

ranchers protect themselves from cattle rustlers. John Rolfe Burroughs, Wyoming Stock Growers Association historian, names the participants as John H. Durbin, Thomas F. Durbin, and Charles F. Coffee, charter members of the Livestock Association of Laramie County, Wyoming, plus Van Tassell and a fifth man whose name has been lost to history. That organization later grew into the Wyoming Stock Growers Association, formed to plan cattle roundups and protect ranchers from cattle rustling. Van Tassell did not join the WSGA officially, however, until 1878 and did not assume any official role in the WSGA although he remained an active member throughout his life.

According to an early day employee, Fred Croxen, Van Tassell's Running Water Ranch near Lusk was begun in 1876. The house and barn were built with the same type of materials used to construct buildings at Fort Laramie. The ranch also boasted a secluded water well, hidden in the barn behind the saddle room, so men and horses could have protected access to water in the event of an Indian attack, Croxen recalled in an article in the *Lusk Herald.* The ranch had been one of Moore's original holdings in what is now Niobrara County. Another ranch, located about twenty-three miles northwest of Cheyenne on Pole Creek, became known as Van Tassell's home ranch. In 1880, Van Tassell secured ranch holdings near the town now bearing his name.

In 1883, Mary Moore Van Tassell died of tuberculosis, having been an invalid for a number of years before her death. Her husband inherited her property. According to Lemmon, Van Tassell had an eye for lonely and attractive women, but he also watched for opportunities. Mary had predicted that Van Tassell would one day marry Louise Swan, daughter of the wealthy stockman Alexander Swan, and her prediction came true just three years later. At the time of the wedding, Louise was twenty-two and Van Tassell was forty-one. Following an elegant wedding and a reception at the home of the Swans, the couple honeymooned in California. Alexander Swan gave his daughter a stone residence resembling a castle on the corner of Nineteenth and Ferguson Streets in Cheyenne.

Sadly, the newly married Van Tassells never lived in their beautiful, castle-like house. Alexander Swan could not afford to pay for the construction of the house, and contractor Robert W. Bradley assumed ownership instead. David D. Dare, a photographer and businessman, purchased the house, which became known as the Castle Dare. But Dare could not pay for the mansion either, so Bradley and his family lived there. The Van Tassells moved into a house built by J. B. Thomas.

In 1886, the Chicago & Northwestern Railroad crossed the Nebraska border into Wyoming, and the new depot near Coffee Siding, east of Lusk, was christened Van Tassell in honor of the man who owned so much of the surrounding property. But the name irked Van Tassell, who was apparently somewhat embarrassed to be so honored, according to writer Jim Newsome, because he had acquired the property through marriage. Van Tassell "treated the community like an illegitimate child." Rather than having supplies shipped to the new, more convenient depot, Van Tassell continued to have his supplies delivered to Cheyenne.

The harsh winter of 1886–1887 devastated Wyoming's cattle industry. Swan and Van Tassell found themselves among the ranks of ranchers who had once prospered and now faced huge debts. Van Tassell's liabilities were estimated at $150,000. Although it appears that Van Tassell loved money and sought opportunities to gain wealth, he also possessed strong enough character to confront financial difficulties. Van Tassell refused to ignore his tremendous obligations and eventually paid off "every cent of his debts," according to Flynn.

By the end of the 1880s, the Van Tassells's life regained some of its former elegance. When R.S. and Louise Van Tassell attended the inaugural of Francis E. Warren as territorial governor in April 1889, Louise wore a "wine colored robe en traine," according to the *Cheyenne Daily Sun*'s report of the event. By then, R.S. was a member of the prestigious Cheyenne Club and the Fort D.A. Russell Officers' Club and "patronized the best shops in town," Flynn says. In the late 1880s, Van Tassell's name appeared often in the *Cheyenne Daily Sun*, usually in connection with horses. On May 18, 1889, Van Tassell was reported to have shipped three "large high-bred stallions" from Cheyenne to Converse County. He planned to take the horses to "his large horse and cattle ranch on Running Water, where he has an especially fine bunch of American mares." Among the horses mentioned in the article is Luck's All, a sixteen-hundred-pound Cleveland bay. The five year old "was imported by Indiana parties and is certainly one of the handsomest and best stepping English coach horses that has ever come into Cheyenne," according to the newspaper. Van Tassell traveled with the horses himself to be sure they arrived at his ranch in good condition. Two weeks later, the newspaper reported that Wyoming Territory's favorable climate proved a boon for horse breeding and that horses bred in the territory were "much sought after in all quarters."

A September 21, 1889, report in the *Sun* on horse races listed Limerick, a five-year-old light bay, as winner of both the Cheyenne

Club Cup and the Wyoming Cup. The horse had been bred by Dan Ulman on a Crow Creek ranch, then purchased by Van Tassell and Burhans and Company as a yearling when they bought Ulman's ranch and stock. Van Tassell sold the property back to Ulman but kept the horse, breaking him to drive and working him on a coal wagon. Van Tassell had sold the horse in the summer, but the newspaper reported that he still owned sixty horses sired by the nationally known stallion Tom McKinney, who sired Limerick. Van Tassell's love of horses included a quirk, according to Flynn. He always owned a black saddle horse named Gypsy.

The 1880s also appear to have been a decade of heavy business involvement for Van Tassell. Documents kept by Francis E. Warren indicate that Van Tassell was a stockholder in the Cheyenne, Black Hills, and Montana Rail Company, organized to construct, maintain, and operate a railway with branches and telegraph or telephone lines. Among the organizers of the company were Warren, Alexander H. Swan, Morton E. Post, William C. Irvine, and Charles Anthony. Van Tassell was also a stockholder in the Cheyenne Carriage Company. Van Tassell "is said to have ended up with a finger in every lucrative business pie in Cheyenne," comments Flynn.

Reports from the spring 1891 issues of the *Cheyenne Daily Sun* show that the cattle market was rebounding. On March 24, Van Tassell sold "300 hay-fed beeves at $4.50 a hundred" to a government contractor. This was considered the "prize sale of the season." Not only were cattle values increasing daily, but there was a growing demand for Wyoming polo ponies in the East. On April 3, 1891, the newspaper reported, "Beef is bullion," calling the beef market the best in a decade.

Van Tassell also owned the Wyoming Stock Yards, located at the junction of the Chicago & Northwestern Railroad and the Union Pacific Railroad in Cheyenne. Van Tassell advertised that the yards had good drainage, experienced employees, and room for seven thousand head of cattle. In addition, he kept "good timothy and red top hays on hand" along with "plenty of good water." Van Tassell maintained his Cheyenne stockyard business for forty years. He also operated a stockyard in Green River and sold coal from his Cheyenne headquarters at Fifteenth and Eddy (later Pioneer Avenue)

Streets. According to the *Cheyenne Daily Sun*, an Arizona stockman planned to ship eight thousand steers to Van Tassell's Cheyenne stockyards in 1892 for feeding and branding. The cattle were to be sent on to Montana; their owner had chosen Cheyenne over Denver, where he had branded his cattle the year before.

The late 1880s and early 1890s marked a difficult period for stock raisers because of rampant cattle rustling on the range. On September 2, 1891, the *Cheyenne Daily Sun* reported that Van Tassell had traveled to Fox Creek "to deliver some Wyoming feeders to Nebraska grangers." The report also alluded to the increasing conflicts arising between stockmen and cattle thieves, stating, "In some cases the Nebraska grangers help themselves to Wyoming steers, but Mr. Van Tassell don't [*sic*] do business with them that way." The conflict's most horrifying manifestation in Wyoming had occurred two years earlier, when suspected rustlers and homesteaders James Averell and Ellen "Cattle Kate" Watson had been hanged by several prominent stockmen in northern Carbon County. Ranchers and homesteaders continued to dispute land use rights, and stockmen remained dissatisfied at the leniency of courts in cattle-rustling cases. The issue flared into full-blown conflict in the Johnson County War of 1892.

In January 1892, according to historian Helena Huntington Smith, R. S. Van Tassell, "one of the inner ring of sooners who had long ruled the affairs of the [Wyoming Stock Growers] Association, was sent to Colorado to buy horses for the expeditionary force, a move made to bypass the questions which would certainly be asked if any Wyoming ranch owners started working their horses so early in the year." The "expeditionary force" that Smith refers to was cattlemen bent on invading Johnson County and taking the law into their own hands to stop rustling. Van Tassell reportedly purchased four hundred horses from a dealer in Longmont, Colorado. His connection with the Johnson County War extended to the missing copies of A. S. Mercer's *The Banditti of the Plains*. Mercer, a Cheyenne newspaper man, wrote the book with a strong slant against the cattlemen who invaded Johnson County. The first printing (one thousand copies) of the controversial book sold quickly, and Mercer ordered a second, larger printing from a Denver plant. The second printing never arrived at Mercer's office. Rumors abound, including the possibility of a fire in the newspaper office destroying the copies and the possible theft and destruction of the copies en route. Smith states that one name is specific in the stories about what may have happened to Mercer's books: "[A]n agent of the cattlemen, R.S. Van Tassell, destroyed them…. And through all the hearsay, the persistent smell of burning."

In August 1892, the Van Tassells bought the J.B. Thomas property at the end of East Seventeenth Street where they had been living since 1886. Designed by Cheyenne architect George Rainsford, the property included a mansion, a carriage barn with hardwood floors and, according to historian Gladys Powelson Jones, a greenhouse where "one summer day, friends gathered to pick over two hundred pounds of grapes from the greenhouse vines." The Van Tassell Carriage Barn is on the National Register of Historic Places and currently houses the Cheyenne Artists Guild.

In late 1892 and early 1893, the *Cheyenne Daily Sun* carried reports of Van Tassell's big real estate deal with Chicago millionaire Lesser Franklin. The contract on the sale of the Hillsdale Land and Cattle Company property included 31,400 acres of fee simple and patented land acquired from the Union Pacific Railroad and the government and located twenty miles east of Cheyenne. T.B. Hicks, president of the First National Bank of Cheyenne, and Andrew J. Wright, who represented Massachusetts stockholders in the Hillsdale company, together with Van Tassell, arranged for the sale of the ranch, equipment, and stock for four hundred thousand dollars. Partial payment was made in "choice Chicago real estate, which bids fair to appreciate materially in a very short time." The ranch, established twenty-five years earlier by A.H. Reel, had been owned by Sturgis and Lane as a sheep station before passing into the hands of the Massachusetts owners. According to the newspaper report, Alexander Swan, R.S. Van Tassell, A.R. Converse, and T.B. Hicks owned interests as well; eventually Hicks and Van Tassell gained control of the property. Franklin planned to turn the ranch into a sheep ranch but was to receive one thousand head of fine Herefords and four hundred horses as part of the deal. On March 5, 1893, the *Sun* explained that Hicks, Wright, and Van Tassell struck a deal in

Chicago wherein they purchased seven hundred lots from Lesser Franklin for $390,000 along with 87,000 acres of railroad and government land in Laramie County and an unidentified number of horses and cattle.

Van Tassell's Wyoming land holdings were increasing as well. During his lifetime, he acquired ranches at Islay, North Crow, and Summit in addition to his holdings at Running Water and Pole Creek. Realizing cattle could not survive on the open range without additional hay to feed them during the winter months, Van Tassell began to purchase land along creeks where hay could be harvested. Flynn calls Van Tassell "an early day environmentalist" who was passionate about protecting ranch land.

Van Tassell's first chance to ride with President Theodore "Teddy" Roosevelt came in 1903. William Chapin Deming chronicled the famous ride in his book, *Roosevelt in the Bunk House and Other Sketches,* basing his information on reports from the *Cheyenne Tribune* of May 30, 1903. The president began his famous Wyoming ride following his address in Laramie, Wyoming. Roosevelt rode Teddy, a namesake gray horse, and was accompanied by U.S. Senator Francis E. Warren, U.S. Marshal Frank Hadsell, Deputy Marshal Joe LeFors, William Daley of Rawlins, Otto Gramm and N.K. Boswell of Laramie, Fred G. Porter of Cheyenne, Captain Seth Bullock of the U.S. Army, and W.L. Park, John Ernest, and Arthur Porter of the Union Pacific Railroad. The riders headed toward Cheyenne at nine o'clock in the morning. Roosevelt led the group "at a rousing clip" for the first fifteen miles to Tie City. Once there, the group changed horses at Tom McGee's ranch and headed toward Van Tassell's ranch near Islay. They arrived three hours and forty-five minutes after leaving Laramie and had traveled a distance of forty miles.

At Islay, "the party was joined by those in the president's train, which had made the trip around via the Union Pacific and Colorado & Southern, passing through Cheyenne en route." The Van Tassells provided "a bountiful repast," and the group rested for about an hour after the meal. Upon hearing Van Tassell's full name, reports Charles A. Guernsey, Roosevelt exclaimed, "Oh, you Mohawk Dutchman!" From Islay, the train paralleled the trip of the horse riders.

An account by William Daley in Deming's book says that the last leg of the journey "was made at a more somber pace." Van Tassell rode a buckskin horse. The experienced horseman showed the president a fork in the road leading to a choice of a longer route or shorter, more rugged trail. Roosevelt told Van Tassell, "Lead the way," and Van Tassell chose the rougher route. Some of the riders grew tired before the choice had been made and when the pace increased, "cussed 'Old Van' to a turn." Six miles from Cheyenne, local dignitaries, including Governor Fenimore Chatterton and former Senator Joseph M. Carey, greeted the president and his entourage.

In 1910, Roosevelt returned to Wyoming, spending three days in Cheyenne and then traveling to Francis E. Warren's ranch fifteen miles north of town. Most of the other guests arrived by automobile, but, according to Deming, Roosevelt arrived on horseback at a run, as if he were engaged in a race. Van Tassell was riding with him. Deming writes, "As Roosevelt and Van Tassell drew rein, the former, gazing admiringly at Van Tassell, said, 'The old rascal tried to beat me.'" Roosevelt was about fifty years of age at the time, and Van Tassell was in his sixties. Roosevelt spoke at Frontier Park on August 27, 1910, advocating a monument for artist Frederic Remington. According to Deming, Roosevelt told Van Tassell he wished that Remington had sketched the Cheyenne horseman, and when Van Tassell replied that Remington had sketched him fifteen years before, Roosevelt said, "That's bully. There is no better subject."

Early in February 1909, Louise Van Tassell traveled east and then apparently relocated to Denver, Colorado. Van Tassell's personal check register shows that in August he sent money to the Brown Palace Hotel in Denver to be applied to her account. He also forwarded funds to the Denver Dry Goods Company for her use. By 1911, Van Tassell was sending Louise a monthly allowance of four hundred dollars and covering her bank overdrafts. On January 17, 1912, Louise Swan Van Tassell was granted a divorce from her husband. She accused him of neglect and stated that he never came home. According to Flynn, Van Tassell made no argument. Louise was represented in her action by Cheyenne attorney T. Blake Kennedy who later became a federal judge. Van Tassell's attorney was John Lacey, who also later became a judge.

Van Tassell did not stay away from the romantic field very long. On July 17, 1913, he married Maude Bradley, the daughter of Robert W. Bradley, who had been the contractor for Castle Dare. Ironically, Maude had been raised in the mansion Van Tassell was given as a gift for his second marriage. Maude was thirty-six at the time of her wedding to Van Tassell, who was sixty-eight. The couple was wed in a simple ceremony in the home of Maude's sister. They lived in Cheyenne and entertained at their ranch, spending winters in California.

In 1919, a swinging ranch gate struck Van Tassell and injured his hip, hindering his ability to ride horses. But he continued to manage his ranches until his death in Pasadena, California, on April 12, 1931. His funeral was held in Cheyenne, conducted by the Knights Templar. Although some sources stated that he died in his nineties or lived to be one hundred, he was in his mid-eighties when he died.

In death as in life, Van Tassell exhibited a flair for opulence. He was buried in Cheyenne's Lakeview Cemetery, in a large stone mausoleum. The name "Van Tassell" is engraved in nine-inch-high letters on the lintel of the mausoleum. His third wife, Maude, survived him, living until July 25, 1949. According to historian Agnes Wright Spring, Maude willed the four Van Tassell ranch properties and the mansion in town to the Children's Hospital in Denver, Colorado. The value of the properties was estimated at $700,000.

C.D. Kirkland

Of the photographers in nineteenth-century Cheyenne, Charles D. Kirkland is nearly a forgotten name. A subsequent shutterbug, Joseph Stimson, earned more widespread and long-lasting fame for his contributions to the field through his work as a Union Pacific photographer and other creative endeavors. Kirkland, however, also made important contributions to the photography field, with perhaps his most important breakthrough coming in the darkroom rather than behind the lens.

Born in Bucyrus, Ohio, on the Fourth of July in 1851, Kirkland was educated in the public schools. Kirkland, whose achievements include inventing a special photograph paper, may have acquired his mechanical skills and ingenuity from his father. According to Wilbur Stone's *History of Colorado*, Kirkland's father invented a machine to cut out boots and shoes. Samuel Kirkland died when young Charles was just sixteen years old, and Charles took a job as a paper carrier to assist his mother in supporting the family of eight after his father's death.

Photography intrigued Kirkland at an early age. In 1872, he arrived in Denver and worked in one of that city's photographic studios. His work began to attract attention because he used new methods of working with light. He went into business for himself in 1874, opening a shop on Larimer Street. He moved to Cheyenne in 1877 and worked again in a studio, then set up an independent studio of his own in 1881. Kirkland's unique style soon earned him national repute. Stone states he became known "throughout the entire western country, as the leading photographer of the west." To have a sitting in the Kirkland Studio was a mark of prestige.

Kirkland married Hattie Todhunter in 1883. Hattie was a native of Indianola, Iowa, and the daughter of Lewis Todhunter. Historian Frank Hall, writing in his *History of Colorado*, describes the elder Todhunter as "a prominent attorney and worker in prohibition ranks and well known as a writer."

Agnes Wright Spring credits Kirkland with having taken the photograph of the stage coach *The Wyoming* on its final regular run through Cheyenne to the Black Hills. The Cheyenne & Northern Railroad had been completed in February 1887, thus eliminating the need for the stage coach route. On February 19, 1887, driver George Lathrop drove the six-horse team along the principal business blocks in Cheyenne, then pulled up in front of the InterOcean Hotel. Several men scrambled to sit atop the coach, and Kirkland captured the event on film.

Most of the sketchy information about Kirkland and his Cheyenne studio can be gleaned from the newspapers of the day. On September 20, 1889, the *Cheyenne Daily Sun* reported on an artistic display by Kirkland at the Territorial Fair. Kirkland took a group of pictures "by an instantaneous process," chronicling a hurdler in action. "Mr. Kirkland catches the animal in a number of different positions as he goes over the hurdles and his manner of arranging them is very attractive. A number of faces in his display of large pictures are so lifelike that one is almost inadvertantly [*sic*] brought into addressing the subject." The next day, the newspaper extolled Kirkland's abilities, describing his photography as "containing some of the best photographic work known in this country."

By December, news reports said Kirkland was achieving global fame. He displayed life-size bust pictures at exhibitions in Paris and Berlin and received "highest commendations" for his abilities. "The particular feature which calls forth praise of his work is the remarkable light effect on a black ground which throws the figure to the front." One photograph showed a man who had visited Cheyenne. The reporter thought the picture so lifelike that he said when looking at it, one felt he could "run his fingers through the old man's locks." Kirkland had also displayed an artistic photograph of G. B. Goodell's stallion Belvoir, which looked like "a rare engraving produced by re-photographing the original image on an artificial background."

Kirkland's photos of Cheyenne appeared in an 1891 issue of *Frank Leslie's Illustrated Newspaper*. Included were shots of the Methodist Church, the Union Pacific shops, the Burlington and Union Pacific Depots, a view of Ferguson Street looking north from Sixteenth Street, and Mrs. Erasmus Nagle's house, which was heralded as a typical Cheyenne residence. The *Sun* reported that the first edition of Kirkland's *Magic City Souvenir*, a pamphlet of his photographs, sold one thousand copies in one month. Kirkland planned a reissue of the pamphlet with additional new photos.

As successful as he was becoming as a photographer, Kirkland began to show his inventive side in 1891. The January 24 issue of the *Sun* carried news that he had "learned a secret of inestimable value" and called him a "Cheyenne genius." Kirkland had discovered a new chemical process to create an emulsion for photographic paper "that will materially lessen the labor and expense incident to the production of fine photographs." Although he had thought about the method for some time, he had given up on his project time after time. Then, in 1890, the price of photographic paper increased from twenty-eight dollars per ream to forty-four dollars. Kirkland renewed his efforts to create a cheaper product. His process used lower-grade paper that cost only six dollars per ream. The newspaper reported that Kirkland had worked "ceaselessly during the past three weeks" to find the solution.

Kirkland's new method used less silver and half the baths necessary with the higher-grade paper and so simplified darkroom work. The photographer's discovery generated local interest, especially among amateur photographers. The *Sun* reporter viewed some of the prints Kirkland had created by using his new process and emphatically praised the resulting photos. The pictures turned out clear, with a soft, rich coloring of "tender gold brown and a brilliant black and white." Details also showed clearly. Kirkland "has the field practically to himself," according to the reporter, but Kirkland feared that he'd have to relocate to a larger market area when he placed his emulsion and prepared paper on the market.

One story of a famous client coming for a sitting at Kirkland Studio was reiterated in the February 1891 issues of the *Cheyenne Daily Sun*. English actress Adelaide Moore chose Kirkland over other famous photographers of the day because she found their work unsatisfactory. Kirkland took her picture, made large photographs, and sent them to her in San Francisco. Adelaide's manager, W. B. Moore, wrote a thank-you note to Kirkland, saying Adelaide was "charmed" with them "as they far excel any she has ever had taken." (Soon after, the actress retired from the stage because her career had been a financial disaster.)

Kirkland employed at least one other photographer at his Cheyenne studio and hired a fill-in when he had to be absent. For instance, the *Sun* reported, a photographer named Knapp planned to take "flashlight pictures" at the Cheyenne Opera House on the evening of April 18, 1891, while Kirkland was away in Denver.

In June, Kirkland advertised that color photography was available through his studio, the result of recent experiments with his special photograph paper. The photos were heralded as resembling watercolor paintings. In July, he and his wife traveled to Chicago in hopes of finding a large-scale manufacturer for his photographic paper. None of the offers he received suited him, but he still planned to sell large quantities of the product. Now, the newspaper called him "the premier artist of the west."

By June 1892, Kirkland started manufacturing his paper in Cheyenne. With demand for it rapidly increasing, the *Sun* touted his plant as a "growing Cheyenne industry." Kirkland filled orders from throughout the United States and considered purchasing a building to use in his paper business. Denver must have been a more attractive site for his new enterprise, however, for Kirkland's Lithium Paper Company appears in the 1895 Colorado State Business Directory, located at 9 Sheridan Building.

Kirkland's invention proved timely, for highly competitive conditions existed within the photographic industry. A paper war raged in the photographic industry during the years 1893 through 1895, according to photography historian Reese Jenkins. Three types of papers were manufactured: collodion POP; gelatin POP, of which Kirkland was a manufacturer; and bromide DOP, or developing-out paper.

So how did those competitive national conditions affect the Cheyenne photographer? In August 1899, the Eastman company acquired several paper producers, including Kirkland Lithium Paper Company of Denver. "Kirkland was a minuscule outfit, but with it came the talented Frank Noble," according to Eastman biographer Elizabeth Brayer, "who was sent to Chicago to open a wholesale house and then rose through the Kodak ranks." Eastman thought that the quality of Kirkland's paper "is very inferior and we think that those who sell it will ruin their reputations." The amount that Kirkland received from the acquisition of his company is not known, but shortly afterward Kirkland opened a photography studio in Denver at 1617 Champa.

In August 1902, the *Cheyenne Daily Leader* reported on the Cheyenne Frontier Days committee's need for good photographs of the "most interesting events in the cowboy races." News media throughout the nation clamored for such shots, but few really outstanding photos were available. According to the newspaper, "Mr. C.D. Kirkland says that only two photos of bucking and pitching bronchos had been taken and these were quite old." A sketch drawn by the artist Frederic Remington showing "the horse's feet entangled and the rider's hat in the air" had been reproduced hundreds of times throughout the past five years to promote the Cheyenne Frontier Days events. The *Leader* also explained that "it takes a special camera to do this work and very few persons realize the skill that is required or the difficulties they must encounter." Though local photographers had attempted shots of steer roping, the wild horse race, and bucking broncs, none had been successful and none were interested in trying again. Good photos of the wild horse race, the newspaper opined, "would be worth a small fortune."

Kirkland explained to the newspaper in an article appearing a couple of days later that he had gotten tired of trying to capture the rodeo action in pictures and would not take photos at the current event. He said, "For eight years I went out on the cattle ranges with all kinds of cameras and kodacks [*sic*], and 300 to 400 plates each time, and I tried all sorts of schemes of catching a bucking horse, with very poor success. I would take a kodack [*sic*] in my hands and try to follow the motions of the horse, and pursued my efforts with the vain hope that chance might favor me, but all I got was two poor negatives which have been doing duty in the public prints ever since." The newspaper was careful to include compliments for Kirkland along with his discouraging comments, saying he "has met with success in every field but the one we mention."

In addition to the physical skill needed to capture the action, such photography was expensive. Moving picture apparatus cost a whopping twenty-five dollars per minute to operate. According to the newspaper, Mr. E. T. Nash had tried filming the wild horse race the day before, but his unsuccessful attempt resulted in wasting about one hundred dollars worth of film. In September, the newspaper noted another photographer's achievement in this area. Joseph Stimson had taken several colorful photographs of the Cheyenne Frontier Days celebration.

According to Stimson expert Mark Junge, Stimson purchased Kirkland's Cheyenne studio and equipment in July 1889. Historian Dan Davis says that Kirkland sold his photographs to William G. Walker, who had worked with him in Cheyenne, and the photographs were reissued in Walker's name. The Denver Public Library houses numerous Kirkland photographs in its collections, and the Wyoming State Archives has glass-plate negatives, but it is difficult to distinguish some of Kirkland's work from Walker's as a result of the reissues. Kirkland apparently continued working in his Denver studio through the 1910s. The studio's location changed to 1452 Tremont Place in 1910 and was still located there in 1920. Kirkland died August 20, 1926, survived only by his wife, and was buried in Denver.

Harry P. Hynds

LIFE IS A RISK, but some men and women find risk enjoyable and spend as much time as they can gambling. People gamble on love or in business, as a hobby or professionally. Harry P. Hynds gambled big in all those areas. Though his early adulthood was beset by a tragically shattered romance, Hynds again gambled on love later in life, this time successfully. His business gambles appear to have been successful as well. And, in a way, Hynds gambled on the success of the city of Cheyenne, becoming known as one of its most highly respected philanthropists.

Harry Patrick Hynds was born in Morris, Illinois (some sources say Moline) on December 22, 1860, to Martin and Jane O'Hale Hynds. One of eight children, he was educated in the public schools and apprenticed as a blacksmith, setting out on his own in 1878. "Well built and brawny," according to historian Lee Bowker, Hynds arrived in Cheyenne in 1882. He worked first for Herman Haas, considered the finest blacksmith and wagon maker in Cheyenne, for almost two years. Then he formed a partnership with Jack Elliott. In addition to providing blacksmithing services, Elliott & Hynds also built wagons and carriages. The firm was located on the northeast corner of Eighth and O'Neil Streets.

Hynds was said to enjoy gambling, and Cheyenne's twenty gambling saloons certainly suited his fancy. He also enjoyed boxing and trained for two years before fighting James Lavin in Rawlins, Wyoming, on May 25, 1884. Both managed ten rounds handily, but Lavin's energy waned in the eleventh round, and he couldn't stand up to meet his opponent. Hynds's next fight was with John P. Clow.

Clow knocked out Hynds during the sixth round, and Hynds gave up his boxing career and returned to blacksmithing for a short time. Hynds then gambled on starting his own business, opening a liquor establishment in 1885 at 2004 Eddy Street (now Pioneer).

In the mid-1880s, Hynds began his own saloon and gaming business about the same time that he gambled on love. He married Maud Peet in September 1885. Maud was sixteen and Hynds was twenty-four. The *Cheyenne Daily Sun* in May 1889 listed Maud as traveling to Chicago with her sister, Ruby, to spend some time with friends and relatives. About a month later, Harry himself was traveling on "an extended visit to the east." He planned to spend a week with relatives in Illinois, the report stated, then "take in the Chicago races and then go to New York, where he will be the guest of Nelson W. Wilson of the *New York World*. From the Metropolis Harry will accompany some of the more prominent sporting men in a select party to the Sullivan-Kilrain fight." He'd given up his boxing gloves, but Hynds still enjoyed the sport as a spectator.

During the late 1880s, things looked grand for the couple. Hynds's saloon business prospered. Within the next decade, he purchased saloons and club rooms in Laramie, Rawlins, and Salt Lake City.

Hynds soon became notable for his generosity with his time and his money. He served as a member of the Alert Hose Company, the volunteer fire department in Cheyenne. And in 1886, he donated a cross to top the bell tower of the Academy School, a Catholic school built by contractor M. P. Keefe.

In 1888, Hynds opened the Capitol Saloon at 1610 Ferguson Street (now Carey Avenue). The saloon was reportedly the first business to have an outdoor electric sign when electricity came to Cheyenne. The twenty-foot sign stood perpendicular to the building and contained a thousand electric lights. According to historian Shirley Flynn, the ground floor served as the bar, the second floor contained the gambling hall, "and proper ladies didn't speak of what took place on the third." Hynds catered to the higher class gamblers, according to historian William Howard Moore, and the Capitol Saloon was considered the best and most expensive restaurant in Cheyenne. Hynds had connections with Ed and John Chase, influential gamblers and hotel keepers in Denver, the Black Hills, and Cheyenne.

Harry P. Hynds, a gambler and gaming house owner with a love for sport who became a respected philanthropist. (Courtesy Wyoming State Archives)

Those connections enabled Hynds to enter the gambling business. But in the same year that Hynds opened his saloon, the territorial legislature introduced a bill to prohibit gambling and require violators to pay stiff fines. The bill failed. Moore writes, "More than anyone else, Hynds came to symbolize the power that Wyoming anti-gambling reformers liked to ascribe to their enemies." Hynds, who favored gambling, whiskey, and the Catholic church—considered anathema to some prominent Republicans—continued to oppose anti-gambling measures throughout his life. In January 1891, the *Cheyenne Sun* noted that Hynds would soon occupy a new building. By the middle of February, the place was open and deemed "the finest establishment of the kind in the west."

Hynds's business interests extended beyond his clubs. Also in early January 1891, the paper reported that Hynds (along with A. J. Schilling) had "located the Golden Crown claim in the Silver Crown district" (in Laramie County). Hynds traveled a good deal, apparently in connection with his investments outside Wyoming. In June 1891, for instance, the newspaper noted, "H. P. Hynds, [and] Ed Towse returned from Salt Lake, Ogden, San Francisco and Portland." In July, Hynds and his wife were reported to be leaving for Salt Lake for a month, undoubtedly keeping track of Hynds's business ventures there.

Boxing continued to be a favorite sport of Hynds's, if not always a lucrative one. The *Sun* reported in early January 1891 that Hynds lost two thousand dollars on the Jack Dempsey-Robert Fitzsimmons match when Dempsey was knocked out. Hynds often combined his inspections of possible investments in gold mines, real estate, and the oil business with sporting events. In June 1892, the *Sun* reported that Harry Hynds, Charles Hynds, Phil Kerrigan, Samuel Atkinson, and others planned to travel to Rock Springs for a prize fight between Tommy Hogan and a boxer named Reese. Hynds backed Hogan, who lost, and the newspaper explained, "Hynds only says that he hates to lose his money when betting on the winning man." Hynds believed that Reese fouled Hogan often and poor refereeing led to Hogan's loss. Dubbed "the state's leading sporting man," Hynds was slated to travel to New Orleans in August to see the "three great fights to be pulled off there next week."

If the fights were rough, the gambling establishments occasionally offered more glamour. In September 1892, an actress in the production of "Nothing But Money" stopped at Hynds's place to gamble. The *Sun* report states, "She was escorted and chaperoned. The presence of the party somewhat startled the habitues of the place and all gambling was stopped for a few minutes." Just two months later, Hynds purchased the Diamond Saloon in Laramie. In 1895, he donated the third story of a building he leased in Salt Lake City to an athletic club.

Hynds soon faced a dramatic turning point in his life. He and his wife moved to Salt Lake City in early 1896. Maud had been described as "a wayward girl" prior to their marriage. She had associated with people who "were not the best," but she had improved herself through her marriage. In Salt Lake City, Maud enjoyed the rewards of her husband's affluence and was said to have made many friends through her charitable treatment of the poor, something her husband was also respected for doing. Hynds seems to have spent considerable time away from home, tending his several businesses, and Maud grew lonely in their elegant mansion.

One of Hynds's business trips led to tragedy. Hynds returned home from Butte, Montana, a day earlier than planned, on the early-morning train. After purchasing some cigars, he took a cab home. His key did not work in the locked door, so he had to ring the buzzer. Maud answered the door in her nightgown and greeted him with affection but appeared nervous. Hynds soon noticed some oddities—the smell of cigarette smoke, two empty beer bottles, and glasses. When questioned, Maud explained she'd been visited by a lady friend the evening before. She stood before a closet as if hiding something. When Hynds opened the closet, he found a man— Walter Dinwoody.

Dinwoody and Maud had been suspected of being intimate for more than a year, and his friends had tried to dissuade him from seeing the married woman. She had visited him almost daily at his family's furniture store. After a servant identified Dinwoody for Hynds, Hynds ordered both the man and Maud to leave. When Dinwoody spoke a term of endearment to Maud, an enraged Hynds drew his revolver and shot him. Hynds then called to a passerby to fetch a physician and the police. Dinwoody died at the hospital, and both Hynds and Maud were arrested. A few days later, Maud turned her considerable amount of property over to her husband and took the train to Cedar Rapids, Iowa, her hometown. She was not heard from again.

Hynds stood trial in Salt Lake City, pleading justifiable homicide. According to Moore, Hynds had some help from friends in high places. Willis Van Devanter, who served in 1896 as Wyoming's Republican chairman, let Senator Francis E. Warren know of Hynds's predicament, explaining that Hynds controlled Cheyenne's first ward primaries. Van Devanter asked Warren to write a letter supporting Hynds, whose Capitol business block in Cheyenne happened to be one of Warren's largest customers in his Cheyenne Light, Fuel, and Power Company. Following his acquittal, Hynds returned to Cheyenne to resume his business there.

Warren had advised Hynds "to divest himself of some of his gambling investments in view of recent agitation over the issue," according to Moore, referring to the anti-gambling movement which continued to gain strength. In 1899, gambler James Anderson was discovered using marked cards in the Capitol Saloon. Hynds returned the lost money to those who'd been cheated and refused to cash Anderson's checks. Anderson accused Hynds of not paying his debts and took the matter to court. This situation fueled the ire of anti-gambling supporters, including the "mainline Protestants, the Pietists and the Republican landed gentry led by Senator Joseph M. Carey," according to Flynn. Hynds led the Businessmen's Association, which supported gambling. Although Cheyenne editor E. A. Slack took up the anti-gambling cause and sided with Anderson, Hynds continued to declare that he ran an honest establishment. He eventually won the court case. Those against gambling, including Laramie *Sentinel* editor James H. Hayford, contended that gambling disrupted home life and hampered the state's economic development. According to Moore, Hayford spurred the anti-gambling movement in 1888 and again in 1893 by urging the Albany County legislators to vote for repeal of the statute allowing licensed gambling in the territory. Although the repeal measure gained support from the two largest cities at the time—Cheyenne and Laramie—others in the state did not feel as strongly and the repeals failed. Hayford accused Hynds of heading a gambling lobby that defeated the anti-gambling measures.

Hynds stood accused of dishonesty again in August 1900, according to Flynn. This time he was accused of attempting to throw a boxing match between "Kid McCoy" (Norman Selby) and James J. Corbett. Hynds, whose boxing promotions had become national in scope by that time, had first promoted Selby, then switched to backing Corbett. Corbett's wife accused Hynds of requiring a guarantee that the match would be faked. She reported that each fighter put up ten thousand dollars as security. In spite of losing to Corbett, Selby netted one hundred thousand dollars—a healthy portion of the gate receipts—and fifteen hundred dollars per week in royalties on the kinescope pictures of the fight. Though attacked in the national press, Hynds refused to admit any wrongdoing.

By 1901, Hynds's luck was changing. He again took a chance on love, marrying Nellie Gertrude McGuire on April 11, 1901, in Chicago. He was forty-one, she was twenty-two. His net worth was estimated as high as $150,000 at the time of the wedding. The couple lived in Cheyenne at 118 East Eighteenth Street, in a house built by Amasa Converse. Nell was described by a friend as "beautiful and auburn-haired with a vivacious personality and endeared by all who knew her." Nell "was fun-loving and entertained with a generous hand," notes Flynn. Hynds, "described as Cheyenne's first philanthropist," generously supported Saint Mary's Catholic Church. Hynds and his wife also traveled widely, not only to inspect their various investments but also for pleasure. They enjoyed trips abroad and even visited the pyramids in Egypt.

In October 1901, Hynds was deemed by the *Sun* as "one of the luckiest men in the city of Cheyenne" as well as one of the most generous. The luck referred to his purchase of an eighth interest in the Iconoclast Mine in Halleck Canyon, Carbon County, where a rich discovery of copper oxide had been made, "richer than the best ore taken from the famous Rambler mine," the newspaper stated.

In November, Hynds was listed among the many notables attending Cheyenne's first charity ball. In 1902, Hynds gave one thousand dollars to the Cheyenne Elks Club building fund for its new structure at the northeast corner of Seventeenth and Central. Although Hynds was an Elk, he was not a member of the Cheyenne lodge. In appreciation of his generosity, he was given a life membership in the lodge, symbolized by an engraved sterling silver card.

The anti-gambling movement gained its greatest momentum after 1900, spearheaded by a group of activist ministers from Laramie and Cheyenne. An important factor at the time was a court judgment requiring the Albany County clerk to issue liquor and gambling licenses to the saloons in the grading camps of the Union Pacific Railroad at Sherman and Tie Siding, even though the U.P. did not favor doing so. "Boom conditions in the camps brought on wide-open and uncontrollable gambling, drinking, prostitution, claim jumping, and violence," explains Moore, "some of which spilled over into Laramie itself." Cheyenne residents grew concerned that as the railroad work came closer in 1901, the same thing would happen in their town. The Wyoming legislature finally made gambling illegal in 1901, and the law went into effect in 1902. The law was difficult to enforce, however, and many cities and towns in Wyoming resorted to collecting fines from violators rather than trying to eliminate gambling altogether. On the day before the law went into effect, Hynds—whom Moore describes as long a symbol of "the political influence of gambling in Wyoming"—filed a lawsuit to test its constitutionality. The suit moved from district court to the Wyoming Supreme Court, where a decision upholding the law was rendered two years later.

In the meantime, in March 1902, Hynds planned to spend more than two thousand dollars on improvements to the rear room of his saloon so that "private 'solo' or other games can be played as in the big saloons of Denver," the *Sun* reported. On June 10, 1902, the newspaper reported that Hynds put a large scoreboard in his Capitol Saloon, showing scores from National, American, Western, and Union Pacific baseball leagues. The Capitol Saloon also featured telegraph returns of fights.

In April 1902, Hynds sold his half-interest in the Arcade Saloon on the corner of Eddy and Seventeenth to his partner, Phil Kerrigan, and then the next month made improvements on his residence on East Eighteenth Street. On May 13, 1902, Harry and Nell Hynds accompanied his father to New York en route to visit his old home in Ireland.

That summer, Hynds was chosen to referee a fight between Jack Graham and John Flynn on July 4 in Douglas, Wyoming. After that fight, Hynds signed fighter Jack Root, en route from Salt Lake City to his native Chicago, for a fight with George Gardiner in Salt Lake City in August.

The Salt Lake fight appeared in jeopardy for a time. Hynds, together with M. E. Mulvey of Salt Lake, had made the arrangements for the fight to be held during the Elks' carnival there, but the Grand Lodge of the Elks did not want the public to think that they were sponsoring the fight, so the organization nixed the plans. The fight was rescheduled for August 18 at the Salt Palace. Hynds's diplomacy in handling the matter was first noted in the *Salt Lake Tribune,* which reported that "orders for seats from the entire inter-mountain region are pouring in." Hynds and Mulvey were to name the referee, according to the newspaper. But it was Hynds himself who was chosen when all the parties involved found Hynds satisfactory. "He knows the game from start to finish, having been in the ring himself," reported the *Daily Leader,* "and has acted in the capacity of referee in several mills." Telegraphic returns from the fight would be received at the Capitol as well as the Arcade and Tivoli saloons. Root forfeited the match after suffering a broken hand during the fight.

In August 1902, the Cheyenne city council drafted a resolution requiring the operators of gambling institutions to pay fines, pending settlement of the case testing the validity of the anti-gambling law. In mid-September, the gambling ordinance was passed at "one of the most important meetings of the city council this year," according to the *Daily Leader.* As a result, all persons running gambling games in the city would be required to pay fines of one hundred dollars or serve thirty days in jail. Hynds apparently was not concerned about the action. In December, he traveled to Cody to celebrate the opening of the Irma Hotel and to do some hunting. He bagged two bull elk on the trip.

In February 1903, Mayor M.P. Keefe, devoted to cleaning up the town, outlined his anti-vice policy: "Gambling is honorable when conducted by honorable men. I gamble in my every day life. You do. Every businessman does. Every exchange, every board of trade does. In our political career we gamble." He went on to say that he hoped high licensing fees would "wipe out the dives," and leave the "sober, upright men" in business.

In 1904, the anti-gambling test case reached the Wyoming Supreme Court. In the *State ex rel. Hynds v. Cahill, County Clerk, et al.,* the justices responded to the case reversed from District court. The suit, originally filed February 21, 1902, with Hynds as the relator, asked that the Laramie County clerk, treasurer, and sheriff issue him a license to allow faro and roulette to be played in his establishment for three months from that date. The county officials had refused to do so, explaining that the anti-gambling law of 1901 made that illegal. Hynds argued that the law had not been properly enacted by the legislature and therefore was void. The justices unanimously decided that the 1901 law had been enacted properly. The law stood. Hynds's establishments remained in operation until a grand jury probe in 1903 drove most of the gambling in Cheyenne underground. Even then, enforcement of the anti-gambling law was so ineffective that the issue surfaced in Governor Joseph M. Carey's second term in 1913 when law enforcement officials had to be removed from office for not enforcing it.

By 1909, Cheyenne business leaders began to see the need for a new hotel in the city. The InterOcean was no longer large enough to serve the needs of the growing city. In February 1910, the Cheyenne Security Company was formed with the intention of building a hotel. Major investors were Dr. H. W. Bennett, Thomas A. Cosgriff, E. A. Abbott, Fred Warren, and William Dubois, who was the architect for the new building. The cost was estimated at two hundred thousand dollars; the hotel took sixteen months to build. When the Plains Hotel opened March 11, 1911, Hynds and Captain V. K. Hart were the lessees. The Cheyenne Security Company owned the building, and Hynds and Hart owned the furniture and operated the business.

The opening night gala gave Cheyenne residents a chance to dress formally and dance to the music of an orchestra. Journalist Daze Bristol described the hotel as "magnificent." It contained one hundred sleeping rooms, most with baths and all having telephones. (The Plains Hotel is said to have been the first building wired for phone service in the state.) Hynds's Arapaho friend, Chief Little Shield, agreed to sit for a photograph taken by Cheyenne photographer J. E. Stimson. The photograph became a recognizable part of the hotel logo, used on stationery and china, in a tile inset in the sidewalk, and on the hotel sign.

Hynds made the lobby of the hotel as comfortable and plush as possible, installing numerous leather chairs and sofas. Soon the Plains Hotel gained a reputation as a fine hotel. Wyoming legislators gathered there, and the Indian Grill and Cocktail Lounge became known as "the town's elite watering hole," Flynn writes. Hynds soon handled two of the city's finest hostelries. He purchased the InterOcean Hotel and operated it until it was destroyed by fire in 1916.

Early-day Cheyenne attorney T. Blake Kennedy recalled Hynds as an able and honest businessman, very proud of one investment that paid big for him. "After much effort and expenditure," Hynds bought an interest in the Big Muddy Oil Field. When a larger company offered to purchase his interest and those of other individuals to consolidate ownership, Hynds sold his interest for one hundred thousand dollars. He invited Kennedy to the bank so he could show him the check. Kennedy recalls, "It was the first time I had seen a check of this size and Harry was very exuberant because he had anticipated my attitude in looking at it." With a portion of the money, Hynds decided to construct a new building on the site of the old InterOcean Hotel. He retained Kennedy to examine the title abstracts before purchasing the property for thirty thousand dollars. Hynds "wanted to make [the new building] better than any building in Cheyenne and as good as any building in the country of this city's size." He decided on steel and brick construction, with steel doors and windows. Construction costs were high—an estimated $365,000 for the five-story building. Kennedy and his law partner were offered their choice of office space in the new building, completed in 1919.

Hynds also invested in a gas distributing franchise for the city of Casper in the 1910s. By 1919, nothing had been done even though the franchise had been renewed once. Hynds asked Kennedy to organize a corporation for him, with capitalization of two million dollars, so he could be prepared in case a deal came up. Hynds explained that he might not use the company, but Kennedy could take his fees in stock if Hynds paid disbursements. The company was never used, but Kennedy said it paid him good returns. Hynds eventually made a deal with Frank Curtis of the New York Oil Company, which took over the gas franchise and issued stock to Hynds and Curtis for their interest in the Casper gas franchise. Kennedy recalls, "True to his promise, Hynds told Curtis that he was obligated to give me a portion of his stock even though he did not use the company which I had organized for him." Curtis gave Kennedy the same portion he'd received for his share, about two hundred shares, and Kennedy states his interest was sold "at a rather substantial figure" after he was seated as a judge.

In 1922, the Hynds Building, designed by Cheyenne architect William Dubois, was constructed at Sixteenth Street and Capitol Avenue where the InterOcean had been destroyed by fire in 1916. The American National Bank of Cheyenne had opened at the InterOcean's old location in December 1919, and after construction of the Hynds building, the bank located on the ground floor. Kennedy also had offices here after the building was completed. The Hynds Building has deteriorated but still stands in Cheyenne. Hynds also owned the First National Bank Building (now known as the Majestic Building).

In addition to his business ventures, Hynds continued to be generous to the community, both by donating money and by serving himself. He served on the Cheyenne Frontier Days general committee in 1914. In 1922, he gave twenty-five thousand dollars to the Boy Scouts to help build a lodge about thirty miles west of Cheyenne. The Young Men's Literary Club allowed the building to be erected on land it owned, and later transferred the lodge ownership to the City of Cheyenne. (In 1971, Curt Gowdy State Park was created, and the Wyoming Recreation Commission obtained the lease for the lodge and surrounding property from the city. The lodge, rededicated in 1980, continues to be used by the Boy Scouts of America and other groups.)

Hynds also showed many kindnesses to individuals; his employees held him in high regard. *History of Cheyenne* contains a photograph that Hynds took of Oscar McIntyre, who had worked as a jackhammer operator and a dynamite man on the Hynds Lodge. According to the McIntyre family memories, Hynds took the photograph to honor all the work McIntyre had done. The staff of the Plains Hotel gave Hynds a sterling silver loving cup for Christmas in 1912, and the Filipino bell boys employed at the hotel presented Hynds with a pewter loving cup in 1913.

Hynds died March 13, 1933, in San Antonio, Texas. His wife, Nell, asked Hynds's personal driver, Arthur F. Vizina, to drive her to Texas to meet her husband's body as she was not able to be with him when he died. Nell rode with the body on the train to Cheyenne, but Vizina drove "at great speeds to catch the train at every stop on the way home to check on Mrs. Hynds."

Hynds's funeral is said to have been one of the largest ever held in Cheyenne. More than fifteen hundred people sought entrance to Saint Mary's Cathedral where a requiem mass was said for Hynds. A Boy Scout bugler played "Taps," surrounded by the honor guard of eighty-seven Boy Scouts who paid tribute to their benefactor. Nell was escorted by her husband's brother, Dan, and Judge T. Blake Kennedy. Employees served as pallbearers, testament to the high regard in which they held their boss. His net worth at the time of his death was estimated to be more than one million dollars. He owned the Majestic Building, the Hynds Building, the Plains Hotel lease, stock in Producers and Refiners Corporation (PARCO, which became Sinclair Oil), Carbon Oil and Gas, drilling equipment, and oil and gas interests in Texas, as well as his home in Cheyenne on Eighteenth Street.

Hynds was buried in Olivet Cemetery in Cheyenne. Nell survived her husband by twenty-three years. She inherited all of Hynds's property, but under the terms of his will, everything was sold except the Hynds Building and the couple's house. The Hynds building went to a relative on his side of the family.

In the late 1940s, Nell moved to 2800 Carey Avenue. She was considered a woman of high society in Cheyenne, enjoying entertaining and attending parties. She often had young men escort her to various functions, which spurred the rumor mill. She died May 21, 1956, at the age of 76. All of her holdings were sold after her death. She was buried in Olivet Cemetery next to her husband.

George D. Rainsford

Georgeᴅ. Rainsford was enigmatic. Reportedly sent to Wyoming by his wealthy New York family because they could not tolerate his childish behavior, Rainsford eventually became known as one of Cheyenne's prominent architects and earned national and international renown for his fine Morgan and Thoroughbred horses. Horses were always a great passion for him, and they alone had the power to calm his infamous temper.

Born in Vermont, probably around 1856, Rainsford was the son of prominent New York banker George S. Rainsford. Some sources state he was related to England's royal family, others that he was descended from an English earl. A third source found a Rainsford ancestor in Admiral Bliss, First American Navy. Bliss was the son of Commodore Bliss of the British navy. As a child, Rainsford lived in New York and was educated in Europe as a civil engineer and an architect.

In 1879, Rainsford rode over the area near the current town of Chugwater, leading a pack horse. This may have been about the time that he trailed cattle from Texas to Ogalalla, Nebraska, as he is said to have scouted around the country then. He believed that the area near Chugwater would be suitable for horse breeding because of its climate and because it contained a good quantity of limestone, something which helps develop bone in horses. There was also a good supply of water, along with meadows suited for grazing. He chose a location twelve miles west of Chugwater and established his Diamond Ranch there. He probably settled there around 1881 but did not receive his first land patent until a decade later. The area had first been known as Kelly to honor cattleman Hiram Kelly who settled there, but Rainsford requested that the name be changed to Diamond. Though he did not want to serve as the railroad agent there, he offered to build the depot himself and pay one-half of the agent's salary. The Union Pacific Railroad accepted his offer.

Rainsford exhibited a certain elegance in all facets of his life. John Limburg, a Swedish homesteader, built a four-room stone house and a stone stable for Rainsford in 1885. The stable was of the utmost importance because Rainsford valued the comfort of his horses above his own. But he was no slouch when looking out for himself. According to an article by A.R. Bastain in a 1936 issue of the *Chugwater News*, Rainsford claimed to have camped with Indians on his first night on his homestead. The rugged life was not to Rainsford's taste, though. "It was a pleasure to see him drive into town with his spirited horses hitched to a cart or a spring wagon, whip in hand, reins tight and going like a lord, followed by about 15 hounds," writes Bastain. "He loved to put on style and was often referred to as Lord Rainsford. He enjoyed being classed as such for he declared, 'That's what I am.'" Bastain reports that Rainsford "lived about the same whether he made money or not." Local gossip ranged from Rainsford's family paying him to stay away from New York, to his sister financing him, to speculation that his expertise as an architect gained him wealth. His fine horses also contributed to his financial standing.

As early as 1889, the *Cheyenne Daily Sun* reported that Rainsford was receiving horses from the East. One dubbed a "fine trotter" arrived by rail in early August. By early 1891, the Diamond Ranch entered several horses in the Wyoming Futurity Stake. Every breeder included offered one hundred dollars to the winner "if it be the get of a designated sire." Planners intended for the Wyoming Futurity Stake to become "the greatest 2 year-old event ever known in the West," but the event apparently never came to fruition, though Denver was interested in hosting the event at the time.

Rainsford raised, and trained his horses on the ranch, gaining the most renown for his Morgans and Thoroughbreds. He began by raising an annual crop of fifty colts. As he developed home-bred fillies and imported eastern mares of different bloodlines, Rainsford increased his breeding stock. In raising horses, he was reportedly quite particular. Colts were grain-fed and sheltered during their first winter to prevent stunting, then turned on the range so they could be hardened to conditions. They were halter broke during the winter months; however, the horse trainers were not allowed to use ropes for fear the colts might be injured. Instead, Rainsford demanded that the men walk up to the colts in a small pen and put the halters on them. He considered the safety of the colt more important than that of the people working for him. An enclosed round corral with six-foot walls and about a fifty-foot diameter became the training ground for colts. Rainsford also exhibited his impatience in the colt-raising process. If a colt was too mean to be broken, Rainsford shot it rather than waste time trying to train an obstinate animal. Rainsford also believed that keeping a herd of Angora goats with the colts protected them from distemper; this unusual method apparently worked.

Rainsford trained driving stock, fitting them for service singly or in two-horse, four-horse, and six-horse teams that could work single file or in tandem. After training them in Wyoming, he docked the horses's tails, then shipped the teams to his eastern stables. The half dozen employees there—about half the staff he employed in Wyoming—ensured that the teams could work in the city, too. Some horses sold as high as one thousand dollars. He reportedly earned four thousand dollars for one team of four horses trained to drive with their hoofbeats keeping the same rhythm. Prices for his teams ranged as high as seven thousand dollars, and unbroken prize horses raised by Rainsford cost a minimum of five hundred dollars per head.

Architectural historian Herbert Gottfried sums up Rainsford's equine passion, saying, "His first love, other than himself, was probably the Morgan horse." Perhaps Rainsford's most famous horse was a Morgan stallion named Spartan. Some sources state that Spartan earned the first prize at Madison Square Garden in 1883. The National Museum of the Morgan Horse could not corroborate that information but does list Spartan as having earned the first prize in the New Jersey State Fair in 1875 when he was owned by J. Woodruff of New York. Rainsford referred to Spartan and Spartan, Jr. in the handwritten notes discovered by attorney James Vaughn in 1970. He also made references to Shepherd Farm, Bound Brook, New Jersey. This was most likely his eastern stable site. Other horses mentioned were Vicallia, a mixed-breed filly, and Lady Hattie. Red Bud and Emigrant were well-known Thoroughbred stallions kept by Rainsford. Some sources have also noted that Rainsford bred and sold Clydesdales to the Budweiser Brewing Company in the early 1900s; however, a search of the Anheuser-Busch company archives revealed no mention of Rainsford. He might have sold horses to the company in those early years but they most likely were draft horses. (The Clydesdales were not used as show horses until after Prohibition in 1933 when they were presented as a gift to August Busch, Sr.)

By 1900, Rainsford had built his herd to three thousand horses. He had increased his land holdings to include the nearby LL Ranch and the Hill Ranch, which he purchased in 1902. He also added some state and school sections to his property. In the latter part of the 1800s and the early 1900s, though, the federal government cracked down on illegal fencing. Many homesteaders and cattlemen had fenced in government property during those years. For example, alternate sections of land owned by railroads created a checkerboard pattern of ownership on the land, and many property owners fenced in the alternate sections rather than face the more daunting task of fencing around them. Rainsford was one of many forced to take down his fences, and this was said to have discouraged him so badly that he threatened to destroy his livestock. An employee took two hundred horses into the mountains to protect them from the bad effects of their owner's temper, but Rainsford never acknowledged this kindness. He soon sold most of his stock to the U.S. Army. Some were sent to the Officers' Equitation School at Fort Riley, Kansas. Others were sent to cavalry regiments at Fort Robinson, Nebraska; Fort D.A. Russell in Cheyenne; and Fort Reno, Oklahoma's Remount Depot. Rainsford's brood mares with colts were sent to England, and two carloads of horses were shipped to Japan. Horses bred and raised on the Diamond Ranch earned international repute as some of the highest quality horses in the world. All of Rainsford's Diamond Ranch horses were branded with a small diamond on the left jaw.

Another frequently related tale about Rainsford's temper involves his relationship with God. Rainsford and an employee were driving horses from pasture to corral when a bolt of lightning struck and killed two animals. Rainsford is said to have jumped from his horse and, shaking his fist at the sky, cursed extensively at God. He is also said to have drawn a circle on the ground around himself and dared God to destroy him. Historian Agnes Wright Spring reveals much about Rainsford's personality in *Cow Country Legacies*. She writes that Rainsford "possessed the best knowledge of horse breeding, the best sense of architectural proportion and the best command of profanity in the Wyoming of that period."

Bastain says Rainsford once followed a noted bandit who stole one of Rainsford's prized saddles. Rainsford "mounted his surest horse and with a six shooter on his hip followed the trail and got his saddle back," he explains. The handwritten notes left by Rainsford mention a San Diego, California, saddlemaker and also contain a reference to Cheyenne saddlemaker Frank A. Meanea. He was apparently not as careful with items belonging to others. Mrs. Ogden Whipple, a neighbor, once drove her team and wagon to Rainsford's to retrieve sacks that her husband had sent filled with oats for Rainsford's horses. Rainsford, expecting visitors to arrive in an automobile that day, none-too-politely told her to get out of his yard.

Rainsford considered homesteaders peasants and often expressed his feelings of superiority, a fact that did not endear him to many. His attitude toward food is another illustration of his eccentricities. He insisted that food served to him be flawless, and after the dish was cut into and his portion served, it was returned to the kitchen. He did not partake of it again because he disliked leftovers. In addition to a cook and butler who were with him for some time, he occasionally employed homesteaders' daughters as housemaids. One Chinese cook was known to be independent and somehow managed to do as he pleased during the time of his employment by Rainsford. Sources also often refer to Rainsford's tantrums. When things did not go his way, he threw himself on the ground, kicked his legs in the air, and threw dirt into his beard. Once when a woman threatened to throw a pail of water on him to stop his fit, he jumped up and ran away. On horseback, though, Rainsford was much calmer. Bastain says Rainsford's temper often flared when he was crossed, but at other times "he was most courteous and polite, just a prince of a gentleman."

The princely aspect perhaps came out in Rainsford's architectural designs. Gottfried calls him "the most talented architect in Cheyenne's early days, [an] old-fashioned gentleman architect, who designed things as a sideline, something a gentleman could do." In the 1880s, Rainsford partnered with William Augustus Bates in a New York firm known as Bates and Rainsford. "Rainsford was progressive about design," says Gottfried. "In fact, after he left Bates, Bates's buildings never again had the same flair they did with Rainsford in the partnership." Rainsford designed his own town house in Cheyenne at 702 East Eighteenth Street. His city home differed from others in the neighborhood because he attached the stables to the mansion as was done in the East. Rainsford's unique design intrigued others. His home was a frame house with a sharp mansard roof and set-in porches under rounded domes. He soon designed several other houses of the era for the cattle barons and prominent folk in Cheyenne.

Today, the area containing several of Rainsford's buildings is designated a National Historic Site and called the Rainsford District. The nomination form states, "Rainsford is best known for his experiments with varieties of roof shapes and simplified traditional styles. His influence and that of the eclectic vitality of the age is visible throughout the district, reflected in multiple roof and dormer shapes, ornamental windows with tracery, stained, leaded, beveled and etched glass and in an abundance of machine produced ornaments on porches, bay windows, and gable ends, 19th century American equivalents of European folk art." His designs were widely copied and expanded.

Homes designed by Rainsford included those of R.S. Van Tassell at 921 East Seventeenth; Charles N. Potter at 1722 Warren Avenue (formerly Dodge Street); Amasa R. Converse at 118 East Eighteenth; and Samuel Corson at 209 East Eighteenth. The Rainsford District boundaries are Seventeenth Street on the south; Twenty-second Street on the north; Warren Avenue on the west; and Morrie Avenue on the east. The area includes about thirty square blocks of the original city of Cheyenne. Those who lived within the boundaries of the Rainsford District included A.J. Parshall, who came to Wyoming in 1872 and later surveyed the first Lincoln Highway across Sherman Hill.

The Parshall family lived in their home, designed by Rainsford, until 1930. Other famous residents of the district were Nellie Tayloe Ross, the first woman governor of Wyoming and in the nation; Grace Raymond Hebard, a beloved Wyoming historian, professor, and suffragette; Dr. William Crook, one of the state's first physicians; and Judge Willis Van Devanter, the only Wyoming judge appointed to serve on the U.S. Supreme Court. According to Gottfried, the Sturgis House, home of William Sturgis, at 823 East Seventeenth, was actually a Bates & Rainsford design in the shingle style. The house still stands in Cheyenne, and Gottfried hails the home as "an excellent example of the style."

One of his more famous designs was the Cheyenne Club at 120 East Seventeenth Street. The club, now defunct, was one of the most elegant of its day. The building, said to have cost twenty-five thousand dollars, had a wide veranda, a large dining room, a billiard room, card rooms, a reading room, and a lounge. Apartments for members and friends were located on the second floor. The building was taken over by the Cheyenne Chamber of Commerce in 1927 and torn down in 1936. Bastain relates an incident that occurred during the opening gala of the Cheyenne Club, which shows a different side to Rainsford's nature. Contractors and carpenters had rushed to finish their tasks before the opening reception and ball. The porch began shaking during the evening, so Rainsford and several friends, clad in tuxedos, hunkered beneath the porch on their hands and knees to keep the porch from collapsing as the party-goers left. A photograph published in the book *Early Cheyenne Homes, 1880–1890* shows Rainsford driving a four-horse coach in front of the Lawn & Tennis Club at 820 East Sixteenth Street. The tennis club hosted teas and tennis tournaments and likely was a favorite haunt of Rainsford. He did not necessarily design the building, though. His name probably would have been listed prominently in histories, and brief mentions of the Lawn & Tennis Club do not name the designer. William C. Deming, in his *Collected Writings*, describes Rainsford as a man with a "patrician manner and pointed beard," who built homes in Boise when he ran cattle in Idaho.

In October 1902, Rainsford's temper made news. At Denver's Festival of Mountain and Plain, cowboy Thad Sowder competed to retain his title as championship rough rider of the world, a designation he'd earned the year before. After winning the honor in 1901, Sowder joined Buffalo Bill Cody's Wild West show. Rainsford was chosen as one of the judges for the 1902 competition. Rumors abounded that Cody had refused to allow Sowder to enter the contest unless the judges first promised they'd award him the prize. A defeated champion would not be as great a draw to the Wild West as a current champ. One contestant, Thomas Minor, rode eight horses during the first day of competition. Sowder rode only one. Minor had ridden EA, considered "a veritable little demon," during his last effort. Sowder rode Steamboat, known as a picturesque bucker but not considered truly difficult to ride in some circles. Both men rode well, and the *Denver Post* (quoted in the *Cheyenne Daily Leader*) stated that "the judges lacked the nerve to award the belt off hand to Sowder...." Two of the judges, W.J. Wilson and John C. Twombly, voted for Minor. The other three judges were Rainsford, John C. Coble, and D.W. Wylie. After much argument, they decided that a fair compromise would be to make Minor ride Steamboat the next day.

The cowboy did so in fine fashion, but the newspaper reported that Rainsford, Coble, and Wylie insisted he'd held the horse's head to prevent Steamboat from bucking. Sowder was the winner in their eyes. Another argument between the judges ensued, and finally the two men favoring Minor suggested Sowder should ride EA. The three judges favoring Sowder disagreed, and although Sowder was willing to ride again, he'd been ordered not to, so he did not. The judges apparently gathered around Sowder as if he could make the appropriate decision. Charlie Irwin identified himself as Sowder's manager and said he refused to let him ride again as Sowder had been declared the champion the day before. Finally, the directors of the festival made the judges follow the rules, which stated that on the demand of any two judges, a contestant must ride again.

Sowder rode EA. However, some judges and audience members thought he touched the saddle horn to reseat himself during one of the bronco's particularly spectacular bucks, so yet another argument occurred. Sowder denied this, explaining he'd reached for his quirt and accidently hit the saddle but didn't hold it to pull himself back into position. According to the newspaper report, "Mr. Rainsford became highly indignant when asked if he had seen the trick and refused to answer the question. He also made several foolish threats of dire vengeance if anything of the kind be published." Rainsford was identified as Sowder's employer before Sowder earned the championship title. (Sowder was reported to have purchased both EA and Steamboat to take them along on the Wild West Show's European tour.) He offered to ride again to settle the competition question but said business engagements precluded him from doing so for a year.

Some cowboys were so disgusted by the judges' behavior at the festival that they pledged to boycott the event the next year. Businessmen had begun to withdraw their support of the festival following the 1901 event. The rodeo was eventually abandoned entirely in 1912 to allow Cheyenne Frontier Days the rodeo spotlight. Sowder rode for President Teddy Roosevelt on the chief executive's June 1903 visit to Cheyenne. That event was touted as Sowder's chance to prove himself world champion, and he gave a fine ride.

A news item from the *Cheyenne Daily Leader* states that Rainsford was appointed Laramie County's game warden in early January 1903, and census records indicate that Rainsford remained in Wyoming as late as 1910. Mortgage records dated 1922 indicate that Major Paul Raborg purchased the Diamond Ranch, and Percy S. Hoyt purchased Rainsford's Cheyenne home. Hoyt was a bit eccentric himself. The organizer of Cheyenne's Fire Department was said to have drunk only champagne. He promoted the Boy Scouts by traveling throughout Wyoming in his private rail car.

In later years, Rainsford divided his time between New York City and Daytona Beach, Florida. In New York, he resided at the Hotel Plaza during the summers and wintered in Daytona at the Princess Issena. A bachelor, Rainsford had sworn off women because he didn't wish to be bothered with such nonsense, but, even so, Bastain reports Rainsford employed a nurse during his last fifteen or twenty years. Bastain states, "Singular as it seemed, as head strong as he was, she managed him like a child, and it was by her care and his obedience to her that his life was so prolonged." Bastain records his last visit to the state in 1930.

James Vaughn explains that the handwritten references and notes he discovered were written as late as 1935, the year of Rainsford's death. Vaughn writes, "One gets the decided feeling of a well educated man who had been reduced to the circumstances of a man most of whose friends had long since predeceased him." George Rainsford arrived in Florida on November 10, 1935, and died in Daytona Beach on December 26, 1935, at the age of 79. His body was shipped by train to New York. His funeral was held at the Chapel of the Intercession on Broadway and 155th Street in New York, and he was buried at Trinity Church Cemetery.

Elwood Mead

Children often build boats to float in the waterways. As one youngster played along the banks of the Ohio River in Indiana in 1860, those childhood delights grew into a deeper desire. Elwood Mead's childhood fascination with water remained throughout his life. The water code he established for the young state of Wyoming set the standard around the globe and remains basically intact today.

Elwood Mead was born on January 16, 1858, in Switzerland County near Patriot, Indiana, to Daniel B. and Lucinda Davis Mead. Daniel was a farmer who raised tobacco, corn, sheep, and cattle. The farming life interested Elwood, but he disliked the isolation of rural life. As a child, he read voraciously the books in his paternal grandfather's library, an extensive collection that some considered the "largest personal library in the state," according to Mead biographer James Kluger.

Mead loved the outdoors. As a teenager, he worked in the summer as a rodman for the county surveyors until he finished school. He wanted to go to college to escape from the rural solitude. In 1877, he began classes at West Point, but a bad case of malaria forced him to return home. The next year, he entered Purdue University in Lafayette, Indiana. This choice worked better. His thesis, "Tobacco," drew on his farming experiences as well as his college courses. He graduated in June 1882 and was recognized for his special work in agriculture and science.

After college, Mead worked for the Army Corps of Engineers as an assistant engineer on the project surveying and improving the

Wabash River. Though he lived in Indianapolis, his heart remained in Lafayette. He had fallen in love with Florence Chase, daughter of local banker and lawyer Hiram W. Chase. Mead married Florence on December 20, 1882. They honeymooned in Fort Collins, Colorado, where Mead's former professor, Dr. Ingersoll, was president of Colorado State Agricultural College (now Colorado State University). Ingersoll invited Mead to teach math and physics there.

The choice of Fort Collins proved fortuitous for Mead for the first large-scale irrigation system in the West began in Larimer County, Colorado, and Mead became fascinated with the system. Though water in the territory had been regulated through legislation, the laws were not enforced until a dispute between the cities of Fort Collins and Greeley erupted over water appropriations in the 1870s. In 1876, Colorado's state constitution upheld the principle of prior appropriation of water, that is, the first person to ask for a water appropriation gets preference on the right to that water. Mead was so interested in the irrigation activities that he began helping state engineer E.S. Nettleton with Fort Collins's appropriations. He worked as a part-time watershed engineer while assisting Ingersoll and Professors A.E. Blount and James Cassidy in creating an agricultural experiment station.

According to Kluger, Mead stood about five feet, seven inches tall, "debonair and approachable." He was a popular professor. He and Florence lived in the dorm with the students and were the first faculty members to attend student dances. His classes intrigued the students, and he used practical methods. One of Mead's physics lessons included "measurement and flow of water for irrigation." He remained at Fort Collins for three semesters and then returned to school himself, earning a degree in civil engineering from Iowa Agricultural College at Ames in 1883. Then he returned to Lafayette and earned a Master of Science degree from Purdue in 1884.

Despite, or perhaps because of, his continual hunger for knowledge, Mead remained undecided on his career at age twenty-six. He considered an invitation from his father-in-law to join the law firm, but he tried only one case, which he lost. In July 1885, he returned to Colorado to learn more about irrigation. Though he was unsuccessful as a lawyer, his legal background added to his broad knowledge and helped Mead build his career. He worked again for state

Elwood Mead served as the first territorial engineer, creating the Wyoming water code, which affects the use of the state's water today. (Courtesy Wyoming State Archives)

engineer Nettleton and in the fall gained a position on the faculty of Colorado State College (now the University of Northern Colorado) as Professor of Irrigation Engineering, the first position of its kind in the country. Mead's students delved into the history of irrigation and water laws of other countries. His own research into these areas helped him suggest improvements to Colorado's water laws. Mead also had his students conduct field experiments, showing them how to gauge the water flow of streams and examine irrigated fields. One project included surveying on campus to decide how best to drain streams flowing through the area.

During the three years Mead was working these two jobs—professor and assistant to the state engineer—his reputation as an irrigation expert grew. In a speech before the Farmers' Institute in Fort Collins in 1887 titled "The Ownership of Water," he expressed his view that water rights should be attached to the land. Mead feared a "water-right aristocracy" because ditch companies had engaged in speculative building. The ditch companies believed they could influence land values by holding the water rights because the cost of water increased with the cost of land. This would ensure them grand profits. But in 1888, the Colorado Supreme Court ruled that the ditch companies were only common carriers and could not own the water diverted through the ditches. It is unknown what influence Mead may have had on this decision.

In 1888, Wyoming Territory's political leaders were considering statehood, and they sought Mead's advice. According to Mead's "Recollections of Irrigation Legislation in Wyoming," Fort Collins attorney Gibson Clark, who lived in Cheyenne at the time, told him about a bill to create the office of Territorial Engineer in Wyoming. J.A. Johnston of Wheatland, chairman of the committee on irrigation and water rights, also believed that a territorial engineer was needed. At that time, Wyoming had nine different water districts and "considerable litigation looking to the settlement of the priorities and amounts of water rights, but there was nothing in the law which coordinated the work on different tributaries of a stream or created a record which would show the extent of the state's irrigation development." Mead learned through reading the *Denver Republican* that he had been appointed and confirmed as territorial engineer of Wyoming Territory.

Mead confided to Francis E. Warren, a leading Republican in the Territory, that he was afraid that his youth might hamper his ability to do the job. But Warren encouraged Mead, and the men began a friendship that lasted until Warren's death. Not all Wyoming Territory political leaders were so encouraging, however. Territorial Governor Thomas Moonlight's letter offering Mead the position was written after Mead had seen the newspaper article. Moonlight said that he had not written sooner because he thought the bill would fail, and he did not want to raise false hopes. The appointment put Mead in an awkward situation with Professor Ingersoll, who did not understand that Mead had not sought the job. Mead traveled to Cheyenne to tell the governor that he could not accept the position until he finished the college term. Moonlight told him privately that if he had known that Mead was so young he would never have offered him the job because he was certain the young man would fail. Assurances from Warren and other prominent Wyoming Territory residents convinced Mead otherwise.

Residents of the territory had learned the importance of water during the harsh winter of 1886–1887, when thousands of open range cattle died of exposure and thirst during a series of fierce blizzards. Governors Warren in 1885 and Moonlight in 1887 referred in their annual reports to the need for water for livestock on the open range. Mead hoped to turn the territory into an agricultural commonwealth, using water to irrigate small farms with grazing lands attached and thus preventing the tragic cattle losses ranchers had suffered in the years before. The territory then could become self-sufficient, able to grow its own food as well as sustain livestock and attract more settlers.

As territorial engineer, Mead first had to straighten out the tangled water rights issues in Wyoming. He began the arduous task of examining more than three thousand claims, organizing them so ditches diverting water from certain streams were grouped together and arranged in the order of priorities. "The first thing which was manifest," wrote Mead, "was that the virtue of self-denial had not been conspicuous on the part of claimants. If the amount of water claimed had existed, Wyoming would have been a lake." The task was made more difficult because water measurements were not standardized; claimants used source inches, agricultural inches, California inches, and miner's inches while territorial law recognized only the measurement of water in cubic feet per second. Mead also found that claim locations were not clearly defined. Occasionally they were missing entirely or given in the vaguest terms. A claim for Wagon Hound Creek, for instance, was located "at the place where I now stand." Even with these challenges, Mead believed the chief problem was how the judicial system handled claims. County clerks were responsible for recording water claims, county surveyors measured the ditches, and district judges fixed the rights. Few judges had experience in this facet of the law, however. One judge's decree on a creek mentioned only six rights of the forty-two actual users of water and granted rights to individuals regardless of location or use.

In 1888, the City of Cheyenne made one of the first requests to the territorial engineer to adjudicate the waters of a stream. District Judge William Maginnis, recently appointed to Wyoming Territory from Ohio, had decreed that the first right to water from Crow Creek belonged to the city, and Cheyenne requested that the seventy-five ditches above the city be regulated so enough water could flow into town to meet requirements. Mead found that not one of the seventy-five ditches was named or located in the decree. "Instead," he wrote snappishly, "the decree made grants of water to individuals who might live in Cheyenne, on their farm, or in Hong Kong." He asked the judge how he should decide which head gates to regulate so the city could receive its water. The judge told Mead to look up the individuals and determine from them where they wanted to use the water. One grant inexplicably gave a user twenty times as much water as another without indicating why. Mead explains, "I told the Judge I knew something about the opinions and prejudices of irrigators and that if I attempted to give one irrigator twenty times as much water for the same acres as I gave another, it was probable that I would be lynched, and his reply was that if I did not carry out the decree he would see that I was jailed!"

Mead sought help from Attorney General Hugo Donzelmann (spelled in some sources as Donzelman). Donzelmann prepared a letter to the judge, explaining that the decree did not conform to the law and did not provide enough information for the territorial engineer to prepare instructions for the water commissioner. Further, if settlers could agree among themselves on a priority list of appropriations and ask Mead to act accordingly, he could. Donzelmann's help gave Mead a good starting point. From the testimony given in the city's case, Mead created a list of ditches, priorities, and acreage irrigated so he could help direct the commissioner in doing his job.

Mead took the unpopular stand of advocating public control of water. Early irrigators in the territory had built their ditches without having to ask anyone for permission. The belief that water rights were similar to homestead filings persisted, and settlers "looked on the stream as they did on the air, as something to be enjoyed without any limitation from a public authority, and to be taken just as they shot game or fish." Mead wanted them to understand that the public regulation of water meant that streams would be less likely to run dry and users below could also have access to water.

Some irrigators, convinced that Mead was right, asked him to submit a code of laws to be included in the new state constitution. Again, this task was not an easy one. Mead feared that attorneys would oppose his constitutional proposal because the litigation over water rights had provided them with much profitable business. Under his plan, litigation would be reduced because control of water rights would be given to the state. Mead credited the Cheyenne law firm of Lacey and Van Devanter with helping his proposal become part of the constitution and gave special credit to attorney Willis Van Devanter for supporting the measure. Mead's ideas on water laws were adopted for the state constitution almost as he proposed them. Article VIII, which defines the Wyoming water code, passed with only two negative votes to thirty-five affirmative ones at the constitutional convention held in the fall of 1889. The next year, the state legislature passed a bill allowing constitutional measures to go into effect. Future water appropriators were required to file applications for diversion of water with the state engineer. The engineer had the power to refuse applicants if he determined that the request would harm the public interest. This again did not make Mead popular. He recalled the circulation of handbills around Cheyenne that asked, "Do you want to live under a czar?"

The "Wyoming system" of a comprehensive water code eventually served as a model for other western states as well as parts of Canada, Australia, South Africa, and New Zealand. Though California and Colorado had pioneered in forging western water law, Wyoming's achievement was in giving the state full control of water.

In Mead's first biennial report to the governor for 1891–1892, he outlined the operations of the state board of control (formed in 1891), the adjudication of water rights, the creation of water districts, and the supervision of water appropriators. Mead reported impressive progress, including appropriations on the water of thirty-five streams, compared with appropriations on only six streams that had been settled under the territorial law.

In 1891, Warren—then serving as one of the fledgling state's senators—introduced the Arid Lands Bill in Congress. Warren's bill required that funds received from the sale of federal lands be used to build irrigation projects for those lands. Settlers would be limited to 160 acres of irrigable land. Mead favored this plan because he believed that the states could be more effective developers of their lands than the federal government. He spoke in support of the bill at the First National Irrigation Congress in Salt Lake City that year. He continued to support the concept of cession of federal lands even after the bill's failure and, according to Kluger, despite the fact that members of the National Irrigation Congress remained divided over the issue for the next several years.

In 1894, Senator Joseph M. Carey of Wyoming introduced a bill asking that one million acres of land be ceded to each state if that land was irrigated and settled by farmers within three years. The Carey Act made Mead's position awkward. Kulger explains that Mead was friends with both Carey and Warren, even though the two senators had by that time become extremely bitter toward one another. Mead suggested that Carey's bill be amended to allow ten years for irrigation rather than three, and the changed bill passed August 18, 1894. Although Mead supported government control of water, he opposed having the federal government build irrigation works because he disliked the waste and delays inherent in federal projects. He also believed that the federal government would focus on larger areas and ignore smaller ones. Mead created a state program for the Carey Act in Wyoming and worked with the U.S. Department of the Interior to see that the requirements for the program were properly met.

In his second biennial report to the governor as state engineer, Mead explained that legislators had been reluctant to pass laws limiting rights to water. Because water was "a gift of nature," Mead believed the title to it should "remain in the public," as was explained in the state constitution. "To recognize the right of an appropriator to sell water or to divorce it from the conditions by which it was secured," Mead wrote, "is to make of water a speculative commodity…. It separates the ownership of water from the ownership of land…."

In 1896, the state engineer's office approved six private irrigation projects, the largest being Buffalo Bill Cody's irrigation company in the Big Horn Basin consisting of five hundred thousand acres. Mead surveyed the Cody canal and ran a line along Heart Mountain over what was known as the High Line Ditch. At that time, the project involved 43,000 acres; $36,000 had been spent.

Mead continued his methodical work in creating order in Wyoming's water system. In his report to the governor for 1895–1896, "The Adjudication of Rights to Water," he wrote, "At the outset of its labors the Board [of Control] has had to deal not only with conflicting interpretations of our laws but with problems which no law can prevent being both perplexing and difficult." Though he explained that land boundaries were easy to fix, he admitted that water was harder to define clearly. "We can fix no boundaries to ownership in the stream nor can we give a patent to the snows which may or may not fall next year, nor to the waters which flow to-day and are gone to-morrow," Mead wrote. "The stream we deal with to-day is not that of yesterday, and the supply which meets the demands of this month will not be the same next month or next year. Yet the waters are of value and must be divided. The irrigated home is important and its productiveness must be made secure, not for this year only, but for next year and for all time." He explained that the board's most important ruling had been in limiting rights to water. He noted that several rulings of the board had been questioned, but he argued again that "rights to water for irrigation *belong neither to the canal builder nor the land owner, but attach to the land reclaimed and are inseparable therefrom.*" In making his case for the importance of board rulings, he drew on his earlier research of water laws in the histories of foreign countries.

In 1897, Mead proposed "that the millions of acres of public grazing land in Wyoming be given to the state to lease and the proceeds used to finance irrigation projects," according to Kluger. Through this plan, settlers could buy 160 acres of irrigable land and rent for a penny an acre an additional 2,560 acres of adjacent land to be used for grazing. The remaining lands were to be used to prevent overgrazing by cattle and sheep, and Mead hoped that this would stop the bitterness between the cattle and sheep raisers. Although Mead's ideas earned favorable comments in the media, no action was taken.

The year 1897 was rough personally for Mead. His wife, Florence, died of a toxic goiter, leaving three children younger than seven. Mead realized, too, that he had achieved as much as he could in his profession in Wyoming. By now, he had become more amenable to the involvement of the federal government in building irrigation facilities and decided that he wanted to become more involved. As a result of Senator Warren's influence, Mead was given a job as a part-time consultant to Secretary of Agriculture James Wilson. When Congress approved the re-establishment of the Division of Irrigation in Wilson's department in 1899, Mead resigned as Wyoming State Engineer and moved to Washington, D.C.

In Washington, Mead was placed in charge of irrigation investigations for the Office of Experiment Stations in the Department of Agriculture. This job proved difficult for Mead because his views differed from those of the president's advisors. Kluger explains that Mead wanted the states to have control of their irrigation potential, but the federal government actually became even more involved. Eventually, in 1902, the Reclamation Act passed, creating the U.S. Reclamation Service. Mead felt dissatisfied in his new position and began seeking other opportunities. He taught a special course at Harvard and a six-week course at the University of California at Berkeley in 1901, where he was appointed Professor of the Institutions and Practice of Irrigation.

Following his return to Washington, Mead suffered an accident. He had attended a baseball game and was transferring from one trolley car to another when he fell beneath one. The car ran over his right arm, and he lost that limb. Kluger states that "Mead accepted the misfortune with characteristic good nature, writing [Dr. Wheeler, president of the university] that 'if I understand my field, I can do as well without any hands as with both of them.'" Mead went to Atlantic City to recuperate.

He continued with his duties, surveying water rights and studying methods of irrigation in the West. He learned to write with his left hand and published his book *Irrigation Institutions* in 1903, which drew on his experiences with irrigation and contained a full chapter on irrigation in Wyoming. In 1904, Purdue University presented him with an honorary doctorate in engineering, the first honorary degree conferred by the university.

Mead decided that he wanted to return to university teaching full-time so he would have more time for research and writing. But this was not to be. The University of California could not match his three-thousand-dollar annual government salary. The situation worsened when San Francisco suffered an earthquake in 1906 and budgets were restricted. According to Kluger, the university president asked Mead to relinquish his one-thousand-dollar stipend that year with the excuse that Mead had not paid enough attention to his duties. Discouraged with governmental politics, Mead consulted for private firms in New York and Boston and considered going to work in the private sector.

Though he was restless in his work, Mead found time for romance. On September 28, 1906, he married Mary Lewis, a nurse who had worked at the hospital where his arm had been amputated. Though the beginning of a second family brought promise, Mead's career appeared to have stalled. The situation in Washington had not improved. The University of California could not afford to pay Mead the salary he required. Then officials in Victoria, Australia, offered him a position as head of the State Rivers and Water Supply Commission. They doubled his salary to six thousand dollars, and Mead agreed to go for six months. The family sailed for Melbourne on October 11 and arrived in November.

Mead's job consisted of advising Victoria officials on irrigation problems and settling interstate water disputes. Though he had planned to remain in Australia only six months because he did not want to make long-term commitments that far away from the United States, he found that he liked it down under. Kluger explains that the position allowed Mead a chance to test nearly all his ideas about reclamation. In January 1908, Mead recommended that the state of Victoria enlarge canals and reservoirs to provide a more stable water flow. The cost was estimated at twenty million dollars and included a 7.5 million-dollar reservoir that was to be the largest in the world. The government officials liked Mead's ideas, and he decided to stay in Australia for five years to supervise the project.

Mead served on both the State Lands Purchase and Settlement Board and the Water Commission, and the legislature decreed that both board cooperate in the matter of irrigation districts. By 1910, most of Mead's suggestions to combine irrigation, immigration, and denser settlement to help build the economy were in use, and he traveled to Italy, Denmark, the British Isles, Canada, and the United States to recruit settlers.

Throughout his time in Australia, Mead wrote numerous articles for technical and popular periodicals about irrigation, mainly focusing on irrigation methods in Australia. Mead's regular correspondence with his son Tom, who remained in the United States to attend college, contains descriptions of Mead's projects, information about financial affairs, and messages of personal encouragement for the young man.

On October, 19, 1911, Mead wrote, "The most important news this month is that you have a new brother who is now four days old but who is already able to fight for his grub." The new addition was named Elwood Lewis. Mead also noted that they had a garden, which provided peas, potatoes, turnips, spinach, asparagus, artichokes, maize, tomatoes, melons, and beans.

In early February 1912, Mead encouraged Tom to come to Australia. Since he realized his son's plans were undecided, he asked Tom to cable him his thoughts as soon as he received the letter. Mead instructed Tom to send the cable simply to "Watercom, Melbourne." Tom decided to continue in school.

When no openings in California befitting his experience seemed forthcoming for Mead by the beginning of the year, he began to believe he might live the rest of his life in Australia. In early February, he wrote to Tom, "I am as well satisfied with what I am doing as with anything I have ever done. We have a comfortable home here and I dread the turmoil and unrest that goes with pulling up and settling down again, besides I have reached the age when one begins to think of ceasing all work rather than beginning anew, and unless there is an assured prospect of a comfortable income I am not going to change."

Mead was overseeing thirty projects in Victoria, working long hours, and traveling throughout the state, according to Kluger. The

University of California offered him the position of Professor of Rural Institutions, creating an unsettling bout of indecision for Mead. He liked Australia but resigned his position to accept the new post, which halved his salary to five thousand dollars per year but provided the opportunity to remain a consulting engineer in Australia for part of the year. When the Australian government requested that he stay, he asked to delay his arrival at the university until May 1914 when the irrigation season ended. By late November, his dilemma remained unresolved. He wrote to Tom explaining that while the children preferred to return to the States, he had received numerous commendatory letters from settlers and businessmen and he planned to stay. Yet in his next letter, he admitted that he had not decided what to do.

In February 1914, he again traveled to the United States at the urging of the Victorian government to study irrigation developments and straighten out his plans. University President Wheeler agreed that Mead could return to Australia for two to three months per year as a consultant. Then Secretary of the Interior Franklin Lane invited Mead to direct the Reclamation Service. Mead declined the offer and decided to stay in Australia for one more year.

That fall, the university increased the salary offer, and in April 1915, Mead tendered his resignation to the Australian government. The following month, the Meads sailed for San Francisco. Overall, the impression he had made on Australians had been good, according to Kluger, and the government gave Mead a silver boomerang decorated with a gold kangaroo in appreciation of his services. Mead considered his years in Australia the "most fruitful experience" of his life. He had been able to set into motion his ideas on irrigation and to show that they worked.

More papers, articles, and speaking engagements were part of Mead's work when he returned to California. He became very involved with state government, beginning in 1915 when the governor appointed him as chairman of the state Commission on Colonization and Rural Credits. The intensive survey that the group initiated and prepared focused on thirty-two private land settlement plans in the state. The group collected detailed information from settlers on those properties, asking about the size of the farms, the amount of capital owned when the farm was purchased, the purchase price, terms of sale, improvements made before and after the sale, the amount of acreage being cultivated, number of head of stock raised, and the amount of debt. The commission also asked for detailed comments and consulted bank officials, county agents, and managers of the colonies as well as agricultural college faculties with regard to the private land settlements. The study became the foundation for Mead's plans to colonize California by using what he had learned in Australia.

In 1916, Mead submitted his plan to the governor. It required the state to purchase a ten-thousand-acre tract divided into two hundred regular farms from twenty to one hundred acres each. Also included would be one hundred two-acre farm plots and three hundred acres for schools, public buildings, and a townsite, along with a manager to direct operations, collect payments and give agricultural advice. The land would be prepared and irrigation ditches built prior to settlement, and settlers would need to meet certain criteria, including agricultural experience and access to $2,500 in cash.

Mead's proposal was not universally liked. Real estate agents opposed it because they felt that the plan restricted land agents and private companies and they disliked the government intruding in the normal course of business. But California lawmakers liked the idea, according to Kluger, and the bill passed in 1917 with an initial appropriation of more than a quarter of a million dollars. The solons set up the Land Settlement Board, and Mead was selected as the chairman. In 1918, Mead supervised the purchase of more than 6,200 acres near Durham but found that the appropriation fell far short of what was needed. The early settlers borrowed nearly one hundred thousand dollars more from the Federal Land Bank so the board could construct irrigation ditches as the land had cost nearly twice the legislature's appropriation. The first farm unit at Durham opened in May 1918 and the remaining units were opened by November.

The project appeared successful, and the second project at Dehli, in the northern end of the state's San Joaquin Valley, would be modeled on the Durham community. Mead wanted to expand on his idea and provide farms for soldiers when they returned home from service in World War I. Although he had hoped to earn national support for his idea, funds were not forthcoming from Congress. In 1919, California passed a second settlement bill, set up a million dollar revolving fund, and sent $125,000 to Durham, the first community, with preference to be given to veterans. The American Legion disliked the measure, arguing that most soldiers did not have enough capital and qualifications to meet the requirements, and using funds for only one settlement was unfair because tens of thousands of California residents had served their country during the war.

The Dehli settlement consisted of 8,400 acres costing $800,000. According to Kluger, the price was considered high for its time and unusual also because most of the land came from one seller, Edgar M. Wilson. The preparations for settlement, such as leveling the land and building an underground concrete pipe irrigation system, raised the total cost per acre to four hundred dollars. The settlement board created a factory to build the pipe and employed settlers to install the irrigation system so their wages could supplement income until their farms produced crops. The first unit at Dehli opened on May 1, 1920, and the rest followed over an eighteen-month period. That same year, Mead published his second book, *Helping Men Own Farms.* The book drew on his experiences in Australia and used Durham as an example of planned settlement. Although Mead's book garnered favorable reviews, the two settlements were not as successful as he had hoped.

Even so, private land companies asked Mead to direct their operations, and railroad colonization departments used many of Mead's ideas in their own projects. Kluger concludes that the special advantages settlers received as part of the two "demonstrations" led to their downfall. He writes, "Mead had observed how preferential treatment in federal reclamation opened the door to more and more concessions and threatened to make water users 'wards' of the state. He never seemed to recognize that this same consequence applied to his own scheme." He also failed to recognize the farmers' love of independence.

Despite these disappointments, Mead himself was not defeated. He was appointed the Commissioner of the Bureau of Reclamation on April 3, 1924. His articles on reclamation, irrigation, and agricultural development continued to appear in magazines as diverse as *Country Gentleman, Sunset, Review of Reviews, Agricultural Engineering,* and *Engineering News-Record.* In December, Mead was appointed to the International Water Commission. In the late summer and fall of 1926, he visited Haiti and Cuba to consult on irrigation and hydraulic development.

Though his work took on worldwide significance, Mead never entirely severed his ties to Wyoming, and his writing of the Wyoming water law is considered his most important contribution to the irrigation field. In 1925, during his time at the Bureau of Reclamation, Guernsey Dam in Wyoming was begun. Charles A. Guernsey in *Wyoming Cowboy Days* writes that Mead once told him that the dam was successful from the beginning of its operations in 1927. According to William C. Deming in the August 16, 1927 issue of the *Wyoming Tribune-Leader,* Mead and Guernsey had selected the dam site on the North Platte River, and the two men conducted the first survey for the dam. "Nearly forty years later, Elwood Mead, as Commissioner of Reclamation, was able to crystallize Charles Guernsey's dream...."

Mead continued to write articles for various publications, including those already mentioned as well as *Scientific American,* the *New York Times,* and *Encyclopedia Britannica* through 1935. He was a member of numerous professional organizations, including the American Society of Civil Engineers, American Society of Engineers, American Society of Agricultural Engineers, and the British Institute of Civil Engineers. He also served on numerous governmental committees, including the water resources committee of the National Resources Committee. The Subsistence Homesteads Program of President Franklin D. Roosevelt's New Deal followed Mead's theories on planned community settlements..

Arguably, one of Mead's greatest achievements during his service as Commissioner of the Bureau of Reclamation involved Boulder Dam in Nevada. The Boulder Dam, dedicated by President Roosevelt on September 30, 1935, was part of the $165 million Boulder Cañon project, which also included the All-American Canal and the Grand Coulee project in Washington state. Yet Mead did not ignore Wyoming. He visited Casper in 1934 and toured the

Casper-Alcova project with the editor of the *Engineering News-Record* and H. W. Bashore, the chief engineer in charge of the project's construction. The Casper-Alcova project was first proposed in the early 1900s. According to the *Casper Tribune-Herald*, Mead supported the project from the beginning. Some believed that his suggestion to implement the Seminoe power plant phase of the project helped overcome the many setbacks that plagued it from its inception and turn the work into a successful venture.

Elwood Mead died after a short illness and complications due to a blood clot on January 26, 1936, at his home in Washington, D.C. with his family in attendance. He was seventy-eight years old. Three days later, his funeral was held in Washington, with pallbearers selected from the employees who had worked the longest period of time with Mead. He was buried in Abbey Mausoleum at Arlington, Virginia. His wife, Mary Lewis Mead, and sons, Tom, Arthur, and John, survived him as did daughters Lucy and Sue and seven grandchildren. In his honor, all work on reclamation projects halted for several minutes during his funeral.

The *Reclamation Era* of February 1936, a publication of the U.S. Department of the Interior, contained many tributes to Mead. Among them was a note of condolence to Mary Mead from President Franklin D. Roosevelt, who called Mead "one of the country's outstanding engineers." Mead's assistant in the Bureau of Reclamation, Mae Schnurr, called him "a kindly friend and counselor who made of each associate a competent and loyal assistant." On January 28, 1936, the House Committee on Irrigation and Reclamation passed a resolution acknowledging Mead's work in reclamation. On February 6, 1936, Secretary of the Interior Harold L. Ickes announced that the reservoir formed by recently completed Boulder Dam would be renamed Lake Mead in honor of Elwood Mead.

Joseph M. Carey

An Easterner traveling to Wyoming Territory as a young man and making his mark on the formation of his adopted home—this description applies to many men in Wyoming history. They heeded the call of diverse careers in the livestock industry, the railroad industry, the merchant's trade, and the political arena to name a few. Among them was Joseph Maull Carey, one of the best-known statesmen in Wyoming's history. Carey influenced the territory and the state through his political career as well as through his involvement in agriculture, industry, and community. Carey eventually became known as one of Wyoming's "Grand Old Men," a designation he shared with two other well-known Wyoming politicians, Francis E. Warren and John B. Kendrick.

Joseph Maull Carey, of English-Scotch heritage, was born January 19, 1845, in Milton, Sussex County, Delaware, to Robert H. and Susan Davis Carey, the third boy in the family that would eventually have five sons and two daughters. Joseph Carey received a public and private school education. He attended Fort Edward Collegiate Institute, Fort Edward, New York, and Union College in Schenectady, New York. In 1865, he traveled to Philadelphia to study law with B. F. Temple, W. L. Dennis, and Henry Flanders. He graduated from the University of Pennsylvania in 1867, earned admission to the bar that same year, and began practicing law in Philadelphia. At this time, he also began his political speaking career, stumping for the Pennsylvania governor in his re-election bid in 1866. In 1868, he promoted the Republican cause in New Jersey, speaking throughout the state.

Carey arrived in Wyoming Territory in 1869, when President Grant appointed him U.S. attorney general for the Territory. In this capacity, Carey prosecuted territorial cases for counties that had not yet elected county attorneys. After holding the position for two years, Carey resigned to accept an appointment as Associate Supreme Court Justice for the Territory, a position that he held until 1876. During this time, he served also on the U.S. Centennial Commission. In 1876, Carey also served as commissioner of the territory at the World's Fair in Philadelphia. Because of Carey's work in the judiciary, people addressed him as "Judge" throughout his life.

Carey seems to have been involved in Wyoming politics from the beginning. In one of the odder incidents in Wyoming's political history, a bill proposing that Wyoming's capital be Laramie rather than Cheyenne was introduced into the Territorial Assembly. The bill passed the House by one vote. When the bill came before the Territorial Senate, the number of absentees was quite large. One explanation was that the Cheyenne members stayed away so there would not be a quorum. The other explanation, according to Wyoming historian T.A. Larson, "was that Judge Joseph M. Carey's party for the legislators the night before had left some of them in no condition to conduct legislative business." The six members who were present passed a bill declaring the seats of those absent to be vacant, including that of President Francis E. Warren. The members then passed the capital bill and returned it to the House. Territorial Governor John Campbell vetoed the bill, whose legality might have been found questionable had he approved it. Cheyenne retained its capital city status, first bestowed in 1869 by Governor Campbell and approved by territorial lawmakers.

In 1875, Carey's legal career placed him in the center of a political storm when Governor Campbell resigned to become U.S. consul in Basel, Switzerland. Carey had been one of Campbell's good friends. Wyoming Territory's Republicans, who had argued among themselves for several years, further divided over whether Carey should be dismissed. According to Larson, Laramie banker Edward Ivinson wrote to the U.S. attorney general in Washington, D.C., to complain that Carey was not well versed in the law and did not decide issues fairly. The attorney general then sent U.S. Marshal

Gilbert Adams to interview ten citizens about Carey's reputation. They all supported Ivinson's opinion. As Larson writes, "All liked [Carey] personally; all questioned his ability as lawyer and judge." In Carey's defense, seventeen of the twenty lawyers practicing within territorial boundaries wrote to the Washington officials in his support. Though he was not ousted, he was not reappointed when his term ended.

In the mid-1870s, Carey partnered with his brother Robert to form the J.M. Carey & Brother Livestock Company. Reportedly, the Carey brothers took up the first water rights for irrigation in the North Platte Valley. "In time he built up one of the most valuable cattle outfits in the West," writes historian Agnes Wright Spring, "with headquarters near the present town of Glenrock." Among the nineteen ranches with more than one thousand head of cattle listed in the *Cheyenne Leader* in 1875, J.M. Carey & Brother topped the list, with six thousand head on Crow Creek branded with the "CY" brand. The company took part in the first cattle round-up in the North Platte Valley. Joseph Carey later partnered with Dr. John F. Carey, another brother, in the livestock business. Joseph, who retired from the Territorial Supreme Court in 1876, eventually bought out the interests of both his brothers.

T.A. Larson describes Carey as a large, strong man and a "rugged individualist," terms applicable to each of the three of Wyoming's Grand Old Men. In a series of editorials he wrote in 1873 for the *Cheyenne Leader,* Carey urged churches to find ways to increase attendance and help the downtrodden. He was among the "surprising number of business, professional and political leaders" who were members of the Masons. About half of the territorial lawmakers belonged to this order, in addition to several lawyers and newspaper editors. On September 27, 1877, Carey married Louisa David of Dubuque, Iowa. Louisa's father, Edward, served as surveyor general of Wyoming Territory. Louisa and Joseph Carey had two sons—Robert Davis, born in 1878, and Charles David, born in 1881. Although Louisa was not active in politics, historian Cora Beach described her as "keenly interested in those things which touched upon the welfare of the territory and state, and [she] was devoted to the furtherance of the success of her husband and sons, in their life work. It would seem that her greatest influence was achieved through social contacts and hospitality, in which she was and is, adept."

Carey kept his hat in the political arena. He served as mayor of Cheyenne from 1881 through 1885, focusing on improvements in the water and sewer systems. In 1881, Carey also worked to help create Cheyenne's Opera House. A group of prominent local citizens met on April 16, 1881, to discuss this cultural improvement to the city and, in Carey's words, "to establish and maintain a public building, a hall for the promotion of literature, art, science, music and all kinds of useful knowledge including that class of scientific and dramatic representations which are of an elevating character." Other trustees were William W. Corlett, Tim Dyer, Thomas Sturgis, F. E. Warren, M. E. Post, A. H. Reel, Isaac Bergman, and Henry Hay; among them, they raised fifteen thousand dollars. Warren sold a lot on the corner of Hill (later Capitol) Avenue and Seventeenth Street to the group for twenty-five hundred dollars. A bond issue later brought the public into the venture.

According to Spring, the cost of the Opera House construction was estimated as high as fifty thousand dollars. Capital stock in the opera house venture was set at twenty thousand dollars with shares priced at fifty dollars. The two-story building was made of brick and tile with gray stone trimmings and lighted with gas manufactured in its own interior. The lower floor, rented to the library, became a good source of revenue, and the library hall was also used for lectures and dances. On February 28, 1882, a grand ball celebrated the opening of the new building. Women enjoyed the chance to dress formally, wearing silks, satins, and oriental cashmere and carrying hand bouquets. Tim Dyer prepared a stately banquet for the occasion.

On May 25, 1882, Cheyenne residents enjoyed the opening night opera "Olivette." Again, the festivities bespoke luxury. Guests were given white satin programs printed with blue ink and scented by pharmacist George W. Hoyt. In 1884, the famous actress Lily Langtry appeared on the opera stage. Other performers appearing during the Opera House's heyday included Grace Hawthorne, Sarah Bernhardt, and Charles Dickens, Jr., who gave a reading.

Joseph M. Carey, one of Wyoming's best-known politicians, introduced the bill for statehood while serving as territorial delegate to Congress. (Courtesy Wyoming State Archives)

A notorious event during Carey's term as mayor shows a seamier side of western culture. It was also apparently the only time that Carey's talent for public speaking proved useless. In 1883, Henry Mosier was lynched—hanged from a telephone pole at Nineteenth and Eddy (later Pioneer) Streets. He was accused of murdering a man and wounding another in an attempted robbery three miles north of Cheyenne. According to Charles Guernsey, Mosier had left the Black Hills with two other men headed to southern Colorado.

They traveled from Fort Laramie to Cheyenne, camping the last night near Camp Carlin, not far from Cheyenne. Mosier hit each of the two men on the head with an ax while they slept. Believing that he had killed them both, Mosier rode away. One man recovered sufficiently to identify Mosier, who was caught in northern Colorado and brought back to Cheyenne. Charles Guernsey writes that Mayor Carey was called from his home "and expostulated from a box near the [telephone] pole being used but it was too late and [his speech] fell on deaf ears as to both Mosier and the crowd."

Carey overlapped his term as mayor with service to another organization, the Wyoming Stock Growers Association. Carey served as president of the WSGA from 1883 through 1888, one of the most prosperous eras for the Wyoming cattle industry. Larson estimates that Wyoming's cattle numbered 1.5 million at that time, each worth thirty dollars or more. More than five hundred people attended the group's annual convention in 1884, including representatives of the Chicago commission houses, transportation interests, and suppliers of Texas longhorns. When the WSGA honored its treasurer, Thomas Sturgis, that year, they presented him with a gold-lined Tiffany sterling punch bowl and two sterling silver candelabra.

During the 1880s, Carey's political career was on the rise. In 1884, Wyoming Territory citizens elected him to the Forty-Ninth Congress as the territorial delegate. (Francis E. Warren had declined the nomination to the post, preferring an appointment as territorial governor.) Carey wrote to the Secretary of the Interior in January 1885 approving Warren's appointment, saying in part, "[W]hile the Territory has had many good officers sent here, so many miserable fellows have, from time to time, crept in that the people are sick at heart. They do not want a sick man or a politician sent from elsewhere." Carey also admitted that Warren was so well known that the Democrats would not likely try to have him removed.

Busy as he was with public life, Carey did not neglect his home life. In 1885, the Careys built an elegant house at 2119 Ferguson Street (now Carey Avenue). The three-story mansion, constructed of cut stone and brick, had bay windows, large porches, and ornate trimmings. The interior decorations included fireplaces, frescoed ceilings, crystal chandeliers, parquet floors, and a gold-embossed wallpaper design. The home was considered one of the most elaborate of its time. The Carey mansion was at least once threatened by fire, according to information contained in the book *Early Cheyenne Homes*. Young Robert and Charles Carey decided to learn how to smoke on the third floor of the house but ran outside to play when they heard someone coming. The house caught fire, and Louisa Carey, panicking, telegraphed Joseph in Washington to tell him the house was on fire and to ask him what to do. His straightforward answer? "Put it out."

During the first session of the Forty-Ninth Congress, in 1886, Carey introduced twenty-seven bills and joint resolutions, including bills to improve and repair the penitentiary at Laramie, to establish a new land district in the territory, to enlarge the jurisdiction of probate courts in the territory, to set the number of Council and House representatives for the territory, to allow the completion of Fort D.A. Russell, and to allow the erection of the capitol in Cheyenne. He advocated the admission of an additional Supreme Court associate justice to the territorial court, a land grant for a hospital for the insane, and the leasing of school lands. He also urged amendment to the act providing for the sale of desert lands in certain states and territories, and an amendment to land grants provided for universities in Dakota, Montana, Arizona, Idaho, and Wyoming. Carey's impressive work as a territorial delegate for the first session fills a half-page in the *Index to the Congressional Record*.

Carey's primary objective during his early years as Wyoming's territorial delegate, according to historian George Paulson, was to "try to stop unfavorable land legislation. [Carey] endeavored at the same time to secure favorable land laws for the West. A concomitant task was to educate the Eastern members of Congress about the unique problems pertaining to Western land."

In late June 1886, Carey spoke to the House of Representatives on behalf of protecting public lands. Upset by the negative attitude toward cattlemen spouted in the House, Carey defended his fellow stock raisers. He commented that the Wyoming Stock Growers Association was probably the largest organization of its kind in the world, explaining that the association represented "at least one hundred million dollars of wealth invested in cattle, horses, and sheep in the arid regions of the United States." Members in the WSGA hailed from twenty-five states and territories, he said. Further, Carey pointed out, "The men who conduct this business are just as honorable and upright, have as much business honor, and love their country just as well as the members of this House."

Carey defended cowboys, who various members of Congress believed to be scalawags. "I do not believe that you can find among any class of men engaged in any employment in the East fewer dishonest men than among that class of men in my country that we call 'cowboys,'" he said. "They are too fond of fair play to interfere with any class of settlers. They come from too intelligent a class to be made the dupes of their employers if their employers should attempt to use them for dishonest purposes. They live a free and generous life, and as they grow older drift into other pursuits. In my country it is not a disgrace to be called a 'cowboy.'"

In 1883, Carey himself had filed on a 160-acre timber claim twenty-five miles north of Cheyenne. He planted thirty thousand trees—including white ash, white elm, and box elders—in 1885. According to Larson, Carey testified that all the trees died because of drought and hail even though he had irrigated and cultivated them. He planted twenty-seven thousand cottonwoods, and again most of these trees died. Still, Carey did not give up easily. He continued his tree-growing attempts for many years, and after 1896, Carey estimated he had between one thousand and twelve hundred growing trees, but only about four hundred of those were healthy. He earned his patent in 1896 but believed the requirements of the 1873 Timber Culture Act were impossible to meet in the arid regions of the country.

On July 19, 1886, Carey again addressed the House of Representatives, urging passage of a desert-land law. Federal land policy, he argued, had made it "possible for every man who had the money to go into the market and buy a piece of land, or if he wanted to go out West, to buy public land at $1.25 an acre, or make settlement under the homestead law. Our theory has been that it is best for every man to control and own his home. This policy has caused the people of these United States to love their country, to take a deep interest in its welfare, because they are part and parcel of it."

On February 27, 1888, Carey introduced the most important legislation of his life in the House of Representatives—a bill to admit Wyoming Territory as a state. The bill did not proceed further. Colorado's Senator Teller introduced a similar bill in the Senate in March, but that bill languished for more than a year in the hands of the Committee on Territories. During that time, Carey, always a proponent of settlement, offered pioneers the opportunity to buy land in the new town of Casper. In the fall of the year, the J.M. Carey & Brother company offered for sale alternate lots in the newly platted town. The Wyoming Central Railroad owned the other lots and had built track into the city that year so the town could serve as a terminal for shipping cattle. The first passenger train arrived June 15, 1888, before the town had actually been surveyed. Larson explains that Carey's lots sold at low prices, but even so, buyers did not jump at the chance to purchase the land in the frontier town.

In autumn of 1888, Carey sought re-election as the territorial representative against Democrat Caleb Perry Organ. In this campaign, Carey's public speaking skills again proved useful. Carey, according to Larson, "could speak at great length, cogently and effectively, though making no attempt at flowery oratory" even though his copious use of statistics caused local newspapers to complain that his speeches were too dry to be of interest. Organ, on the other hand, who had little public speaking experience, had another man speak in his stead. In this race, the question of statehood played only a small part, according to Larson. Republicans supported the measure, while Democrats generally opposed it. Carey handily gained the seat, winning by nearly three thousand votes.

In 1889, as public enthusiasm for the WSGA waned, Carey urged the group to promote the cattle business and to allow small herd owners to join the association. This was a controversial proposal because of the tensions between large and small operators. Owners of large cattle herds often grazed their herds on public lands, and conflict ensued when homesteaders selected their claims from those lands. Those who owned large herds suspected the smaller operators of keeping strays from the large herds as their own; they also resented the homesteaders' presence on what the large stockmen considered their grazing properties. The harsh winter of 1886–1887, when many producers lost most of their herds, also had a detrimental effect on the stock growers' organization. Despite Carey's plea, the stockmen did not embrace his idea, and smaller operators did not rush to join the WSGA.

Meanwhile, in Congress, the statehood measure continued to be discussed. In December 1888, Democrats offered an omnibus bill, hoping to trade three Republican states for the admission of New Mexico. A separate bill to admit Wyoming as a state was also introduced. In February 1889, the Republican territories of Washington, Montana, and the Dakotas were admitted, but the Wyoming statehood bill still did not proceed to the House floor. Congress adjourned before taking action on the admission of Wyoming, but this gave territorial residents time to write a constitution and vote to approve it, enhancing the chances of statehood when the bill next came under consideration by Congress. Territorial Governor Francis E. Warren, appointed to his position in March, emphatically urged territorial citizens to support statehood in his inaugural address of April 9, 1889.

Carey and his wife, Louisa, attended the inaugural celebration for Warren. According to newspaper reports, Warren rode in a four-horse landau, with Carey and District Judge Micah Saufley following in an open landau, and Warren's wife and children behind them. The newspaper also made mention of the women's attire at the elegant inaugural ball. Louisa Carey, for example, known for her dignified appearance, wore a "Worth gown, rose point petticoat, court train of cream colored moire antique with reverses of brocade satin moire, waist decollete with deep beretra of point lace, hair worn high, dressed with apple blossoms, pearl necklace, diamond ornaments."

On the day of Warren's inaugural, the *Cheyenne Daily Sun* interviewed Carey, who enthusiastically endorsed statehood, saying, "Since the first agitation of the state question I have taken no middle ground. I am in favor, as is well known, of state government at the earliest possible time." He believed that ninety-five percent of the voters of the territory favored statehood, and he approved of the state government formation bill, saying it provided equal representation to all parts of the territory. Carey explained, "Wyoming has reached that condition when she can be compared to a boy made of the right material who is just approaching his majority and who has in him the elements of a strong man; he rejoices that he is about to cast off the disfranchisement of his minority. He does not dread or shirk the responsibilities of a mature manhood. So with Wyoming. She has the strength, she has courage and does not stand in fear of the responsibilities that would arise under state government."

In September 1889, a Constitutional Convention was held. An especially hot issue was the question of continuing suffrage for women. The debate ended in the decision to grant women suffrage even though some believed that the territory ran the risk of being refused admission because of this provision.

While most historians have written of Wyoming's statehood movement as popular and nonpartisan, Carey's correspondence with Territorial Supreme Court Chief Justice Willis Van Devanter indicates that partisan politics were very much at work. Democrats realized that their original opposition to the statehood movement had proved to be an error and that, if statehood were gained, Republicans would probably become the governmental leaders. As a result, according to historian Lewis Gould, the Democrats "did as little as possible for statehood." The Republicans, meanwhile, dared not upset voters by acting in any highly partisan fashion because the Constitutional Convention was hailed as a nonpartisan effort. The result was general apathy. "Regarded as a politician's movement," Gould comments, "the effort for the admission of Wyoming aroused little enthusiasm until it was on the brink of success."

On December 20, 1889, two days after a presentation on behalf of statehood in the U.S. House of Representatives, Carey wrote to Van Devanter, saying, "I have made good head way in the State matter, and so far as the Republicans are concerned the way will be comparatively smooth. If the prominent Democrats of the Territory do their duty, we will get into the Union." The *Cheyenne Daily Sun* reported on Carey's speech, calling it a "very complete and exhaustive argument for the admission of Wyoming." Despite Carey's remarks before Congress, his good press, and the apparent support of the residents of the territory, voter turnout (though favorable) in

November for the special election held to ratify the Wyoming Constitution was light.

On January 24, 1890, Carey wrote to Van Devanter, that the statehood matter was progressing, saying, "I am making a point every day and from the present outlook the bill will go through the Senate very soon with little or no opposition." Carey also admitted, "I feel that I am receiving but little assistance from the people of Wyoming in this fight.… Now I do not care whether a man comes here from Wyoming Territory, but I am entitled to the assistance of the press and of the Wyoming Legislature in this fight. I am far ahead of the others in the fight, though I have had to go it single handed." Carey thought that the statehood bill would pass through the Senate "with little friction," but noted that he thought he could get the bill through the House by a Republican vote only, if it were necessary to do so.

In February 1890, Delegate Carey addressed the House Committee on Territories regarding Wyoming's statehood. The bill passed through the committee favorably, even though the minority leader on the committee, William Springer of Illinois, "disapproved of Wyoming, woman suffrage, and the admission of new Republican states," according to Gould. In early March, Carey wrote to Van Devanter, explaining Springer's attempt to organize opposition for the Wyoming statehood bill. Nevertheless, Carey remained optimistic. On March 15, he wrote that the "state matter, up to this point is in the best possible shape." On March 24, 1890, Carey also mentioned his own political career possibilities, saying, "Just as soon as I can get time I will write you very fully and candidly and without mental reservation, about the political preferment for myself in case the State bill should become a law."

On March 26, 1890, Carey addressed the House of Representatives regarding H.R. 982, the bill providing for Wyoming's statehood. His remarks included lengthy references to the Ordinance of 1787, which controlled the development of federal lands northwest of the Ohio River. He spoke of Wyoming's resources, including grazing interests, forests, and minerals, and explained the territory's advances in education, institutions and banking interests, financial matters, postal services, and railroad building accomplishments. In response to questions about woman suffrage, Carey said, "Woman suffrage is not a new question. It is not repugnant to the Constitution of the United States." He noted that New Jersey became a state with woman suffrage, although the privilege was revoked in 1807. He closed by saying, "Many of yours are old and powerful States. Wyoming, young and enterprising, rich in resources, with Western ambition and strength, will hasten to overtake you, and at your side bear a State's share of the burdens and responsibilities of the Republic."

With statehood imminent, Wyoming Republicans hoped to control the congressional seats that would come with admission. Carey was an obvious choice to fill one of them, and Van Devanter had apparently indicated that he felt Carey should announce as a candidate for a Senate seat soon. Carey explained, "I have never wanted to consider myself a prospective candidate for the Senate or any other place that would be open by reason of Wyoming becoming a state." But he left the door open, stating, "I do not expect to stand in anybody's way, while I do expect to assist in carrying the new state into the haven of the Republican Party." He suggested that Republicans should run an offensive campaign and put the Democrats on the defensive side. By June, Carey commented that "It looks to me as if the Democrats in Wyoming are doing just what I imagined they would do, exhausting themselves now, making fools of themselves."

After the House voted to admit Wyoming, the Senate passed the bill on June 27, 1890. President Benjamin Harrison signed the act on July 10, 1890, making Wyoming the forty-fourth state.

Several celebrations of statehood occurred soon after the bill was made law. Carey's arrival in Cheyenne sparked the fifth of such festive events. The *Cheyenne Daily Sun* on July 27, 1890, carried enthusiastic reports of Carey's return to the new state he'd helped create. Residents "of every class and degree" and "[m]echanics, artisans, business men and professional men left their avocations and rushed to the depot" to greet him. Carey was whisked to a nearby carriage after enjoying a hearty round of handshaking. An impromptu parade consisting of the Union Pacific band and members of the Grand Army of the Republic escorted him to his home. The band played, "Marching through Georgia," and bystanders cheered and sang all along the route. Upon his arrival, the marching line separated into two ranks, flanking Carey as he walked from the carriage to his house. According to the newspaper report, "On his reaching the portico, three times three rousing cheers filled the air, the band struck up anew and the judge with evident surprise stood gazing upon the audience around him." After a time, when the crowd quieted, Carey gave his remarks.

He said in part, "I am happy that the auspicious day has come when I can rejoice with you, and we can rejoice together over what has been accomplished—the realization of our most daring hopes and proudest anticipations." He credited the people with earning the achievement of statehood, saying, "I am with you today to take you by the hand as a citizen, a neighbor and as one of the people, to help uphold the destinies of our state and to labor for its welfare with you, until it shall be one of the best, proudest and greatest states of our common country." The crowd broke into cheers again and then dispersed for the afternoon. That evening, the Union Pacific band again serenaded the Careys, who were "visited by hundreds of their neighbors and friends who assembled to pay their respects and extend their congratulations." A Republican caucus followed in a local saloon because Republicans were anxious to plan for the first state election, slated for September.

Carey ran for U.S. Senator and was elected to that office by the legislature in November. Francis E. Warren was elected to the other senatorship on the seventh ballot. He resigned as governor, and Amos Barber became acting governor of the new state. Senate terms were decided by lots in Washington, with Carey drawing the longer term of four years and Warren slated to serve for two.

In the 1890s, according to Larson, Democrats began referring to Carey and Warren as "Me and F.E." Both Republican leaders were in their mid-forties, and although the Democrats tried, "they could not find two men in the Democratic Party with the prestige and ability of Me and F.E." The two Senators from Wyoming became "conservative spokesmen for western interests."

In 1891, both Senators voted against the free coinage of silver, even though the measure had popular support in the west. Carey believed that the United States should stick to the gold standard until all the nations of the world came to agreement on rationing silver in accordance with the current gold standard of the United States or through an international monetary congress. Both Carey and Warren attracted the attention of the press through their vote on this issue. According to Larson, the Republican papers defended the senators' unpopular stance by arguing they would have preferred free coinage of American silver but they did not want this privilege extended throughout the world.

In Washington as in Wyoming, the era signified opulence, and Louisa Carey's refined social skills proved helpful. In February 1891, Mrs. Carey and Mrs. Warren welcomed four to five hundred callers at an afternoon reception at the Arlington Hotel in Washington, D.C. Guests included Mr. and Mrs. Theodore Roosevelt, Mrs. Leland Stanford, many senators and their wives, and military personnel. The women's attire again earned press coverage. For the reception, Louisa Carey wore a "court train of garnet velvet over petticoat of silver gray brocade, with silver passementaries." Mrs. Warren dressed in a "court train of black velvet with point lace and diamonds."

Later that month, Warren introduced the Arid Lands Bill in the Senate, advocating that the government transfer arid lands to the states. Although the Senate adjourned without taking action on the bill, Carey called it "one of the most important measures that has been before congress in years."

In May 1891, on his return to Wyoming, the *Sun* reported him in "excellent health and high spirits" and quoted him as saying that his distillery-fed beeves at the Chicago stockyards sold for more than seventy dollars per head. Similar cattle of his had sold the previous fall for twenty-seven dollars per head, according to the report. Later in the month, Carey, along with Warren and State Engineer Elwood Mead, attended the Trans-Mississippi Congress in Denver. The congress passed resolutions favoring the arid land bill and free coinage of silver.

While in Wyoming, the Careys focused on home life and the family's agricultural interests. Louisa Carey escaped serious injury in early July when the horse pulling her carriage fell into an open trench. Louisa was badly frightened but not hurt and the horse was rescued. Apparently the senator had not accompanied his wife on this particular outing. On July 30, 1891, the *Sun* reported that Carey and his brother Robert had stopped in Wheatland en route to Cheyenne from the CY Ranch in Natrona County to view the new government experiment station established by the University of Wyoming.

Carey's dream of successfully irrigating arid lands also began to blossom. In August 1891, the *Sun* carried information on the Wyoming Development Company, which had been formed in 1883, with Carey as president. Others involved in the company's formation were William C. Irvine, Horace G. Plunkett, John W. Hoyt, Morton E. Post, Francis E. Warren, and Andrew Gilchrist. The company was organized with one million dollars capital. According to the news report, the objective was "to reclaim the land by conducting water through a canal from the Laramie river, tapping that stream at a point twenty miles from the edge of the farming tract, then distribute the water through laterals. It was a grand colonization scheme." Each settler would have "a generous farm, with pieces of meadow and grazing thrown in." As a result, "[t]his portion of the territory would become self-supporting, and while a considerable town would grow up on the land everything would be tributary to Cheyenne." Though the newspaper claimed that Carey and Gilchrist had been discouraged at times, the situation looked brighter now, with seventy-nine patents covering fifty thousand acres having been issued at the land office. The company had title to the tract of land beneath the irrigation ditch, and it was ready to welcome settlers to the new colony of Wheatland. The project was not immediately successful, but by 1900 the community of Wheatland began to thrive.

In August 1892, the *Sun* carried an editorial about Senator Carey showing a gentler side to his personality. The newspaper explained that Carey returned annually to Milton, Delaware, where he was raised, "and kept alive the affection for friends and associates of his youth. Senator Carey thinks no better people ever lived than those among whom he spent the days of his childhood." Perhaps this was a precursor to the coming political campaign and was meant to help soothe feathers Carey had ruffled when he again voted against free coinage of silver in July 1892. According to Larson, Carey and Warren evoked the wrath of Democrats and Populists by voting against the measure, and the two senators "were hanged in effigy in Ogden, Utah, as enemies of the West."

In the election of 1892, even though he was not seeking re-election himself, Carey campaigned for the Republicans, speaking throughout the state and generating much enthusiasm. At a mid-October appearance in Rock Springs, according to the *Sun*, the Republican candidates enjoyed a fete with a parade "nearly a mile long, with 150 torches, which illuminated the entire city. There were ladies on horseback, in carriages and on foot. Twenty handsome young ladies were dressed in neat uniforms and drilled to perfection, [and] attracted great attention." At the October 20 campaign rally at the Cheyenne Opera House, several hundred men stood and ladies filled four boxes to listen to the speakers, addressing the crowd on the "stage profusely decorated with flags and pictures of [President] Harrison." At the final campaign rally in Cheyenne in November, Carey served as chairman of the meeting where "a perfect storm of applause greeted him."

Carey's most important legislation during the second half of his term was the Carey Act of 1894. Under this act Larsen writes, "a million acres of government land were given to Wyoming to be reclaimed by irrigation. Wyoming offered to prospective settlers cheap land, water for irrigation, and a share in the canal. Settlement could actually be regulated by the state, and the public could be protected against speculation in land and water." Also in 1894, Carey earned a personally satisfying award. He was made honorary chancellor of his alma mater, Union College in Schenectady, New York, and awarded an honorary Doctor of Law degree.

In 1894, though Carey again wanted to serve as U.S. senator, he didn't gain any votes in either the Republican caucus or the public voting. Francis E. Warren and Clarence Clark, an Evanston attorney, were elected as Wyoming's senators. This was partly due to Carey's stand on silver—he had been criticized for being a "gold bug" because of his unpopular loyalty to the gold standard. Warren, an astute politician, reverted to the will of the people on the silver issue.

According to Larson, editors E. A. Slack of the *Cheyenne Sun* and James Hayford of the *Laramie Sentinel,* two of the most influential Republicans in the state, threw their support to Warren. Carey retaliated by purchasing the *Wyoming Tribune,* although his efforts by this point were too late to assist him in winning the campaign. Perhaps having the outlet of newspaper ownership and thus a public mouth-piece with which to criticize the winning faction assuaged Carey's disappointment. Carey's enormous popularity during the statehood movement had faded fast. Gould states, "Within four years (of Wyoming statehood), a combination of circumstances, including the Johnson County War, the Democratic victory in 1892, the silver issue, and the superior political skill of Francis E. Warren, cost Carey his Senate seat." Carey and Warren broke ties with each other over this political upheaval. Sadly, their deep-seated animosity lasted for twenty-five years.

Carey's temperament had also worked against him. Speaker of the Wyoming House of Representatives Jay L. Torrey explained he'd had "pleasant" personal and political dealings with Carey in the past but said, "Senator Carey seems to have a very unusual conception of his relationship to the people of Wyoming." T. Blake Kennedy, an early-day lawyer in Cheyenne, who later gained notoriety through his work as a judge during the Teapot Dome scandal of the 1920s, recalled that Carey was "possessed of a peculiarly vindictive disposition and temperament oft-time akin to a school girl." Kennedy wrote, "He took to heart any opposition to himself and punished those who had opposed him in an exceedingly icy manner." But Kennedy also complimented Carey's oratory skills, saying he was "perhaps the most astute and effective stump speaker that Wyoming has produced."

The early 1900s apparently were mostly quiet for citizen Carey. One of the most disappointing events of this period involved the Opera House. The Careys had refurbished the opera house in 1892, installing new scenery, painting the walls of the auditorium, repairing the seats, carpeting the floors, and renovating the boxes. But in the 1890s, Cheyenne was cut off from the direct Union Pacific route between Salt Lake City and Denver. Theatrical troupes could play both of those cities without missing a night's performance if they took the direct route rather than stopping in Cheyenne. As a result, fewer productions were held in the city. Then, on December 7, 1902, fire destroyed the Opera House. According to Jean Bastian's account in *History of Cheyenne,* the blaze began beneath the stage. High winds and a broken gas main accelerated the flames. Although a portion of the building remained standing, the glory days of the Opera House were over.

Carey and Louisa soon found another social event with political overtones to enjoy when they entertained President Theodore Roosevelt in their home during Roosevelt's visit to Cheyenne in 1903. In early June 1903, the president enjoyed the hospitality of Wyoming citizens and rode on horseback from Laramie to Cheyenne, where he was feted with a parade and a wild west show in the tradition of Cheyenne Frontier Days. On the Sunday morning of his visit, Roosevelt rose early, took breakfast in his rooms, and attended services at the First Methodist Church. After church, he was driven in a carriage to the Carey home. The *Cheyenne Daily Leader* of June 1, 1903, gave credit to Louisa Carey, saying she "proved herself a charming and accomplished hostess and the dinner proved a most enjoyable affair for the President and the other distinguished guests." During the event Roosevelt reportedly donned an Indian warbonnet hanging on the newel post and performed an impromptu war dance. According to Robert D. Carey's recollections, the guests at the luncheon included Washington dignitaries James Wilson, secretary of Agriculture, and, surprisingly, Francis E. Warren. The two Wyoming politicians apparently set aside their differences during the president's visit.

Joseph Carey continued publishing the *Wyoming Tribune* until 1904, when William C. Deming took over ownership. Despite Speaker Torrey's comments that Carey had an odd view of his political relationship to the people of Wyoming, Carey would soon again enter public service on behalf of the state. The Republicans had enjoyed a long run controlling politics in Wyoming, and Francis E. Warren was generally recognized as the spark plug of their efforts. Larson explains that not everyone liked Warren's political machine, as it became known, and Joseph Carey proved instrumental in the Democrats' efforts to reduce Warren's power. In May 1910, Carey, still a Republican, announced his desire to become governor of Wyoming. Though he still had many friends within the Party, Carey realized that to win the nomination he'd have to support the Warren party line. Rather than do so, Carey declared his candidacy as a Progressive Republican, following those who had been disappointed in

President Taft's governing of the nation. At the Republican state convention just five days later, W. E. Mullen, a Sheridan attorney and Wyoming's attorney general, earned the gubernatorial nomination over Carey.

All appeared lost, but Carey's dream of holding the governor's seat was not yet dashed. The Wyoming Democratic Party, realizing that it had no strong candidate for the governor's seat, approached Carey. Carey agreed to run after a suitable platform had been drafted. The platform, according to Larson, included support of election reforms, state-run conservation of natural resources, good roads, and an eight-hour working day for women and children under age eighteen. The Democratic platform also supported passage of a law to limit the influence of lobbyists and the elimination of the leasing system at the state penitentiary.

Carey again hit the campaign trail, using his public speaking skills to his advantage. The Democrats astutely referred to him as the "Grand Old Man" and the "father of statehood," drawing on Carey's impressive earlier work in Congress. That he had authored the 1894 Carey Act became a selling point as well. In November, Democrats swept the state offices, with Carey defeating Mullen by 5,851 votes. Larson called Carey's election "a great personal triumph." Although the Democrats won state offices for the first time since 1892, the legislature went solidly Republican in both houses. And, even though her husband had been elected governor, Louisa Carey refused to move from her home into the governor's mansion. Instead, the Carey mansion served in this capacity during the years 1911–1915.

In his message to the legislature on January 12, 1911, Carey said he had "but one object—that of assisting in building up the State." He stated further, "Believe me when I say that I strive not to build a party machine and that I have no other object today than advancing the growth of the State and the honor of her people." He called his objective "an industrial constructive policy." He urged the legislature to forego partisanship concerns and accept the items he'd campaigned for.

According to Larson, he managed to work well with the Republican legislature. Lawmakers approved the direct primary system, which Carey said, "destroy[s] the convention system, root, body and branches." They reapportioned legislative seats by population and created seven new counties: Campbell, Goshen, Hot Springs, Lincoln, Niobrara, Platte, and Washakie. But they took no action on Carey's recommendation that lobbyists be licensed.

Carey's request for a type of campaign finance reform, in which candidates would be required to publish their campaign expenses and limit their expenditures, gained some support. The legislature also passed a law limiting candidates' expenses to twenty percent of their annual salary in office and sent the voters of the state an initiative and referendum amendment. Though a majority of voters in the 1912 election favored the system, the total votes were not high enough to pass the bill.

In 1912, Carey's name was suggested as a possible replacement for F. E. Warren in the Senate, but Carey did not express interest in the position even though he might have enjoyed defeating Warren. The year marked another acrimonious political campaign in Wyoming, this time with the Progressive Party as a strong competitor against the Democrats and Republicans. According to Larson, Carey began leading the "insurgents" in Wyoming as a Bull Moose Progressive. But the Warren machine was firmly entrenched in Wyoming and supported Taft. In the presidential election, the Progressive Party split the results, and Democrat Woodrow Wilson defeated Taft. Wyoming remained Republican, although Democrat John B. Kendrick had made a strong showing in his bid for the U. S. Senate.

On January 14, 1913, Carey delivered his opening message to the legislators. He welcomed two women—Anna B. Miller and Nettie Truax—as representatives at this session. He asked lawmakers for amendments on bills that had been passed in the previous legislature, saying that while the substance of the laws passed made good legislation, they needed some refinement.

Carey also asked for a Blue Sky Law to eliminate fraud perpetrated by companies selling worthless stocks, but the legislature did not pass such a bill. He also urged lawmakers to support the Board of Immigration, thereby encouraging settlement of Wyoming's lands, but some legislators believed Carey wanted only to promote his own Wheatland project through this board. Lawmakers did not appropriate funds for the board. Carey also requested that the state be allowed to exchange its poor lands for better ones owned by the federal government. The lawmakers passed a bill approving the cession of all vacant and unappropriated lands to the state. Carey also reported to them on the progress of the Carey Act.

The legislature also gave the governor power to remove county officers who did not perform their duties in enforcing laws against gambling, prize fighting, and illegal sales of intoxicating liquors. However, the lawmakers added the stipulation that the county commissioners must have been found guilty by a district judge and the charges stated in writing first. Carey again asked legislators to create a nonpolitical tax commission to study taxes and revenue as he was concerned about high taxation, but the legislators did not comply with this request.

In 1913, he asked lawmakers to support the state fair by allowing sufficient appropriations for its continuance and "to enable the State Fair Commission, with the assistance of the Governor, to take steps to acquire the actual ownership of the lands where the Fair improvements are located, with the view of its becoming state property."

According to Larson, Carey's 1913 address "stood second only to his 1911 message in its far-reaching proposals for reform. The legislature left much undone, more indeed than in 1911." Critical time had been lost in the earlier re-organization of the House and the hullabaloo over the Senate election. This term, Carey vetoed sixteen bills and cut recommended appropriations by nearly four hundred thousand dollars. None of his vetoes was overridden. According to Larson, the most important veto was Carey's disapproval of the creation of the new county of Shoshone, which would have been taken from the northern part of Fremont County. A similar bill to divide Fremont County had failed in 1911, and Carey found evidence that Republican leaders in the state threatened to divide Fremont County in the event that county residents elected Democrats to the legislature. They had. The 1913 bill had passed both houses along Party lines.

Carey did not seek the governor's office again, but a reconciliation of sorts occurred between Progressives and the regular Republicans in 1914. Democrat John B. Kendrick won the gubernatorial seat, defeating Hilliard S. Ridgely, a lawyer who espoused the political views of Francis E. Warren. Some of the bitterness of the 1912 campaign faded, but it wasn't until 1918 that the feud between Carey and Warren ceased. That year, Carey's son Robert sought the governor's seat in Wyoming. When Warren supporters threw their weight behind the younger Carey, the two older politicians were able to reconcile their differences. The Carey Progressives joined the Republicans, and the younger Carey won the gubernatorial position, defeating Acting Governor Frank Houx by five thousand votes. Joseph Carey became the only Wyoming governor to carry the distinction of also being the father of a Wyoming governor.

Joseph Carey died February 5, 1924, at the age of seventy-nine. He'd suffered a lengthy but undisclosed illness. State offices closed and business was suspended on February 8, the day of Carey's funeral. Businesses in Cheyenne closed during the afternoon for the funeral. A public memorial service was also held on February 10 at the Capitol. The banner headline run on the evening edition of the *Wyoming State Tribune* and *Cheyenne State Leader* on February 6 stated, "The passing of J.M. Carey brings to Wyoming sorrow as profound as that of Woodrow Wilson to the nation." (The former president's funeral had been held that same day.) The newspaper referred to Carey as an "empire-builder, statesman, philanthropist," remarking that he "held more high offices of public trust than any other citizen, and in each employed ability unsurpassed by that of any other who has held any of these offices." He was buried in Lakeview Cemetery in Cheyenne. Louisa, their sons, Robert and Charles, and their wives, as well as Joseph M. Carey III, Robert's only son, were all buried in the Carey plot at the cemetery.

Asa Shinn Mercer

AMONG THE WEST'S nineteenth-century pioneers, one man led a life as rugged as the seas he sailed on and the foreign mountain tops he climbed. His name is linked forever with the romance of transporting young East Coast women by ship and around Cape Horn to Washington Territory so they might become brides of the men who lived in that western outpost. But his romantic image is tarnished by his involvement in a frontier fracas in Wyoming. Asa Mercer played an important role in the Johnson County War of 1892, and his book, *The Banditti of the Plains*, remains a classic in western literature.

Asa Shinn Mercer, of Scottish heritage, was born in Princeton, Illinois, on June 6, 1839. According to Bartlett's *History of Wyoming*, he was the first white child born in Bureau County, the youngest of fourteen children born to Aaron and Jane Dickerson Mercer. Not much is known of Asa Mercer's early years, but he completed his college degree at Oberlin College in Ohio in the early 1860s and then traveled to Washington Territory to visit his brother, Judge Thomas Mercer. He enjoyed his surroundings so much he decided to stay. He is credited with helping found the University of Washington, and he served as its first president.

Linnie Marsh, who chronicled the university's presidents in an article for the *Washington Alumnus* in December 1910, states of Mercer, "The plans for a territorial university struck him as very laudable. He donned rough clothes and went out to grub stumps." In May 1861, the cornerstone was laid, and then building "proceeded as rapidly as circumstances would allow." By September, two structures—the president's house with dormitory space and the school building itself—were ready for use. Marsh writes, "Mr. Mercer had inspired such confidence among the commissioners and the townspeople that he was chosen principal of the university to teach for a term of five months. He was to receive for his services two hundred dollars and all tuition fees." In November, the board selected Milton Gatch (then president of Willamette University) as its new president, but Gatch declined the offer. Mercer was teaching all the classes. He had thirty students, about fifteen percent of Seattle's population at the time. He taught mathematics and Latin but also taught lower level classes in reading, writing, and arithmetic.

The territorial legislature opposed this upstart university, and the chairman of the board, Daniel Bagley, was accused of the "squandering of lands and funds." A committee of councilmen and representatives was sent to investigate. Mercer gave them a cordial welcome and had a brass band play. Mercer "completely won the sympathies of the visitors for the school and its promoters" during the speech he gave, according to Marsh. Bagley showed the investigative committee that all was proper with his bookkeeping. Soon, the legislature incorporated the university and chose Bagley as head of the Board of Regents.

After the first term, Mercer took charge of a private school on the grounds, teaching "all branches of the primary, grammar and high school grades" with assistance from Mrs. Virginia Calhoun. Mercer, during his time as a teacher, had noticed that there were few women in the territory, a fact that concerned him. Marsh states he thought such conditions led to "a variety of evils—unsettled condition of the male population, marriages with Indian women and a general low moral tone." The legislature approved of Mercer's plan to bring women settlers from the East Coast, and the governor promised him funds, as did bachelors in the Puget Sound area. He left for New England in January 1863.

Once there, he promoted his plan and gathered funds to procure a ship that would transport the women from New York to Seattle. Writer Flora A. P. Engle recalls that Mercer's idea attracted the attention of persons who might otherwise have never considered re-locating to the West Coast. In 1864, Mercer addressed a group of Lowell, Massachusetts, citizens in Mechanics Hall and "pictured in glowing terms the wonderful financial advantage that would without doubt accrue to any and all young ladies who would leave their New England homes and migrate to Washington Territory." Engle states that Mercer did not mention marriage but instead focused on the financial gain people could make embarking on such an adventure. The offer was an attractive one, though, because Lowell's economy depended on southern cotton. With the cotton held in the South instead of being shipped North during the war, the cotton mills had been forced to close. Ten "well-educated and accomplished young ladies, ranging from fifteen to twenty-five years of age," agreed to travel with Mercer. According to Engle, the young women were from "some of the best and oldest families in the city." Their parents approved.

The group set sail from New York, traveling to Panama and San Francisco before reaching Washington Territory. After a short stay in San Francisco, they completed the last leg of the journey by riding on "barks, brigs and full-rigged ships that carried lumber from our mill ports to San Francisco" as a steamer sailed only monthly. Some rode the bark *Torrent* and some rode the brig *Tanner*. The group arrived in May 1864 after two months' travel on board ship. Mercer arrived in Seattle to discover that he'd been nominated by King and Kitsap Counties to serve as their joint representative on the territorial council. He gained the seat easily and served on several committees, including claims, counties, education, elections, engrossed bills, enrolled bills, and federal relations. He was chairman of the roads and highways committee. He completed his term in January 1865.

Also in 1865, Mercer published a promotional pamphlet extolling the virtues of the territory entitled *Washington Territory: the Great Northwest, her Material Resources and Claims to Irrigation. A Plain Statement of Things as they Exist*. This apparently was his first publication and perhaps piqued his interest in writing as he continued to try to promote the territory. The pamphlet included much statistical information and sections on lumber, minerals, fishing, whaling, grazing lands, fruit, and trade. According to historian Charles W. Smith, only the final sentence refers to immigration of women to Washington Territory "and should dispel the notion…that Mercer's sole purpose on this trip was to import a cargo of young women." Mercer planned another more ambitious immigrant sailing, this time hoping that he could entice President Abraham Lincoln into backing the project. Marsh states Mercer had written to a friend that he had sat upon Lincoln's lap as a youngster and believed the president would most certainly come to his aid. But by the time Mercer arrived in New York, Lincoln had been assassinated. Mercer did not win the approval of Lincoln's successor, Johnson. However, Edward Everett Hale of Massachusetts provided funds, according to Marsh. Though the idea initially attracted many, the press impugned the reputations of Puget Sound men, and Mercer came under attack for his part in the plan. The group of interested persons decreased to about half its original size. Marsh also states that Ben Holladay, who owned the steamer *Continental* on which the Mercer group would sail, demanded full payment. This demand conflicted with their earlier agreement. Holladay was the president of the California, Oregon, and Mexico Steam Ship Company at the time.

A letter written to Mercer by Holladay on October 17, 1865, states: "In the event that we conclude our arrangement with the Govt of the U.S. for the purchase of the steamer "Continental" we will take five hundred passengers for you, as proposed, from New York to Seattle, Washington Ter. for the sum of Fifty thousand dollars (50000)."

The ship had most recently been used for transporting soldiers. According to Engle's first-hand account, not much was done to make the steamer comfortable for passengers. She suspected only a partial fumigation of the ship had taken place prior to their boarding. Her account seems to reiterate the possibility that Mercer had a conflict with Holladay over money. She explains that Mercer had to borrow money to meet his expenses, and "when it was whispered from one member of the party to another at the New York hotel where we were gathered together that on the next morning bright and early all were to be in readiness to board the steamer, small wonder that it was also whispered that our leader thought of slipping away leaving a few of his bills unpaid."

Mercer did apparently manage to pay Holladay. His receipt for funds received, dated January 3, 1866, also attests to the greatly diminished load of passengers and the lack of creature comforts that would be provided on the journey. According to the document, Mercer paid eight thousand dollars for the passage of seventy-five passengers from New York to San Francisco. Conditions of the agreement included only three or fewer passengers to a stateroom, "which they are to take care of and keep clean and in good order themselves and wait on themselves in every way. They are also to keep the cabin clean and do everything necessary for the good order and cleanliness of the Steamer under the direction of the Captain." The receipt explains, "The ship only furnishes provisions and has them cooked and stateroom accomodations [*sic*]. The bed linen to be washed and kept in order by the passengers." The fee per passenger appears to have risen slightly. The first agreement would have been one hundred dollars each for transport, but according to this receipt, passenger fares were almost $107 instead.

Engle's account concurs with the description of the spartan accommodations in the agreement as well as the reports that Mercer had evoked the ire of some. She traveled with her mother and brother on this second expedition. Engle remembers that the food was bad and in short supply, stating, "fried salt beef was brought to the table, also tea steeped in salt water, and for seventeen days in succession the principal dish at dinner was beans only slightly parboiled." The meals nearly caused a mutiny because Mercer began the trip dining at the Captain's table, where much better food was served. He soon changed his mind and began eating with the other passengers. Engle says this poor fare may have been a blessing in disguise because none of the passengers grew ill during the three months' trip. Two babies were born on board, and only one death occurred when a deck hand drowned in an accident.

On March 4, 1866, after the *Continental* negotiated the Straits of Magellan and then stopped, Mercer left the ship with L.A. Treen, John Wilson, and an unidentified seaman. Carrying a revolver and a hand ax for protection, the men climbed "what seemed to be the highest mountain in Tierra Del Fuego," about three thousand feet. Once situated on the mountain peak, they could see the Antarctic Ocean.

They cut a small pine tree from below timber line, fixed it for a flag pole, and attached strips of red, white, and blue bunting to represent the American flag. In honor of the occasion, Mercer gave a speech, telling the men his many predictions for the future and showing his flair for promotion. Among his predictions was that Alaska would prove to be a prime lumbering and fishing area, with much treasure to be discovered in mining there. He said, "[R]ecognizing the fact that gold (money) is the thing most men are putting forth their greatest efforts to secure, I am led to say that if the position of the North Pole is ever found, it will not be by scientific exploring ships, but by the hardy miner pushing North step by step, as he delves in the frozen earth in search of the yellow treasure." Once the trekkers were satisfied that their mission had been completed on the mountain top, they returned to the ship to sail on toward Washington.

Shipboard romances also blossomed, even a couple for Mercer himself. He had fallen for one young woman but his feelings were not reciprocated, and then he fell in love with Annie Stephens of Baltimore, who did return his feelings. Four weddings took place after the ship reached its destination, and one of those was Mercer's.

On May 1, 1866, the ship arrived in San Francisco and the Mercer group stayed in two local hotels. Some decided to remain in California, but the others traveled up the coast on the brig *Sheet Anchor*. Engle states that the food was good on board this vessel and calls the journey "an exceedingly pleasant affair." On June 1, they landed at Admiralty Lighthouse and many settled on Whidby Island. Engle eventually became the assistant light-keeper at Admiralty Head, marrying local farmer William P. Engle and remaining a Washington resident after his death in 1907.

After the arrival of this second expedition, Mercer moved to Oregon. He continued his promotional activities and is credited with building the first grain wharf in Astoria, according to Smith. Some sources also credit Mercer with shipping the first Oregon wheat to England, but others recognize Joseph Watt for that accomplishment. Smith says Mercer was definitely active in maritime trade, however. His article reproduces several letters that mention Mercer's "Line of Oregon Packets," sailing ships that departed monthly from New York to the Columbia River. Rufus Ingalls, the assistant quartermaster general, wrote to Mercer on February 10, 1868, that he had served for several years as quartermaster in Oregon and Washington Territory and stating, "I can bear testimony to the necessity, convenience and economy of such a line."

Not everyone supported this plan, however. Mercer wrote to the editor of the Portland *Oregonian* in mid-August 1869, promoting direct trade. He explained, "A year and a half ago, I went to New York fully convinced that the time had come for Oregon to assume her place among the States, as one having an important commerce. Keeping that conviction constantly alive, in the face of two monster lines of opposition, I have succeeded in establishing a line of sail vessels between New York city and Portland, Oregon." The opposing factions were California interests and Oregon merchants themselves who "have stood by quietly looking on, saying nothing against us, but withholding the very support which we grievously need, and which they could readily give us." According to Mercer, Oregon at the time produced five million bushels of wheat, and he felt that the farmers could produce twenty million bushels if they could reduce the cost of getting the crops to a shipping point. He concluded, "[W]ould you develop Oregon, you must first look to the interests of the farmer; make his labor remunerative, and as the result will have a million cultivators of the soil, and no unproductive land."

In 1875, Mercer published another promotional pamphlet, *The Material Resources of Linn County, Oregon, embracing Detailed Descriptions and Business Directory*. It was seventy-two pages, with a forty-four-page business directory, among other information. His efforts at promotion did not go unnoticed in political circles; the Oregon governor appointed him to serve a one-year term as "A Special Commissioner of Emigration for the State of Oregon." The next governor accorded him a similar honor in 1876 as "Honorary Commissioner of Emigration to Oregon." Mercer published another promotional booklet in 1876. *The Material Resources of Marion County* was eighty pages and included a map of western Oregon. Mercer also was the publisher of the *Oregon Granger;* however, it is unclear whether he began publishing that paper upon his arrival in Oregon and before the publication of these pamphlets or later.

In 1876, Mercer moved to Texas and became a newspaper owner and publisher there. According to Smith, he began his newspaper career there with the *Sherman Courier,* which he published for three years. Then he moved to Henrietta to publish the *Henrietta Shield.* He also owned and operated the *Wichita Herald,* the *Vernon Guard,* the *Bowie Cross Timbers,* and the *Mobeetie Panhandle.* In 1883, he sold these papers and moved to Wyoming Territory.

In Cheyenne, he continued his love of journalism, publishing the *Northwest Live Stock Journal.* The first issue appeared November 23, 1883. According to historian Lewis Gould, Mercer's paper was funded largely by the Wyoming Stock Growers Association during the first six years of its existence. He received advertisements from the group in return for his work for the WSGA "as well as the Association's blessing for Mercer's frequent efforts to achieve government employment." Toward the end of the 1880s, Mercer began purchasing printing equipment, apparently planning to resume his journalism activities in Texas. But his plans fell through, and Mercer defaulted on his payments. Because the stockmen were running into difficulties during the end of that decade as well, Mercer's source of financial support dwindled.

The frustrations between stockmen and homesteaders peaked in July 1889, with the lynching of Ellen "Cattle Kate" Watson and James Averell on the Sweetwater River. Watson and Averell had been suspected of rustling cattle, and the stockmen in the area, disgusted with lenient court decisions that let rustlers go free, took matters into their own hands. Mercer, in his *Northwest Live Stock Journal,* showed his allegiance with the cattlemen, advocating "freer use of the hanging noose." The *Laramie Boomerang* of August 31, 1889, quoted Mercer as saying, "Cattle owners should organize and not disband until a hundred rustlers were left ornamenting the trees or telegraph poles of the territory. The hanging of two culprits merely acts as a stimulus to the thieves. Hang a hundred and the balance will reform or quit the country. Let the good work go on and lose no time about it."

Gould reports that Mercer wrote to Senator Francis E. Warren in May of 1890, asking to be appointed a World's Fair Commissioner, stating, "If you give me this place, I will show up western stock interests in a way that will do us all good." Warren appointed him as an alternate to the position, giving the delegate spot to A. C. Beckwith. Because Beckwith did not want to attend the meetings in Chicago, Mercer took his place. The position's small salary was not enough to stave off Mercer's creditors, who had begun seeking recompense through the courts in 1892. But Mercer owned no Laramie county property that could satisfy the judgments.

Mercer apparently traveled quite a bit in 1891. The *Cheyenne Daily Sun* reported that World's Fair Commissioner Henry Hay left for Chicago on the afternoon of March 28, 1891, while A. S. Mercer, "the energetic alternate, started yesterday." The commission was slated to meet on April 7. In mid-June, the newspaper noted that Mercer had returned from a trip to Texas and reported on his enthusiasm for that state's "unprecedented growth" as a result of state ownership and control of lands there. In early July, Mercer and his two daughters returned from the East. The girls had been attending a seminary at Toronto, according to the newspaper.

Mercer is probably best known in Wyoming for his connection with the Johnson County War. In April 1892, a group of Wyoming cattlemen, together with hired guns from Texas, raided the county in an effort to rid it of cattle rustlers. Nathan Champion and Nick Ray, considered rustlers, were killed. President Benjamin Harrison sent the U. S. Cavalry in to restore order. Mercer wrote an editorial opposing the cattlemen in the July 8, 1892, issue of the *Live Stock Journal,* claiming that he had posted bail for E. H. Kimball, editor of the *Douglas Graphic,* who had been arrested on charges of libeling the stockmen. John W. Griffin, a Cheyenne hotel owner, actually provided the bail, according to Gould, although Mercer may have offered his help. Kimball's arrest, in fact, played a crucial role in Mercer's switching sides "from cattlemen's mouthpiece to settler's champion." This action caused the cattlemen to withdraw their support from Mercer and his paper. The circumstances "thus cover[ed] his shift in allegiance from the stock growers to the Democratic Party with a cloak of martyrdom."

In late August, Mercer accused Stock Growers President John Clay of sending his employees to the cattlemen's raid. C. A. Campbell, a Clay employee, strode into the newspaper office to demand a retraction that same day, When none was forthcoming, he struck Mercer. The incident provoked some sympathy for Mercer, who was fifty-five years old. Campbell was younger, but Mercer, according to Gould, exaggerated the vehemence of the attack.

In September, the *Cheyenne Daily Sun* reported that Mercer was campaigning in Casper and Douglas for Democratic gubernatorial candidate John Osborne. This, too, led to controversy. The paper reported that in exchange for Mercer's political support, Osborne had paid a "long past due note of Mercer's held by a Cheyenne bank" and it was not known how much more Osborne would pay for Mercer's services. A correction claimed that J.J. Hurt loaned Mercer the sum of three thousand dollars to pay the note.

On October 13, 1892, an editorial in the *Cheyenne Daily Sun* called Mercer a turncoat and took him to task for his abrupt about-face on cattlemen. "Having by his murderous suggestions and constant bad advice worked up sufficient feeling to make possible the Johnson county invasion," wrote the editor, "he then ignominiously (after a few cattlemen had withdrawn their advertisements from his paper) sold out, body and breeches" to the Democrats. "Mercer now prates about the settler, the small ownership of land, etc." The piece concluded, "As a grand turncoat and all-around dead beat A.S. Mercer is chief."

In retaliation, Mercer printed what became known as the Dunning confession on the next day. George Dunning had been one of the Texas raiders who escaped after the fight at the TA Ranch. His confession implicated prominent Wyoming Republicans in the invasion. The editorial noted that the confession had been printed in the *Live Stock Journal* "on the order of the state Democratic central committee." The story was a bit longer than two pages and contained an affidavit signed by Dunning. The *Daily Sun* noted that the confession blamed Republicans for the entire Johnson County incident and stated, "The worst features of the 'confession' are its criminal libels and the certainty that it will be spread beyond the state. For these reasons only, refutation is necessary." The newspaper criticized Mercer for holding the "sensational 'confession' of a criminal" for seven months, explaining "[t]he value of a good newspaper item lies largely in its early publication."

The Republicans, of course, were outraged. Willis Van Devanter, state chairman of the Republican Party, wrote an editorial in the *Sun* to try to deflect the harm. "One of the lines in the *Stock Journal's* heading over the Dunning 'confession,' is 'Republican Rottenness Fully Exposed.' Of course, the story has no political mission."

Those refuting Dunning's claims included Acting Governor Barber, Judge J. W. Blake, and Attorney General Charles Potter. "Senators Carey and Warren, who are absent from the city, have already made public declarations on this subject, disclaiming all knowledge of our connection with the invasion. Citizens who know the prominent men and Republicans, would not require of them a denial of any sort." Barber wrote to the *Sun* in a letter published October 18, 1892, claiming that he "neither directly nor indirectly had any knowledge or intimation of the cattlemen's expedition to Johnson county until after the expedition was on the road at some place between Casper and Buffalo, and I never in any manner assisted, encouraged or acquiesced in this expedition...." Potter denied any involvement in the invasion, directly or indirectly in either personal or professional capacities. Blake stated that he "never in any manner approved of this deplorable affair, and [has] been greatly grieved to know that it occurred." Warren spoke in Sheridan, Wyoming, saying "He who says I contributed one cent towards, or had any knowledge of, or in any manner approved of that invasion of Johnson County, utters a lie as black as human tongue can articulate." Carey was at Saratoga, Wyoming, but publicly stated he had not participated in and had no knowledge of the raid.

On October 22, 1892, the *Daily Sun* reported a mishap apparently unrelated to all the rest of the brouhaha. Asa Mercer, Jr. had fallen from a high school building window and was badly bruised. The Mercers' luck appeared to have gone entirely bad. Just three days later, while he was in Chicago as an alternate World's Fair Commissioner, Asa Mercer was arrested on charges of libel against John Clay. Clay sued, according to the *Sun*, because "the cattle rustlers of Wyoming had been referred to as 'the anarchists of the plains,'" and Mercer's editorial dubbed Clay "a bulldozing foreigner." Clay admitted that he had connections with foreign capitalists but insisted he was a United States citizen. He knew nothing of the stockmen's invasion in

Johnson County because he was in England at the time, and he did not know about the libelous statements until someone showed him a copy of Mercer's newspaper. The hearing date was scheduled for October 26, 1892. The *Sun* reported, "It will be noticed that this case has nothing to do with the Dunning 'confession' paper. Mercer attacked Mr. Clay and C.A. Campbell in August." Mercer's bail was set at five thousand dollars, which he was unable to pay.

On November 1, 1892, the *Sun* reported that a sheriff's sale was planned for the debts and mortgage of the *Northwest Live Stock Journal*. But the sale did not take place. Annie Mercer showed she held a prior mortgage in the amount of twenty-two hundred dollars, and because that took precedence over other mortgages, she saved her husband's business. When his case was called for trial in Chicago, Mercer did not appear. His lawyer reported that Mercer's wife had fallen ill in Cheyenne. Despite Mercer's financial disasters, including seizure of his assets, fourteen hundred copies of the Dunning confession had already been printed. By Christmas Eve, the *Sun* reported that Clay's suit was dismissed "on the ground that there was lacking evidence to prove that Mercer circulated in Cook county [Illinois] papers containing the objectionable article."

Pioneer John Hunton claimed he had visited with Mercer in Cheyenne after the invasion, around the time the cattlemen were brought to Fort Russell. Hunton was quoted in the *Daily Sun* as saying Mercer's plan was to have the stockmen travel in small groups of four or five "with a rope and piece of bacon on the saddle," to get the rustlers without any problems. Because the cattlemen opted to travel by railroad and wagons, Hunton said that Mercer's feelings appeared to have been hurt that they didn't use his idea. "In view of the course afterwards pursued by Mercer, the speeches he made during his campaign, his present position and his denunciation of his former associates, all these things make Mr. Hunton's statement strange reading...," the newspaper wrote.

In March, Mercer reaped a reward for his support of Democrats. Albert New of Evanston, the chairman of the Democratic State Committee, appointed him state statistical agent for the Agricultural Department with a salary of six hundred dollars per year. Though he and New, along with Governor John Osborne, discussed beginning a new newspaper in Cheyenne, that plan did not materialize. Mercer's newspaper (now called the *Wyoming Democrat)* went out of business that summer, and he spent the summer in Chicago at the World's Fair. His luck was not holding for he was implicated there in an award-selling plot.

That winter, Mercer wrote the book for which he is probably most famous, *The Banditti of the Plains.* (He took the title from a previous best-seller called *The Banditti of the Prairie.)* The book was controversial from the beginning. Sources agree on the controversy but differ in the exact retaliations against Mercer because of it. The book's release corresponded with the ending of the Wyoming Republican State Convention in August. The book took the view that the cattlemen had been wrong to invade Johnson County.

Although Mercer's place of business was said to have been destroyed by fire and numerous copies of the books destroyed—most probably by irate cattlemen—"no evidence has been found to support the stories of book burning, injunctions, or personal threats against Mercer," Gould writes. His view is echoed by Helena Huntington Smith. "There is no getting away from the conclusion that something untoward happened to Mercer's book," she writes. "It was suppressed, but no one can say with certainty how or when—the last and biggest Mercer mystery." She continues, "It is an awe-inspiring thought that if these willful men had simply kept their hands off the press—more specifically if they had refrained from attacking Kimball and Mercer—*The Banditti of the Plains* would never have been written."

Mercer and his sons toured parts of Wyoming on a door-to-door sales campaign after the book's publication. One shipment of five hundred copies was said to have been sent to Sheridan, but the salesman was threatened in Buffalo and left the state without selling them. The books remained in the Burlington railroad station until 1909, when they were apparently sold by a local stationery shop. This, Smith says, accounts for the first printing. When a second printing of several thousand books was ordered from Denver, Mercer never received them. "Either it was destroyed by a well-timed fire in the newspaper office, or it was seized and burned en route, according to the family's recollections," Smith says.

Legends about the book are numerous. That books were stashed in hiding places in houses is one. Historian Agnes Wright Spring told N. Orwin Rush that she had looked into buying the law library of the late attorney Hugo Donzelmann. The woman in charge of his estate told Spring that after the cattlemen discovered publication of the book, Donzelman had managed to get several copies and kept them in his basement. When he hired a janitor to burn them, the janitor kept a few and sold them on his own. (Copyright copies were apparently never deposited with the Library of Congress.)

By 1894, Republicans were looking forward to other political battles, and the Johnson County invasion no longer came to the forefront. According to Gould, "The Republicans, under the leadership of Warren and Van Devanter, crushed the Democrats in the election of 1894, banishing the invasion as an issue in Wyoming politics."

Mercer remained as state statistician until June 1895, when a reorganization of the Agriculture Department eliminated the office. He then decided to homestead in the Big Horn Basin near Hyattville, Wyoming. He wrote a few more books there, including *Big Horn County, Wyoming, the Gem of the Rockies,* 1906; *The Pioneer,* 1913; and *Indian Chief Washakie, and the Big Horn Hot Springs,* 1916. Mercer reportedly had an operation for cataracts in 1910 and later lost most of his vision. He continued his promotional work, apparently, gathering eastern capitalists for oil and mining ventures and becoming president of the Valley Development Company of Basin, Wyoming.

He died at the home of his daughter, Janet Webb, in Buffalo, Wyoming, on August 10, 1917. He was survived by three sons, two daughters, fourteen grandchildren, and three great-grandchildren. "[I]n his passing," remarks Bartlett, "Wyoming lost one of its brightest and most honorable men, one whose field of activity was large and whose memory will be forever cherished...." No mention is made of the Johnson County War, and in Mercer's obituaries, no mention of that incident is made either. But, of course, his book *Banditti of the Plains* is listed.

Senator John B. Kendrick wrote a letter to Mercer, ironically on the day of Mercer's death, saying, "Our State is most fortunate in that it includes a man of such ripe experience, mature observation and sound judgment that enables him to glimpse the great possibility of the development of the State of such, and of its different communities."

Estelle Reel

Estelle Reel exhibited a few quirks, including writing her own obituary and changing her will monthly. She titled the final version of her obituary "A Woman Who Held Many Offices in Her Time," and wrote of herself, "In all her life she seems to have been a pioneer." In many regards, this was true.

She was the first woman elected to state office in the nation when she became Superintendent of Public Instruction in 1894, winning by large margin over Democrat Arthur J. Matthews. This was a befitting turn of events for the nearly five-year-old state, which had granted women the vote in its territorial days. (Another Wyoming woman, Minnie Slaughter, had been appointed Superintendent of Public Instruction in 1890 to replace her father, John Slaughter, who was ill.) Reel would later earn a presidential appointment as National Superintendent of Indian Schools—the first and only woman to hold that position. That appointment also made her the first woman to receive Senate confirmation.

Born in Pittsfield, Illinois, in 1862 to physician A.L. Reel and his wife, Jane R. Scanland, Reel attended Chicago, Saint Louis, and Boston schools. Details of her early life are sketchy, but it appears her parents died when she was young, and Reel made her way to Wyoming in the mid-1880s. She taught school in Cheyenne for several years before being elected twice as Laramie County Superintendent of Schools. In her first election, she garnered the largest majority of votes ever received by a candidate in Wyoming at that time. She directed several annual county teacher institutes, earning praise for her organizational skills. Teachers from Wyoming, Colorado,

Nebraska, Utah, and Mississippi attended her training sessions in Cheyenne.

After enjoying success in those endeavors, Reel decided to hit the campaign trail in 1894. She prepared an informational pamphlet with an attached photograph of herself and mailed it to all the voters in the state. As a result, newspapers reported that Wyoming's cowboys, admiring her pretty face, rode as far as sixty miles to vote for her. Since dances often followed political rallies and Reel was the only female candidate, newspapers also attributed Reel's ability to capture votes to her graceful dancing skills.

The Democratic *Cheyenne Leader* pronounced Reel "as competent to be state superintendent as county superintendent." The fact that 300 of Wyoming's 367 schoolteachers were female and eleven of twelve county superintendents were women also aided Reel in her political bid.

Campaigning presented its own set of difficulties for a woman in frontier times. On swings across Wyoming's 97,000 square miles, journeying by stagecoach, on horseback, and in wagons, Reel traveled with the other Republican candidates—all men. Wyoming's governor, Democrat John E. Osborne, questioned the propriety of the matter. The *Cheyenne Sun* in 1894 quoted Osborne as saying, "which of the distinguished male quintette assumes responsibility for Miss Reel is not apparent." The newspaper retorted that Wyoming women could travel the state without being accompanied by a guardian. Rumors also circulated that Reel had agreed to marry her opponent if she lost. But the gossip died quickly. He was already married.

Reel won voter approval partly through her success as county superintendent of schools for Laramie County and partly through her being "one of the best promoters of herself one could possibly be," according to historian Marian Ross, who knew Reel. She modestly told one newspaper, "I did no stump-speaking. I simply went through the state and met people, you know. It was mere chance I was elected." Yet she told another reporter that she spoke at many political meetings and campaigned hard, saying, "Work? I should say I did."

Winning the position of Superintendent of Public Instruction put Reel in charge of Wyoming's schools and also placed her on two

Estelle Reel, the first woman elected to public office in Wyoming, sent campaign pamphlets containing her photograph to voters throughout the state, prompting numerous cowboys to ride as far as sixty miles to cast their ballots. (Courtesy Wyoming State Archives)

important boards—the Land Commission and the Board of Charities and Reform. Her annual salary was two thousand dollars, an amount some considered exorbitant for a woman. Her duties included preparing a biennial report to the governor on the condition of the state's public schools and performing clerical tasks for the Board of Charities and Reform, which operated the state's hospitals and prison. In this capacity, she toured state institutions of Colorado, Nebraska, and Illinois with other board members and spoke at the National Prison Congress in New York City, earning a bronze medal for outstanding service from that organization.

Reel's land board duties also included clerical work in addition to collection of state land rentals. In March 1896, Reel reported that land rentals increased by seven hundred dollars per month during her first year in office. She favored restrictions on land development to prevent speculators and land corporations from "grabbing up our lands," which she felt should be settled by farmers and ranchers. Reel's report to the governor for the year ended March 31, 1898, showed that Wyoming's 3.6 million acres of school lands had earned rentals of $12,617.55 on 301,812 leased acres. Reel hoped that the schools could become self-supporting rather than tax-reliant.

At the time Reel was superintendent, male teachers earned fifty-eight dollars per month and females only forty-five dollars. As it was widely known that Reel supported equal pay for equal work, rumors circulated that she would seek the governor's seat in an attempt to rectify the unequal pay issue. She squelched these rumors, most pointedly in a letter to the *New York Sun* in 1896, in which she said that the idea of a woman running for the position was "not worthy of serious consideration." She noted that women held nearly half of the state's voting power and argued that they were happy with the right to vote and the chance to persuade the legislature that equal pay should be given for equal work. She concluded, "[Women] will not attempt to encroach upon offices which should always be filled by men, one of which is the Governorship."

Reel campaigned for William McKinley in his presidential bid in 1898. In return, she was rewarded with an appointment as National Superintendent of Indian Schools, the first woman to hold the post. Reel attended McKinley's inauguration, purchasing a one-thousand-dollar Parisian gown for the occasion and accessorizing it with a fifty-dollar hat. The gown cost about as much as a man's wages for two years.

In her new position, Reel exercised general supervision over Indian schools and school-aged Indians under the control of the federal government, which appropriated a budget of three million dollars. She advocated a uniform course of instruction for the Indian schools, wrote a textbook on the subject, and traveled throughout the West visiting the schools. Her book *A Course of Study for the Indian Schools of The United States—Industrial and Literary* was commended by other educators. The course, prepared with the help of Commissioner W. A. Jones, was created to help Indians become self-supporting.

She conducted the Colorado Springs Indian Institute in July 1898 as her first official duty. An active member of the National Education Association (NEA), Reel soon persuaded that organization to hold annual conventions in conjunction with Indian School Institutes. Indian students displayed craft items and schoolwork, and, at one institute, the eighteen-member school band and the Girls' Mandolin and Guitar Club from Perris, California, performed. In her report to Congress dated October 20, 1899, Reel wrote that summer institutes were "a great benefit to the Indian teachers (many of whom are isolated from civilization), who thus meet and exchange ideas that prove most helpful in their vocation."

In her first three years as superintendent of Indian schools, Reel logged 65,900 miles, most by train but more than two thousand by wagon. During her first year alone, she visited schools in Lawrence, Kansas; Chilocco, Oklahoma; Santa Fe, New Mexico; Perris, California; and Carson City, Nevada. She also inspected the Lincoln Institute in Philadelphia and the largest Indian school in the United States in Carlisle, Pennsylvania.

By 1902, Reel felt encouraged by the "great change that has gradually come over the older Indians in their attitude toward the education of their children and the white man's civilization generally." The conditions of Indians at home, she said, showed the value of educational work and the advantages of "inculcating in them a proper appreciation of the blessings of a civilized life."

Despite progress, and although Presidents Theodore Roosevelt and William Taft reappointed Reel to her position, Congress eliminated funding for the position in 1910. That year, Reel, in her late forties, married Washington rancher Cort Meyer. The couple, who had no children, lived near Toppenish, Washington.

Reel was "not noted for her kindness and generosity," Ross says. However, "one of the nicest things she ever did" was keeping an orphaned Aleut girl during the summers. The girl was attending Indian schools in Oregon and Washington.

Ross says that after Reel's eyesight failed, she decided that eggs were expensive and told her husband to eat only one egg for breakfast rather than his preferred two. She scolded him if she heard two eggs crack. The family physician, present at one of these egg-cracking sessions, reported Meyer winked at him when he cracked two at once, making only one sound.

Meyer died at age ninety in 1947. Reel died in 1959 at age ninety-six. A marker stands as a memorial to the Meyers on land they bequeathed to the Toppenish Garden Club for a pleasure resort but which is now privately owned. And, as her obituary attests, Reel is remembered for her pioneering efforts in education and politics.

Willis Van Devanter

In 1884, an Indiana lawyer pulled up stakes and, together with his wife, moved west to Cheyenne, Wyoming Territory. While many sought the West as a place to begin anew, Willis Van Devanter traveled west hoping to increase his opportunities. The twenty-five-year-old attorney could see broad possibilities for himself on the frontier as the legal field grew in response to land settlement questions raised by the constant influx of people seeking their own dreams. An ambitious man and a hard worker all his life, Van Devanter was a goal setter and an achiever, a man passionate about the law and political to his core. He achieved glorious success in his field, attaining the position of justice of the U.S. Supreme Court, the only Wyomingite to be appointed to that position. During the period of 1884–1897, according to historian M. Paul Holsinger, Van Devanter "played a powerful major role in the affairs of the territory and the state of Wyoming."

Willis Van Devanter was born on April 17, 1859, in Marion, Indiana, to Isaac and Violetta Spencer Van Devanter. The first of eight children, Van Devanter was influenced in his love of the law by his father, a lawyer who served as provost marshal of his congressional district during the Civil War. Van Devanter attended local public schools and then Indiana Asbury University (which later became DePauw University). He was a good student who especially enjoyed history, mathematics, Greek, and Latin. But Van Devanter was not just a bookworm. He also enjoyed working on his grandfather's farm during the summers. According to family history, by the age of fourteen he was placed in charge of the farm and managed to produce better crops than more experienced neighbors.

In 1879, Van Devanter entered the University of Cincinnati Law School. There he attended daily lectures presented by the six-man faculty; as a senior he participated in a required weekly moot court. He served as librarian during his senior year, a position which helped him soak up even more information about the law. Experience as class president provided Van Devanter with political skill. His twin loves of law and politics, fostered first by his father's example and then by his college experience, remained with him throughout his life. Van Devanter graduated second in his class of sixty-five in 1881.

Following graduation, he returned to Marion, joining his father's firm of Lacey and Van Devanter. He soon was chosen to fill a vacancy in the prosecuting attorney's office for the Twenty-Eighth Indiana Judicial District. He compensated for his lack of experience by studying cases thoroughly and taking extra time to prepare for them. When his father retired, Willis Van Devanter set his sights on the professional opportunities offered by the opening of the West for settlement and considered moving to Arizona or southern California. Then in 1884, John W. Lacey, a partner in the firm and Willis's brother-in-law, was appointed chief justice of Wyoming Territory by President Chester A. Arthur. Van Devanter's best opportunity for frontier work appeared to be there. So, with his wife, Dellice (Dollie), whom he had married the year before, Van Devanter moved to Wyoming. The connection with the chief justice of the territory proved helpful, and Van Devanter exhibited his deftness at networking so necessary for a man seeking legal work and political clout. Author David Burner writes that Van Devanter "was always good at making important 'connections.'" Those connections strengthened the young attorney's chances for success.

Van Devanter opened his law office within a week of his arrival, soon partnering with Hugo Donzelmann and Charles W. Stewart, two older attorneys. But the partnership broke up quickly, apparently due to personality conflicts.

One of Van Devanter's easier cases illustrates the untamed aspects of the area he'd chosen for his practice. Dan Parker and Bill Brown were accused of being highwaymen and charged with mail robbery before U.S. District Judge John Riner in mid-April 1891.

They had robbed a stage passenger of $150 on Muddy Creek sixty miles south of Rawlins on December 20, 1889. The outlaws were also accused of taking a registered letter from a mail sack. Van Devanter, together with U.S. Attorney B.F. Fowler, argued on behalf of the government. The prosecution relied on testimony of the stage driver and a freighter who had seen the incident and identified the accused men. According to the newspaper account, the defense attorneys A.C. Campbell and C.E. Dodge had "no evidence at all." Brown and Parker were convicted and sentenced to life in prison. Despite the additional efforts of their attorneys, the robbers were denied a new trial.

Van Devanter realized that travel throughout the territory would also be necessary to his success. He traveled by horseback or stagecoach and was sometimes one of the first lawyers to appear in court sessions in many of the more remote outposts. The bulk of his legal work consisted of drafting mortgages, wills, deeds, contracts, and partnership agreements and serving as a notary public. But, as Van Devanter had expected, the West offered new challenges for those in the legal profession. As the land was settled and the railroads crossed the country, new legal questions arose regarding land rights. The chance to grapple with such disputes suited Van Devanter. The capital city of Cheyenne, with its ties to railroads and the booming cattle industry, served his interests well.

The work was not easy. In a speech he gave in Cheyenne in 1933, Van Devanter remarked, "The Wyoming Bar was strong because the drones didn't come this way and those with any pronounced weaknesses didn't live long. Wyoming had no system of jurisprudence and as a result drew on the whole line of the best decisions. This practice made lawyers out of lawyers. They studied and they studied profoundly."

Some of Van Devanter's "most important and prestigious" clients were cattle companies, according to Holsinger, including the Swan Land and Cattle Company. In the fall of 1885, Van Devanter purchased one-third interest in the company for his father-in-law for twenty thousand dollars. Dividends had been as much as ten percent the year before, so it appeared to be a clever investment. That same year, Van Devanter made a savvy political connection by offering his assistance to Territorial Governor Francis E. Warren. Warren, the first resident of the territory to hold the gubernatorial seat, began accepting the young attorney's legal advice. A close and lasting friendship between the two men ensued. Warren often referred to Van Devanter as "Van."

Warren, a staunch and powerful Republican, invited Van Devanter to help Republican leaders create legislation authorizing the construction of a capitol building. The young attorney drafted an appropriation bill. "The bill he prepared was an elaborate one," Holsinger explains, "consisting of 55 sections, the chief provisions of which were that $150,000 should be spent to begin construction of the present capitol in Cheyenne, and another $50,000 to establish a University in Laramie." The bill passed both houses of the territorial legislature. Holsinger states, "For the rest of his life Van Devanter never ceased to be proud of the small yet extremely significant role he played in the creation of both the capitol building and the university."

In March 1886, Warren charged Van Devanter, along with Isaac P. Caldwell and J. W. Blake, with the responsibility of revising the laws and statutes of the territory. Van Devanter drew heavily on his in-depth knowledge of the Ohio statutes. His work on this project had great influence. The revised statutes were voted into effect in 1888 and used in 1889 by the Constitutional Convention to create Wyoming's new state constitution and laws.

His interest in politics remained strong, and Van Devanter decided to seek public office. On October 2, 1886, he and ten others were selected as delegates to the Territorial Convention at the Laramie County Republican Convention. In Rawlins, on October 6, Van Devanter was nominated as a candidate for the Territorial House of Representatives. According to Holsinger, he campaigned vigorously, traveling extensively throughout his district and emphasizing that he was the only attorney in the territory to have been nominated as a candidate. This work paid off handsomely: Van Devanter's twenty-three-hundred-plus votes led the Republican ticket, outshining even the popular Joseph M. Carey who won re-election as the territorial representative to Congress that year. Under the territorial laws, elected candidates had to wait fourteen months

Willis Van Devanter, an attorney who defended the cattlemen in the trial for the murders of Nick Ray and Nate Champion (the event that sparked the Johnson County War), became the first U.S. Supreme Court Justice from the State of Wyoming. (Courtesy Wyoming State Archives)

to take office. Thus Van Devanter earned his seat but did not begin his term until January 1888.

During the spring and summer of 1886, Van Devanter struggled with personal issues. His father-in-law died away that fall. In September, Van Devanter sold his family's cattle company stock to Alexander Swan for twenty-four thousand dollars in promissory notes but, surprisingly, did not obtain a mortgage, largely due to

Swan's prominence in the territory and the cattle industry. Van Devanter probably hoped, as many local ranchers did, that the next year would bring higher cattle prices. But Wyoming's weather conspired against them. The winter of 1886–1887 was one of the worst ever for Wyoming's cattle industry. Some cattle companies lost as much as ninety percent of their herds. The resulting calf crop was poor as well.

On May 28, 1887, the Swan Land and Cattle Company declared bankruptcy. To protect his mother-in-law's money, Van Devanter posted a bond for one hundred thousand dollars and appointed himself receiver for the firm. He worked for more than a year on this project, earning only the company books and an empty fireproof safe for his efforts. He resigned as receiver in June 1888. Despite this failure, his role as a receiver and his legal work with many smaller cattle companies made his name recognizable throughout the territory.

While waiting to take his legislative seat, Van Devanter gained even more political experience and continued building legal clout. Mayor John Riner appointed him as city attorney for Cheyenne in 1887. The position appears to have been a highly respected one as well as lucrative. For his service of a little more than one year, Van Devanter earned $750—more than the mayor.

In 1887, Van Devanter formed a new law partnership with Charles N. Potter. Potter was also a strong Republican and a former city attorney, and the partnership proved profitable for Van Devanter. Seeing the legal opportunities offered through connections with the powerful railroad industry, Van Devanter had tried to gain the Union Pacific Railroad as a client in 1886 when he practiced alone but discovered that the company preferred to deal with larger, more experienced firms. Together, he and Potter were able to attract the business of the Burlington Railroad, a step that helped Van Devanter gain necessary experience to make his services more attractive to the Union Pacific. When John Lacey resigned as chief justice in July 1887 to return to private practice in the firm of Corlett, Lacey and Riner, Van Devanter found himself competing against his brother-in-law for clients in Cheyenne. An ad in the *Cheyenne Daily Sun* in April 1889 boasted that the firm of Potter and Van Devanter "[p]ractice in all the courts of the Territory."

In January 1888, at the age of twenty-eight, Willis Van Devanter took his seat in the territorial legislature and struck out to make a name for himself in political circles. He was named chairman of the credentials committee and helped gather support for Johnson County's Nat Huntington to become Speaker of the House. Van Devanter's apparently unwarranted verbal attack against Herman Glafcke, the Democratic nominee for clerk, drew public criticism. Even so, Van Devanter became a leading spokesman for the House Republicans. He introduced the bill to adopt the Revised Statutes of 1887, which passed easily. Van Devanter was then named chairman of the judiciary committee.

On one issue, Van Devanter split with Republicans to vote against the proposal for a new constitution and the formation of a state government. Van Devanter was one of only four lawmakers casting negative votes. His stand seems odd because statehood was a popular issue, and most politicians favored creating a new state. Perhaps the young attorney was attempting to represent his constituents, who might have been lukewarm to the statehood idea at the time. Whatever Van Devanter's reasoning, he did eventually become a strong proponent of statehood.

The forty-five-day legislative session was grueling because Democratic Governor Thomas Moonlight seemed to be against everything Republicans advocated. Van Devanter supported a bill that appropriated $150,000 for an addition to the capitol and promoted the creation of more public buildings. Though Moonlight disagreed with this bill, the legislature overrode his veto. Van Devanter was also instrumental in the passage of the bill creating Converse, Sheridan, and Natrona counties—another bill vetoed by the unpopular Moonlight and overridden by the legislators.

Republicans gained a prestigious political plum in 1889 when President Benjamin Harrison re-appointed Republican Francis E. Warren to the governorship. Van Devanter served on Warren's inaugural committee, and Republican leaders pressured him to seek the judicial seat held by William MacGinnis. This goal would be achievable only if MacGinnis resigned and President Harrison appointed Van Devanter to the position. Van Devanter was reluctant at first, even reportedly signing a petition favoring attorney W. W. Corlett for the chief justice position. He had begun to campaign for the position with the understanding that Corlett had decided not to, but when he learned that Corlett sought the seat, Van Devanter withdrew. On June 1, the *Cheyenne Daily Sun* applauded his decision and explained that Van Devanter had gained the endorsement of the territorial bar. "In several of the counties the legal fraternity unanimously favored Mr. Van Devanter's appointment and in [Laramie] county over two-thirds signified their desire for his selection as Chief Justice. He is a young man, comparatively, has a desirable and lucrative practice and he appreciates the fact that he has not resided in the territory so long as either of the other gentlemen whose names have been mentioned in this connection [M.C. Brown and W.W. Corlett]. For these reasons he can well afford to step aside as he has done." Corlett had been ill but traveled to New York to recuperate and returned in better condition, according to the newspaper.

MacGinnis resigned in July 1889. No Wyoming resident had yet served as chief justice, and Republican leaders recommended Van Devanter to the president, which may have spurred MacGinnis's decision. Van Devanter was appointed in the latter part of August. The *Sun* called the thirty-one-year-old Van Devanter "conspicuously successful." In an editorial on September 3, 1889, the newspaper gushed, "Quietly, and we might almost say unobtrusively, he has made his way to the front rank of the Wyoming bar, securing a clientele of which any attorney might well be proud. Alike clear and impartial, he never loses his self command nor overlooks the point at issue. His manner is such that he does not arouse antagonism, and yet presses his suit with force, energy and directness. It is natural for him to consider every question upon its merits and he will leave no stone unturned to get at the true solution of a problem. Painstaking, unimpassioned, but with a great persistence he champions a cause with all the forces at his command, and it is not too much to say that he is a natural lawyer." At a reception held in his honor at Cheyenne's InterOcean Hotel, Van Devanter "was the victim of a continuous handshaking from morning till night," yet he "bore his honors with dignity, serenity, and self-poise befitting a supreme judge."

In September, the Constitutional Convention was held. Although Van Devanter was not a delegate, he had a pass to the floor and was instrumental behind the scenes in drafting the document, according to Holsinger. Van Devanter's law firm was also instrumental in helping Territorial Engineer Elwood Mead's proposal for a water code become part of the constitution. That proposal was unpopular among attorneys because Mead's suggestions would substantially lower the necessity for litigation over water rights and give more power to the state. According to Mead's biographer, James Kluger, the firm of Lacey and Van Devanter supported the proposal, which helped it pass by a large margin.

Van Devanter took the oath of office as chief justice on October 2, 1889, in the presence of several Cheyenne attorneys and a few friends, becoming one of the youngest judges in the federal court system at that time.

At the end of the month, Van Devanter participated in the mass meetings held in Cheyenne to campaign for the new constitution for Wyoming's statehood. He served on the speakers' committee, but he also took time for a beloved hobby—fishing—when he visited his former partner and now attorney general of the territory, Hugo Donzelmann at his ranch. Van Devanter also spoke on the subject of the constitution at bar association meetings, an organization he had helped found. Wyoming Territory voters endorsed the new constitution on November 6, 1889.

Each of Wyoming Territory's three Supreme Court justices acted as local judges, presiding over one of three districts, according to Holsinger. The chief justice was required to live in the First District, which included Laramie, Converse, Crook, and later Weston counties. Because the Supreme Court met for only about ten days annually, the cases over which judges presided were largely those on the district docket. Van Devanter took over the district court in Cheyenne on November 12, 1889, facing a "voluminous docket." Among the cases heard were a knifing incident, grand larceny, attempted murders, and cattle rustling. The fate of cattle rustlers had become a sticking point in the territory. The stockmen, backed by the then-powerful Wyoming Stock Growers Association, believed that rustlers should be tried and convicted. But convictions of suspected cattle rustlers were hard to come by, provoking the ire of the stockmen. In a sensational incident in July 1889, Ellen "Cattle Kate" Watson and her lover, James Averell, had been lynched at the hands of Carbon and Natrona County stockmen who believed them to be rustlers. Though many judges let alleged rustlers go free, Van Devanter sentenced three convicted cattle thieves to as much as seven years in jail. According to Holsinger, this was "the first time in over two years that any suspected cattle thief had been convicted." Van Devanter ruled especially strictly in theft cases because, according to Holsinger, he felt the West offered opportunities for everyone and no one needed to steal to survive.

The judge also dealt severely with those showing disrespect for his court. The *Sun* reported he charged a drunk witness with contempt of court and required him to serve twenty days in jail, then recessed the court until the witness sobered up and could give his testimony. Van Devanter also became known for his lectures from the bench, which the newspapers said denoted common sense. On December 5, 1889, the *Sun* reported that Van Devanter sentenced nine persons. The strictest sentence was handed to one of the cattle rustlers, who was required to spend seven years in prison. A bakery safe robber was given a fifteen-month sentence. The report concluded, "The judge then made the collective batch a good, wise and sensible talk on the lessons taught by these sentences, to criminals and to society...." Van Devanter's written opinions are also clear and concise and show that he was so well versed in the law and so comfortable with his knowledge of legal issues that he could come straight to the point without the need for flowery language or legalese.

The Territorial Supreme Court met in late January and early February 1890, the only time the court met with Van Devanter seated as chief justice. The court heard eleven cases, "all of which dealt with minor technicalities in the law." Following the adjournment of the court, Van Devanter worked as a district judge, presiding over cases in Converse, Crook, and Weston counties. He made yet another important connection while he worked in this capacity. After sentencing a man who had wounded Newcastle Mayor Frank W. Mondell, the judge and the politician became good friends. Mondell later served as U.S. congressman from Wyoming.

Wyoming achieved statehood on July 10, 1890. The first general election was planned for September 11. At the August meeting of the Republican State Central Committee in Cheyenne, Van Devanter was nominated, along with H. V. B. Groesbeck and Arthur Conaway, to run for the three Supreme Court justiceships. In a Republican landslide, Francis E. Warren was elected governor, and Van Devanter and the other candidates for the Supreme Court seats earned their places. The justices' terms were to be staggered at four, six, and eight years. They drew straws to choose the chief justice who would serve the shortest term. Van Devanter was selected.

But Van Devanter resigned his position just four days later to return to private practice. Holsinger speculates that the move may have been calculated political plan, in that his name helped the Republicans win elections handily. Van Devanter had many of his political papers destroyed years later, however, so the reason for his decision is unknown. In his legal practice, Van Devanter "devoted proportionally more of his time to cases dealing with political matters than with any other topic. His position in each of these cases depended upon whether or not the Republicans were in control of the state's administration."

Advantages continued to come Van Devanter's way. When Governor Warren opted to become Wyoming's U. S. senator, Van Devanter became the leader of Wyoming's Republican Party. Professionally, he partnered with his brother-in-law, John Lacey. Lacey and Van Devanter soon became a prominent firm in the state because few other firms could advertise the expertise of two former chief justices. And, when the firm was chosen as the legal representatives for the Union Pacific Railroad in Wyoming, Van Devanter finally gained the railroad client he'd coveted for so long.

During the six years of his association with his brother-in-law, Van Devanter defended the railroad in numerous cases. In one case, *Link v. Union Pacific*, the railroad had appealed a case decided in district court in Albany County regarding a land ownership dispute with Cecilia F. Link. Link had asked for a new trial on the basis that she had new evidence, but she could not produce adequate documentation to prove she had title to the disputed land prior to the railroad's title under the land grant acts of 1862 and 1864. Van Devanter successfully argued the case for the railroad before Wyoming Supreme Court Justices Groesbeck, Merrill, and Conaway.

That spring, Wyoming residents watched as tempers flared in northern Wyoming between large and small stock operators. On March 19, Senator Warren wrote to Van Devanter, "I hope matters in Johnson [County] and vicinity may soon mend, but am constantly quaking with apprehension as to what may next happen on account of the stand taken by the rustlers, the cattle growers, and the Live Stock Commission." Warren's anxiety was warranted. In early April, suspected rustlers Nick Ray and Nate Champion were killed at the KC Ranch by cattlemen in an incident that became known as the Johnson County War.

According to Wyoming historian T.A. Larson, on the day before the murders, a six-car special train carrying twenty-five Texas gunmen, twenty-four ranch owners and managers, detectives, and inspectors, along with their horses, wagons and supplies, left Cheyenne and headed to Casper. The men were headed north to clear out the rustlers, taking the law into their own hands. Larson explains that "[p]ositive conclusions are hard to come by" but believes that the Union Pacific officials who furnished the train knew of the intent of the group along with Acting Governor Amos Barber, Senator Joseph Carey, Cheyenne attorneys Willis Van Devanter and Hugo Donzelmann, editor of the *Cheyenne Sun,* E.A. Slack, editor of the *Northwest Live Stock Journal,* A.S. Mercer, and members of the WSGA. Senator Warren may have also been aware of the expedition.

The "invaders" traveled to Buffalo, Wyoming, intending to take over the town and capture the rustlers. Acting Governor Barber wired President Benjamin Harrison who authorized the use of federal troops to prevent further escalation of the conflict. The invaders were captured and held for trial at Fort D.A. Russell near Cheyenne. In July, they were transferred to Laramie for a change-of-venue hearing. Willis Van Devanter was one of their attorneys, serving with M.C. Brown, W.R. Stoll, and Hugo Donzelmann; John Lacey and several other attorneys participated as well. The attorneys successfully argued that the trial should be held in Cheyenne. Defense representatives took two witnesses to the events at the KC out of state and hid them so the prosecution could not gain access to them.

Newspapers of the day pounced on Wyoming's "trial of the century." Van Devanter wrote to Warren a month after the raid to criticize the press for sensationalizing the case. In August, the *Cheyenne Daily Sun* reported on the "sensational session of district court," the Wyoming defendants were released on their own recognizance, while the Texans posted bonds of $40,000 each—more than $1.6 million. The trial was originally set for August 22, but District Judge Richard H. Scott learned that Johnson County was not paying the bills for the prisoners' incarceration, amounting to about one hundred dollars a day. During the jury selection phase, the Laramie County Sheriff had asked the judge that Johnson County be made to pay the expenses. Holsinger writes, "Whether or not Van Devanter suggested this action is today a moot point. Johnson County was bankrupt as everyone well knew and Scott could not force it to pay any part of the bill." Scott set the trial date back to January 2, 1893.

In newspaper accounts, Van Devanter is said to have been disgusted with the behavior of the prosecutors, one of whom had gone on a drinking spree. Though the man had been critical of the accused men visiting the local saloons, he reportedly bought drinks for some of them and would have bribed them not to testify. Though two Texans corroborated Van Devanter's accusations, the prosecutor responded in the newspaper that he'd been joking. The attorneys in the case were supposed to have earned ten thousand dollars for their services. The case certainly became one of Van Devanter's claims to fame and undoubtedly brought his talents to the attention of those in higher positions who could further an ambitious attorney's career.

The Johnson County War had a direct influence on the 1892 election, which was brutal. Van Devanter had been named Republican Party Chairman at the convention in September, according to Holsinger. As state G.O.P. chairman, he made a rather controversial move, offering subscriptions of one hundred dollars each from Republican campaign funds to newspapers throughout the state if those papers would print strong Republican editorials. Though it appeared that he was purchasing newspaper space, Van Devanter required each newspaper to send free copies to non-subscribers. He requested that the Republican names of presidential electors be placed at the top of the ballot in each county, and he sought extra funds from the candidates themselves, dunning Edward Ivinson for ten thousand dollars and Warren for five thousand.

Van Devanter also fought on behalf of the Republicans against Asa Mercer's printing in the *Northwest Live Stock Journal* the George Dunning confession, which implicated leading Republicans in the invasion. Dunning, who was one of the invaders, asserted that the Wyoming Stock Growers Association had offered to pay invaders a per diem fee and a bounty for each rustler killed. Van Devanter wrote to Joseph M. Carey on October 18, 1892, that he had worked with others until three in the morning "in getting up a good 'Sun' and a refutation of the *Stock-Journal's* slander. Am sorry that I could get no definite statement to publish from yourself, but think it all right." (Editor E.A. Slack was out of town at the time.) He sent a similar note to Warren. Van Devanter also asked each man for a thousand dollars for the campaign, explaining, "We are entirely out of money to-day and are seriously in need of it in matters that must receive immediate attention." Copies of the newspaper were delivered to all Cheyenne residences and businesses, and twelve thousand copies were mailed throughout the state.

Senators Warren and Carey were perceived by the public to have been involved in the infamous cattlemen's war. Warren's two-year term was ending, but the newly elected Democratic governor, John Osborne, a Rawlins physician, did not re-appoint him to the seat. The legislature had adjourned without naming a senator, although the solons did approve a memorial to Congress advocating popular election of U.S. senators.

Osborne gained the governor's seat by a majority of nearly two thousand votes over Republican Edward Ivinson. In Wyoming at that time, the elected candidate was allowed to take office upon his election. However, Osborne didn't receive confirmation from the capital, so in early December, he traveled to Cheyenne and had a notary public give him the oath of office. He took the position of governor, but Acting Governor Amos Barber (coincidentally also a physician) accused Osborne of usurpation. Barber stated that the delay in confirming election results was caused by late returns from Fremont and Converse counties, but Osborne believed that there was a conspiracy to change election results and ensure victory for a certain senatorial candidate. On December 8, the canvassing board met and declared Osborne the winner.

In mid-December, the *Sun* reported on the Democratic Party's appeal to the state Supreme Court to compel "the state board of canvassers to count an unauthorized abstract sent from Carbon county by justices of the peace instead of the regular returns submitted by the clerk, the officer designated by law as a canvasser." The newspaper noted that the Supreme Court "had the largest number of spectators it has had for many a day" to listen to the arguments in favor of the Democrats. Van Devanter's arguments to quash the appeal were delayed until the next day, when he spoke for forty-five minutes. On December 18, the newspaper headline asked, "Who is Governor?" The justices had to reserve their ruling until the gubernatorial seat was properly decided because the state canvassing board was required to meet and canvass the returns in the presence of the governor. "It is not known whether it is intended in this proceeding to test the question as to who is properly governor," the editor commented, "but since the statute requires that the state canvass shall be made in the governor's presence, it is highly probabl[e] that the entire question of governorship, will receive the attention of the court, and will probably have to be decided by it in the case of the present litigation."

Van Devanter served as leading counsel for the respondents to the suit and gained positive comments from the press. On December 20, the *Sun* reported that in closing his case, Van Devanter spoke for about twenty-five minutes and "confined himself to the two motions he had introduced." In contrast, the Democratic Party's attorney, Thomas M. Patterson, made a spectacle of himself. The paper states he "magnified this alleged fraud into gigantic proportions" without ever identifying clearly the fraud, but held the floor for an hour and a half. During that time Patterson "shook his fists and rushed up and down the aisles like a calamity congressman. He stood in somebody's hair, pulling this way and that for twenty-five minutes. The person whose hair was intended to be trimmed will perhaps never be known." The next day, the newspaper reported that most of Van Devanter's motions had been retained. On the last day of 1892, the newspaper stated that Osborne's claim to the gubernatorial seat would be settled through the judicial system. On January 1, 1893, the *Sun* reported the ruling of the court favored the Democrats, that the Hanna (Carbon County) precinct was counted, and that the justices of the peace received their election certifications from the House. The three Supreme Court justices agreed and the canvassing board finished its task. Osborne was finally declared the winner.

The new year brought the cattlemen into the spotlight again. The trial for the Johnson County invaders began January 6, 1893. Selection of jurors was difficult. For the defense, Van Devanter examined fifty-three jurors; forty-two were excused for cause. Ten days later, more than six hundred citizens had been examined, and only eleven had been found suitable to sit on a jury. According to Holsinger's account, by January 20, a total of 969 prospective jurors had been turned away. (Eventually, 1,064 jurors were examined and dismissed.) The Laramie County sheriff estimated that only twenty-one hundred jurors were available in the county. The next day, the prosecuting attorney offered to dismiss the charges. But Van Devanter insisted that the trial continue. He knew that if charges were dismissed against his clients in Laramie County, they could be tried in Johnson County. The opposing attorney agreed to a specially picked jury, then Van Devanter approved the dismissal. The jury sat and passed the necessary motions to dismiss, and the trial ended. The cattlemen went free.

Van Devanter's political clout remained strong. His name was suggested as a candidate for U.S. senator—an important position on its own, certainly, but even more impressive at this particular time in Wyoming's history because of the failure of Governor Osborne to appoint someone who could fill the position. Wyoming had gone without a second senator for the past two years, relying entirely on Senator Joseph M. Carey for representation. But Van Devanter continued his work as the state's Republican Party chairman from January 1895 through the summer of 1896 and attended the Republican League national convention in Cleveland in the spring of 1895, supporting McKinley for president.

In March 1896, Van Devanter argued a case before the U.S. Supreme Court. Known as the Race Horse case, it was probably his most famous. In July 1895, Wyoming's legislature passed a law establishing hunting seasons. A Bannock Indian named Race Horse had been arrested in Uinta County by Sheriff John Ward in early October for violating the new law by killing seven elk out of season. Race Horse, who was not able to raise bail, was jailed. Believing that his arrest was illegal, he filed suit in U.S. District Court in Cheyenne. Van Devanter worked on behalf of the state of Wyoming in conjunction with the state attorney general, B. F. Fowler, and another attorney. The Indian's case was based on the government treaty dated February 24, 1869, which gave the Bannocks the right to hunt on unoccupied federal land. Van Devanter and the attorneys representing the state argued that Wyoming's admission as a state pre-empted the treaty within the state boundaries. Judge John Riner decided in favor of the United States and Race Horse.

The Wyoming attorneys appealed the case to the U.S. Supreme Court. Because the other two attorneys had not been admitted to practice before this court, Van Devanter became the lead lawyer. He argued the case on March 11 and 12, 1896, against U.S. Attorney General Judson Harmon. On May 24, the Justices ruled 7-1 for the state of Wyoming. Associate Justice Edward D. White wrote in the majority opinion that the federal government treaty did not give Indians the right to hunt on state lands in violation of state laws. According to Holsinger, "White's decision followed closely Van Devanter's earlier arguments, thus not only giving the state of Wyoming a big boost but giving Van Devanter in his first Supreme Court case an impressive victory."

The case gave Van Devanter additional experience in the issues of land rights and Indian rights, two topics that continued to intrigue him throughout his career. The additional positive publicity helped further his career ambitions as well.

In April 1896, Senator Warren wrote to Van Devanter about the upcoming Wyoming Republican convention in Sheridan: "I am glad…that you intend to have at Sheridan in the delegation from Laramie County a lot of good, conservative men; then our county can with a little diplomacy run things at Sheridan exactly as they like. Of course we want to make the other people think they are at all times having their own way and there is where the diplomacy comes in."

Van Devanter was named as one of six delegates to the national convention when Wyoming Republicans met in Sheridan that year and was unanimously elected as Wyoming's national committeeman. But Van Devanter was not able to attend the convention in Saint Louis. He contracted a severe case of typhoid fever. His illness put him out of commission until October. Wyoming Republicans lost a number of offices in the ensuing election. McKinley gained the presidency, however, and he had pledged to reward those who campaigned hard for him. Senator Warren had repeatedly recommended Van Devanter for higher positions, lobbying McKinley's campaign manager on his behalf. In May 1896, Warren wrote to Van Devanter about his efforts, commenting that "Mr. [Mark] Hanna makes no reference to the portion of my letter wherein I spoke of Solicitor General, Attorney General, etc., and I did not expect he would. I wouldn't if I were in his place under the circumstances, but presuming that he would send the letter to McKinley I wanted to get a nail driven with both of them that we may want to hang something on later in the day." Later Warren wrote, "You may have forgotten it, but two or three years ago you dropped the remark that Solicitor General was a good place."

While Van Devanter was being considered for a prestigious presidential appointment, his association with the railroads prompted criticism. People were concerned that a man who had represented railroads would not be able to remain impartial in cases involving them. Apparently, President McKinley and his advisors had indicated their concerns about the matter. Because Van Devanter was being considered for a position of some eminence within the government, Warren told him that the attorney general "wanted to make some inquiries, chief among which was whether you had been connected with trusts, railway corporations, etc. I explained that you and your partner had numbered the Union Pacific among your clients and they had perhaps contributed one-fifth to one-tenth to your support but that you were no wise in the catagory [*sic*] of corporation attorneys as such." Warren assured the attorney general that Van Devanter's professional business had largely consisted of local matters. "He inquired if you had been in any large land suits or deals for the [rail]road against the government and inquired anxiously if I thought your connection had been such with the road that you could not in case occasion arose feel like pounding that road hard and plenty in decisions or suits...." Because the government was at the time involved in a lawsuit with the Union Pacific, "...the President felt very careful and ticklish about such points."

According to Burner, Van Devanter "was kept quite busy by the Union Pacific. The railroad had been under investigation for many years by Senate and House committees as well as by the Federal Land Office. The charges of criminal activities included fraudulent land surveys of much of Wyoming and of a large portion of Montana, appropriations of coal lands of great value and of land along streams under the Desert Land Act thereby excluding actual settlers. In these years he continued to work for Warren and exerted pressures on the legislature in his behalf." Warren's assurances and the support of Senator Clark and Representative Frank Mondell, who had written to McKinley on behalf of Van Devanter, undoubtedly helped boost his cause. On March 12, Warren summoned Van Devanter to Washington, D.C., for a personal interview at the request of the attorney general.

On March 19, 1897, the *Sun* reported that Van Devanter had accepted an appointment as assistant attorney general. According to the article, he had the choice of two positions—U.S. assistant attorney general or attorney for the Secretary of the Interior. After consulting with Wyoming's delegation in Washington, Van Devanter opted for the assistant attorney general position. The *Sun* expressed regret that Van Devanter had to leave Cheyenne, noting that his "career in Wyoming has been most remarkable."

Ironically, his new position as assistant attorney general placed him in charge of the legal department of the Secretary of Interior's office, focusing on public lands issues. Secretary Cornelius Bliss was not a lawyer himself, and the newspaper predicted that he would rely more upon Van Devanter for legal advice than usually was done. One reason for Van Devanter's appointment was his familiarity with the West. Bliss hailed from the eastern part of the country.

Van Devanter did not sever his Wyoming ties. He became a 32nd Degree Mason, Scottish Rite, as a member of Acacia Lodge No. 11 in Cheyenne in 1897. He remained Wyoming's Republican committeeman from 1897 through 1900 and helped several other Wyoming residents in their bids for national appointments, including Hugo

Donzelmann, who was chosen as American consul to Bohemia; Frank Mondell, who became assistant commissioner of the General Land Office; and Estelle Reel, who became the first woman superintendent of Indian schools for the United States.

Van Devanter served in his position as assistant attorney general until 1903. Historian Larson dubbed him "the legal conscience for the land department." During his tenure, he helped bring the legal affairs of the office up to date and presented lectures at what is now George Washington University. On November 27, 1901, the *Cheyenne Daily Leader* ran a lengthy article containing the Secretary of the Interior Ethan Hitchcock's report to the president. The report was highly complimentary to Van Devanter.

Pleased with Van Devanter's organizational skills, Hitchcock noted that "groundless appeals and motions for review in land cases" had been reduced and the legal work involving public lands had also been greatly reduced. "I cannot commend too highly the able manner in which the affairs of this office have been administered," Hitchcock wrote. He also complimented Wyoming's W.A. Richards for his part as assistant commissioner of general land in opening the Kiowa, Comanche, and Apache lands in the territory of Oklahoma and praised Van Devanter "in the labors devolving upon this department preliminary to and after the opening of said lands." The legal and administrative tasks involved were complex and "too much cannot be said of the masterly manner in which he met them all and discharged the onerous duties imposed upon him."

In March 1902, the forty-three-year-old Van Devanter was mentioned for the Secretary of the Interior post and perhaps even for Secretary of State. Both Bliss and Hitchcock commended his work for the Interior Department. The *Daily Leader* reported that Van Devanter "attracted the attention and won the admiration of President Roosevelt some months ago during a series of conferences on department matters." Van Devanter had not sought the posts, but further career advancements were just around the corner. By late January 1903, the newspaper once again had an opportunity to sing Van Devanter's praises. He had earned a presidential appointment as the U.S. Circuit Court judge for the Eighth Judicial District, which consisted of Minnesota, Iowa, Missouri, Arkansas, Kansas, Nebraska,

South Dakota, North Dakota, Wyoming, Colorado, Utah, Oklahoma, and New Mexico. Although cases were tried in each of the states, the size of the circuit meant that judges worked almost entirely in the court of appeals in sessions at Saint Louis, Saint Paul, Denver, or Cheyenne. Van Devanter would serve with Judges J. Henry Caldwell of Arkansas, Walter H. Sanborn of Minnesota, and Amos M. Thayer of Missouri.

On February 5, 1903, the newspaper reported that Van Devanter's nomination had been sent to the Senate by President Theodore Roosevelt. This presidential appointment was "simply a just recognition of his personal worth." Although Van Devanter had to remain in the Interior Department until his successor could be appointed, he had decided to reside in Cheyenne. Van Devanter was sworn into office in Washington in mid-March and left immediately for Saint Louis to participate in the trial of the Northern Securities Company merger case. According to Burner, Van Devanter's new case load included "jurisdictional disputes, various railroad cases, land claims, questions of negligence, and dozens of like issues that required careful reconstruction of events and invoking of applicable precedent." His work on the Eighth Circuit Court "constituted a rehearsal for the kind of work he would do on the Supreme Court."

Attempts had been made to have Van Devanter appointed to the President's cabinet in 1909 — "a strategy of watch-and-wait as against the do-or-die campaigns" for his appointment to the bench, according to historian Daniel A. Nelson. In January 1909, Warren told Van Devanter that Wyoming would probably not have someone in the White House during their lifetimes, but he believed a Wyoming resident could reach the Supreme Court or cabinet positions. Even though their attempt to get Van Devanter named to a cabinet position failed, Warren felt that the effort had been worth it because Van Devanter's name was now known to the President.

In 1910 President William Taft promoted U.S. Supreme Court Justice Edward White to chief justice and nominated Van Devanter to the court as an associate justice. Senator Warren and Senator Philander C. Knox of Pennsylvania, a former attorney for Carnegie Steel Company, threw their wholehearted support behind the new nominee. Clarence Clark, Wyoming's other senator and the chairman of the Senate Judiciary Committee, along with his brother, D. O. Clark, vice president of Union Pacific Coal Company, also supported Van Devanter's nomination. His appointment was not uncontested, however. William Jennings Bryan was among those who opposed him. According to Burner, Bryan referred to Van Devanter as "the judge that held that two railroads running parallel to each other for two thousand miles were not competing lines, one of the roads being that of the Union Pacific!" Together, Senators Warren and Clark and Congressman Frank Mondell worked to persuade President Taft to appoint Van Devanter. He needed convincing.

In October 1909, Taft appointed Horace H. Lurton to the Supreme Court following the death of Justice Peckham. Though Van Devanter was not considered for this position, he was considered for the next opening that came early in 1910 when Associate Justice Brewer died. Warren wrote to Taft on Van Devanter's behalf on March 30, 1910, stating he'd known Van Devanter since he began his legal practice and "during my twenty-eight years' of practice as an attorney, I have never met with any other gentleman who possessed, in my humble opinion, all the qualifications which go to make up a learned, upright and honest judge."

A snowstorm downed telegraph lines in Wyoming, so Warren wired the President twice to make sure Taft received his recommendation of Van Devanter, calling him "young, strong, vigorous, and reliable, resourceful and industrious to a remarkable degree…versed in mining, milling, water right and irrigation laws so desirable for the west.…"

According to Nelson, Warren literally flooded the wires with requests for aid in securing the position for the judge from Wyoming. He wired Judge J. A. Van Orsdel, who was then seated on the Superior Court of the District of Columbia, as well as Senator Clark and Congressman Mondell. When Warren reached Washington three days later, he went almost directly to the White House to campaign for Van Devanter. Taft felt that the New York circuit wanted an appointment instead, but Warren continued to push for Van Devanter by having others write to the president on his behalf. Warren wanted to remain in the background, but one senator slipped and told the President that he had seen Warren about the matter. It looked as if Van Devanter would not gain this appointment either. By late April, Warren notified Van Devanter that Charles Evans Hughes would probably be appointed. A New Yorker, Hughes did receive the appointment.

The recommendations for Van Devanter continued to pour in. Warren did not give up even though no vacancy existed on the bench, for he believed that with Van Devanter's name foremost in the waiting pile, an appointment would be forthcoming. On July 4, 1910, Chief Justice Melville W. Fuller died. Warren tried to see the president, but Taft was vacationing and would not make appointments until that fall. Another vacancy occurred that summer when Associate Justice William H. Moody resigned in poor health. Warren re-energized his efforts in Van Devanter's behalf, and wrote the president in early September, again mentioning Van Devanter's suitability for the position, although Van Devanter was considered lacking in experience in writing case decisions. The fact that someone from the Eighth Judicial District was due for an appointment increased competition for the position as well.

Early in December, Warren wired Van Devanter that the president thought that he had not worked on enough cases. Van Devanter wired back on December 5, 1910. He said that he preferred his name be withdrawn from consideration because he felt the cases he worked on needed careful deliberation. Warren sent a copy of the telegram to Taft, and this may have swung the balance in Van Devanter's favor. Warren also used political influence on the Democratic president, suggesting that another candidate for the bench supported progressive Republicans who were wreaking havoc with Taft's political agenda. Van Devanter was appointed by the end of the year. Warren announced Van Devanter's appointment formally in a letter December 15, 1910. Warren told the newly appointed justice that the struggle for his appointment had been one of the most challenging of his career.

Van Devanter never played a leading role on the Supreme Court. "He was quiet and rarely appeared in public," writes Burner. "He eschewed controversy and accepted as his own provinces the areas of public lands, admiralty law, water rights, Indian controversies, and corporation law." His work focused mainly on technical issues that bored the other justices. In those areas, however, he "shone in conference as a student of procedure, a tireless worker, and a diplomatic critic of his colleagues' opinions." Van Devanter, skilled in the area of jurisdictional conflict, was selected to draft the Jurisdictional Act of 1925.

One of Van Devanter's most important cases was *McGrain v. Daugherty 273 US 135 (1927)*. The case centered on the Senate's right to subpoena witnesses and was brought by the brother of the U.S. attorney general, who claimed the Senate had overstepped its bounds by incarcerating him for ignoring two subpoenas. (At the time, his brother was being investigated on charges of corruption.) Van Devanter studied the history of legislative power to subpoena witnesses, even researching the practice in Britain and the colonial practice in the United States. He concluded that Congress, in its investigatory mode, had power equal to that of regular courts "unless definite proof can be shown that the investigation's purpose is not to legislate."

Van Devanter, who decided to retire in 1932, wrote just twenty-two opinions in the 1930s, focusing on Indian rights and jurisdictional disputes as well as admiralty law. He'd been hailed as "the foremost intellectual among the conservatives" and managed to get along well with his fellow justices, including Louis Brandeis, who was considered quite liberal. In 1937, President Franklin D. Roosevelt took umbrage with the Supreme Court over his New Deal legislation, and the make-up of the court came into question. Seven of the nine judges had been appointed by Republican presidents. Six of them were past seventy years old, including Van Devanter. The Court Reorganization Bill was introduced, which would allow the president to add one new judge for every judge older than seventy years up to a maximum of six. Though the bill was soundly defeated, Van Devanter resigned. Hugo Black, a Democrat, was named as his replacement.

Van Devanter had been awarded several honorary Doctor of Law degrees throughout his career, including honors from DePauw University, the University of Cincinnati, the University of Wyoming, and the College of Charleston, South Carolina. He enjoyed researching his family's genealogy and studied this history both in the United States and Holland. He also enjoyed hunting elk, bear, and mountain sheep and continued to love gardening, a hobby he pursued in earnest during summer adjournments of the court.

Van Devanter died in Washington, D.C., on February 8, 1941, of a heart attack. He was eighty-one years old and collapsed while visiting his sister, Mrs. Sanford L. Raridan. According to his obituary, he "left the court under provisions of the statute permitting justices over 70 who had served 10 years to retire at full pay at $20,000 a year." His two sons, Isaac and Winslow, survived him, along with three grandchildren. His funeral services were held in the Church of the Epiphany and were conducted by the Chaplain of the U.S. Senate, Dr. ZeBarney T. Phillips. Van Devanter was buried in Rock Creek Cemetery in Washington, D.C., beside his wife, who had died seven years earlier. Additional memorial services were held March 16, 1942, in the Supreme Court building by the Bar of the Supreme Court and the officers of the Court.

According to Justice Charles E. Hughes, Jr.'s memorial address, "He was not a judge of whom the public generally could gain any very sharply defined impression. He was quiet and unassuming, and appeared seldom in public. He made very few speeches even before gatherings of lawyers, and those were of the conversational and unpretentious sort." Hughes eulogized Van Devanter as "a man of simple, unobtrusive religious faith.... Modesty and simplicity were the keynotes of his life."

C.G. Coutant

 Wyoming history often first refer to a bulky, now rare volume found in libraries and archives. *The History of Wyoming from Earliest Known Discoveries*, written by C.G. Coutant and published in 1899, begins with the exploration of Wyoming dating back to Spanish occupation and includes information on French Canadian explorations and the Lewis and Clark and John C. Fremont expeditions. Other topics included in the 712-page volume are the opening of the Overland and Bozeman Trails, the discovery of gold in South Pass, the creation of Wyoming Territory, and the building of the Union Pacific Railroad.

Coutant's book, the first history of the state ever written, was deemed a "Herculean task" by J.H. Hayford, who wrote the introduction. Hayford, who knew Coutant personally, edited the *Laramie Sentinel* in the early 1890s and later served as a district judge in Wyoming. In the book's preface, Coutant himself writes, "I owe it to myself to say that the undertaking has grown on my hands and has become of greater magnitude than was contemplated." Coutant's hopes to produce three volumes were larger than his ability to achieve them. He continued to work on his project, but financial difficulties proved too much to overcome.

❦

Charles Griffin Coutant was born October 16, 1840, in Rosendale, New York, to Gabriel and Mary Ferguson Coutant. Coutant's father was descended from Quakers who came to the United States from France in 1735 and settled in Tillison, Ulster County, New York. "My Father was very proud of being an American of so long standing," Coutant wrote, "and raised his family with that idea."

After being orphaned at seven years old, Coutant lived with an uncle on his farm until he was fourteen. He became fascinated with becoming a newspaperman, so he traveled to New York and got a job as office boy in a publishing house. "[A]fire with the spirit of his work…in a very few years he had become a newspaper writer, all of his spare moments having been given to the obtaining of an education," wrote the *Rogue River* (Oregon) *Daily Courier*. He possessed a great memory and was "a fund of information that was the greatest asset in his professional work, while his fidelity to detail and his accuracy of narrative made his work of the greatest value to the journals with which he was employed." According to Hayford, during Coutant's tenure with the Metropolitan Press of New York City, "he was detailed to examine proposed railroad routes across the continent, and later he followed along the lines of the great trans-continental railways during the period of their construction." Coutant, he states, had been familiar with the Rocky Mountain region since 1859.

At age nineteen, Coutant was stationed in California, covering events there for New York newspapers. He also worked in Mexico and served as a roving reporter during the Civil War. Twenty years later he covered the Indian wars on the plains for the eastern papers. He eventually settled in Kansas and published a newspaper there, where he "became a leader of public thought." Coutant helped organize the Kansas Editorial Association and served as president for several years.

On Christmas Day, 1867, Coutant married Mary Elizabeth Clark of Boston. They raised a family of six children—George, Walter, Charles D., Laura, Georgia, and May. After living in a wide range of places, Coutant moved to Wyoming in 1890, when he was fifty years old and the state was a brand new member of the union. Perhaps his deep pride in being an American melded with his love of words and his writing skills and led to his passion for chronicling the history of this young state.

In September 1891, Coutant became the subject of newspaper stories himself. He had begun a new newspaper called the *Wyoming Commonwealth*. Cheyenne, with a population then around twenty thousand, already had three dailies and two weeklies. The editors of the other papers were none too pleased to see another competitor enter the market. On September 20, John F. Carroll of the *Daily*

Leader wrote an editorial castigating Coutant for his new newspaper, which was being published in the *Stock Journal* office. Carroll writes, "The Kansas colonel was…a booster and a boomer and promoter all rolled into one and what he didn't know about precipitating prosperity upon a community wasn't worth knowing."

Carroll went on to list some of Coutant's money-making schemes. He had interested the Cheyenne Board of Trade in a patented smelting machine, the property of a good friend whom Coutant dubbed the "Inventive Genius." The Board of Trade eventually agreed to give Coutant two thousand dollars worth of town lots, although he had asked for a quarter-section within the city, but the deal fell through. Coutant had issued stock in the ill-fated and fraudulent silver mine at Silver Crown in Laramie County to finance his newspaper. He issued shares of non-assessable stock and a subscription to the *Wyoming Commonwealth* for two dollars each, and apparently was somewhat successful in gaining subscribers. Carroll gave Coutant credit for organizing the State Board of Mines but charged that he had done so only to ensure that his paper had an official capacity. He called Coutant "a Rook, a human bird which preys upon and plucks the pigeons."

Coutant, in fact, suffered great financial woes. His press and type were donated by Will Goetz, a Kansas newspaperman who also loaned Coutant five hundred dollars and became business manager of the *Commonwealth*. When Coutant refused to pay off the loan, Goetz's mother sued. The *Cheyenne Sun* reported that the vice president of the Commonwealth Publishing Company blamed the money problems on Coutant's mismanagement. Coutant left the *Commonwealth* but replied to both newspapers, writing, "The 'Sun-Leader' mongrel is a political combination that is a closed business corporation and editorially, it is a Siamese-twin affair." He suggested that the newspapers be issued from the same office stating, "It is a fraud on the people of Cheyenne to collect double money for the same thing." Ironically, the *Sun* and the *Leader* did merge in 1895.

Coutant left Cheyenne, moved to Lander, and began publishing a weekly newspaper there. While in Lander, he began conducting research for his history of Wyoming. Even though his family was growing at that time and Coutant needed to travel extensively, he was able to balance both responsibilities. He planned to publish the history of

C.G. Coutant wrote the first comprehensive history of Wyoming, and his labor of love, not profitable during his lifetime, is a collector's item today. (Courtesy Wyoming State Archives)

the state in three volumes, using the proceeds from sale of the first volume to finance the next two. Historian John C. Thompson explains, "With this as his plan he collected [money] from subscribers to the history for three volumes." In 1897, Coutant made arrangements with the Laramie Republican Company to manufacture one thousand copies of the first volume. Advance orders amounted to about four hundred dollars, but the publishers sought additional guarantees. Otto Gramm of Laramie City co-signed a note to guarantee the publishers payment for the first edition, and H.G. Balch of the First National Bank in Laramie accepted this at face value. The publishers agreed.

Coutant wrote longhand with a pencil on inexpensive school tablets, a task made more difficult due to the fact that he had palsy.

According to Thompson, Coutant "had a penchant for rotund, frequently tautological composition. Very largely he avoided the use of a single word when three or more might be utilized without conveying any additional meaning." Much of Coutant's inflated prose was edited out of his first volume "but flowers abundantly" in the rough draft of the remaining manuscript. He sent copy to the printers over a ten-month period although they could have completed the work in two months if they had had the entire manuscript to work with. Finally, after more than a year, while Coutant was living in Laramie, the book was completed, but the time delay led to financial loss, and the printer allowed Coutant to take only a few copies. The bank had to pay the printer for the rest. According to historian Alfred Mokler, the bank sold the books to the public at the low price of five dollars each. Even though Gramm paid his note, the bank lost money. So did Coutant. He earned no money to pay himself for his time, his traveling expenses, or to pay his daughter who typed the manuscript. Even so, he did not give up on his dream.

In his preface to the book, Coutant explained his plans for the future volumes. He planned to cover the state's territorial period in the second volume of his work, which he hoped to complete in a few months. That book would have begun with "the history of the founding of Cheyenne, the organization of Laramie County, the founding of Laramie City, the organization of Albany and other counties, together with the commencement of the Territorial Government.... The last book will contain a full index covering the subjects treated upon in the three volumes and these subjects will be subdivided and indexed for the convenience of those in search of information. The index will also give names, battles, incidents and all matter connected with the history of the State, so that the reader will be enabled to find, without delay, any subject, incident or name mentioned in the work." Unfortunately, this work was not completed. (An index was created posthumously by students in historian Grace Raymond Hebard's classes at the University of Wyoming.)

Coutant referred to Wyoming as "the highway where converged all roads leading across the plains to the territories beyond" and couldn't resist voicing his strong opinions on the building of the Union Pacific. He wrote, "The government, anxious to promote the construction of the road, voted a subsidy in land of each alternate section for twenty miles on each side of the road and in addition used its bonds to the company to the amount of $16,000 per mile across the plains and $45,000 per mile across the mountains. At that time it was not believed either in or out of Congress that the road would ever be able to repay the government the amount advanced." He explains, "The only wonder today [1899] is, that private individuals were found who were willing to invest capital in the construction of this road, and it was asking much on the part of the government to even expect that financiers would invest their money in an enterprise which promised so little in the way of returns, over and above the cost of constructing and operating." Businessmen of the day felt that the government should build the railroad even if insufficient private capital could be raised.

"People at this day," Coutant continued, "are inclined to believe that the government did a generous thing toward this enterprise, but it was not so regarded at the time." For example, private citizens, by purchasing railroad lands at $2.50 an acre for settlement, generated funds for the federal government. Citizens who rode the rails paid for the service, generating income for the Union Pacific to pay its bonds. Coutant believed the government gained more benefit by "placing its burden on the shoulders of the pioneers of the west," and should have instead built the railroad and leased it for enough money to provide its maintenance.

Coutant's book contained "numerous inaccuracies," wrote Thompson, but "the Lander newspaperman [Coutant] who accomplished monumental research for this, and two other volumes which were not published, was too canny to repeat some of the alleged historical lore which was supplied him by well-meaning informants." One example was a story related to Coutant by Levi Ashenfelder, a Cheyenne pioneer. Ashenfelder had heard the tale from James Boedan—a story similar to the fable about Androcles removing a thorn from a lion's foot. A Canadian trapper named Peno, wounded in a struggle with a buffalo bull he'd shot, broke his leg when the bull charged him and gored his horse. He eventually crawled to rest near a creek. A large bear came to him with a sliver in his paw, and Peno removed it with his knife. The bear stuck with him for the next several days and led him to a hill overlooking a valley containing a village.

Coutant returned to Cheyenne in 1900. In March, the Coutants traveled to LaSalle, Illinois, to visit relatives. Coutant continued on to Washington, D.C., "to look over some important records in the library of the war department to be used in the second volume of the history of Wyoming," according to the *Daily Sun-Leader*. He told the reporter that he "had no desire to talk politics and in fact, think it is better not to do so." While in Washington, he visited the Wyoming delegation—consisting of Senators Francis E. Warren and Clarence Clark and Congressman Frank Mondell—and spoke highly of all three men. Coutant also met President McKinley during his trip and called the president "a genial gentleman" who "seems to have the happy faculty of saying the right thing at the right time to the right person." When a reporter asked Coutant about the rumor that he was to be appointed to a federal position, he replied that he had not sought such an appointment and that he had never been a political candidate. He added a humorous comment, saying, "[I]t's not likely that at this time of life I would break the record."

By September, the Coutants were living in "a pretty cottage" on 418 East Sixteenth Street. When the city struggled through an epidemic of typhoid fever that fall, Coutant expressed his views in a letter to the editor. Doctors in Cheyenne were in disagreement as to what the disease was when the epidemic first began. Coutant likened Cheyenne's experience to the New York epidemic of 1861 when doctors were divided on the disease. One group there called it typhoid and another typhus. Coutant explained that the twenty-two physicians of Bellevue Hospital were in disagreement, until fifteen doctors contracted the disease. He wrote, "That epidemic taught New York a lesson and sanitary measures became of the first importance." Doctors in that city finally agreed and called the illness typhus fever, tracing it to a boy from Ireland who had it when he arrived in America. Coutant concluded, "Experience has taught me that diseases of the human family are liable to break out in any part of the country when conditions are favorable.... We are only safe when we adopt heroic sanitary measures and this applies with force here in Cheyenne at the present time." The city did clean up its sewers and drainages and later renovated its water system, but the improvements were not due solely to Coutant's letter. Many of the city's physicians and leaders also advocated better sanitation measures.

Coutant served as the Wyoming state librarian from 1901 to 1905. During his tenure, he catalogued the books in the library, a work that the *Sun* called a "stupendous task." Coutant's son Walter who visited his family before accepting responsibilities as the assistant clerk of the U.S. District Court of Alaska, helped his father catalogue the library. Daughter Laura helped as well. She had traveled to Denver to study library management, then returned to Cheyenne to marry her beau, Charles W. Gilmore, at the Coutant home. The *Leader* estimated that the cataloguing job would take three weeks, even with three people working steadily and stated that when the job was done "every book in the library can be found at a moment's notice."

The library had been created by the Second Territorial Legislative Assembly in 1871. It was used mostly by the territory's Supreme Court judges, who influenced the purchase of books under the $250 annual appropriation. By 1889, according to historian T.A. Larson's estimates, the library held more than fourteen thousand volumes. In 1897, the Third State Legislature created the state law library as a separate unit of the state library. This made three units to the state's library: the law library, the main library, and the document library. An 1895 law had made the state librarian an ex-officio member of the Wyoming Historical Society, "charged with custody of all books, manuscripts, charts, maps and other Wyoming historical articles, which were to be deposited in the state library," according to the *Wyoming Blue Book*. By the time Coutant took office in 1901, the position contained much responsibility.

While working full-time and remaining active in community affairs, Coutant continued to pursue his dream of writing the additional volumes of Wyoming's history. The *Cheyenne Daily Sun* in early 1902 reported that Coutant was working on the second volume of the state's history and hoped to send it to the printers by the first of March. The report explained Coutant's hectic schedule, stating, "At present he devotes the early part of the day to his work, as he also does the evening hours after the state library is closed for the day."

Coutant continued to travel, both in connection with his library work and his other pursuits. Some of his travel is documented in the newspaper and included a visit to Omaha on library business. He also visited Cody and Denver. In early 1903, he traveled to Omaha "where he secured rates for the Industrial Convention here next week," according to the *Daily Sun*.

Coutant's removal from office as state librarian in 1905, "following a political turnover, caused quite an upheaval," writes Thompson. Governor B. B. Brooks took office in January 1905, succeeding Acting Governor Fenimore Chatterton. According to the *Wyoming Blue Book*, Coutant left his position in March 1905, but other reports indicate that he moved to Sheridan in 1904 and became editor for the *Sheridan Enterprise,* perhaps forfeiting his office with a healthy dose of political disgruntlement.

By 1907, Coutant was living in Grants Pass, Oregon. After Coutant took a year and a half trip to Alaska, he began work in Grants Pass as editor for what was then the *Weekly Courier* in January 1909. He also worked as editor of the *Daily Courier,* the first daily in the town, from its debut in 1910. Because he could no longer interest publishers in the additional volumes of his gargantuan historical work of Wyoming, Coutant sought solace in the Pacific Northwest.

Although he didn't realize monetary gain and discovered only personal fulfillment from his writing, Coutant's ground-breaking historical work was not in vain. Coutant's widow later sold the remainder of the manuscript to Dr. Grace Raymond Hebard. Dr. Hebard used the information in some of her historical publications. She sold the rest to the Wyoming Historical Department. In 1940, Inez Babb Taylor, assistant state historian, edited the remaining manuscript. Thompson explains that Coutant's manuscript notes contained many more factual errors than his completed book. Thompson believes that Coutant wrote his notes before acquiring in-depth knowledge of the state that would have helped him edit more accurately. Coutant's remaining work was published in the *Annals of Wyoming* in the early 1940s and still serves as an important source for historians and others seeking historical knowledge of the state. In 1942, when Thompson wrote his columns about Coutant, a few copies of *The History of*

Wyoming were occasionally being sold at a price of twenty-five dollars. By then the book had been out of print for many years.

The Rogue River *Daily Courier* called Coutant a man of "magnificent courage." In October 1912, he suffered a stroke at work, which paralyzed his left arm. Additional strokes occurred, but he was able to visit the downtown area on Christmas Day. He never recovered from the strokes, yet he spoke of returning to his work as editor. His obituary states that "even the latest of his writings contained the fire and the vigor that had always been a characteristic of his work."

Coutant died on January 17, 1913, in Grants Pass, Oregon, and was buried in the International Order of the Odd Fellows cemetery. He was seventy-three years old but had never given up his dream of completing his Wyoming history. "Coutant hoped until the day of his death that he would be able to complete the work to which he had dedicated himself," comments Thompson.

His book, though a financial disaster, remains valuable not only because of the important information it contains but also as a marketable antique. Sandy Adams of Adams & Adams Antiquarian Bookstore in Laramie explains that Coutant's book is now considered scarce. When published, the book was mostly distributed to politicians, such as the governor and legislators, and to public libraries. A few copies were given to private individuals. Some people were given copies signed by Coutant. Governor Brooks was given fewer than one hundred copies. He signed the books as the governor of Wyoming and presented them to visiting dignitaries as keepsakes. Some private owners continue to hold onto Coutant's book, according to Adams. As a treasured item of Wyoming history, the owners do not want to part with them. Other copies of the book "went the way of library books," she says, falling into disrepair from use and being discarded. In early 2001, a copy of Coutant's book "in pretty good shape" in Adams's store was priced at $550.

Thompson says if Coutant could have lived long enough to see his work so valued, he would have felt pleased "to know that his efforts resulted in preserving a creditable history of our state for others to enjoy."

Dr. George P. Johnston

AN EARLY DAY newspaper photo of George P. Johnston shows a handsome young man with a handlebar mustache, thick dark hair, a Roman nose, and close-set eyes. During his lifetime, Johnston saw many medical advances and earned honors in his field. Some sources credit him with performing the first typhoid test in the state. The physician, who was granted the state's first medical license, saw medicine progress from kitchen table operations to surgeries performed in sterile hospital operating rooms. His influence on the residents of Cheyenne is still felt today.

George Palmer Johnston was born in Greene County, Ohio, on March 6, 1863, to Thomas P. and Elizabeth Shellabarger Johnston. He was one of ten children. He graduated from Antioch College in 1888, then earned his medical degree from the Medical College of Ohio in Cincinnati and trained an additional year at the National Soldiers' Home in Dayton, Ohio. Following that training, he moved to Cheyenne in 1891 or 1892 to establish a practice. Johnston "made the usual courtesy calls to other physicians," writes journalist Cal Bernstein, "and was surprised when he was told by one to 'get out of Cheyenne and stay out.' Dr. Johnston stayed." He did leave briefly to seek more training, returning to Ohio in 1896 to earn a master's degree from Antioch College. He continued his education with postgraduate courses even after beginning his practice.

Although based in Cheyenne, Johnston's practice spread beyond the boundaries of the state. The doctor, traveling by horse and buggy, visited sick patients as far as seventy-five miles from his Cheyenne home. He treated patients in Kimball, Nebraska; Pine Bluffs,

Wyoming; and the Silver Crown mine area near Cheyenne. In 1897, the *Cheyenne Daily Leader* reported him as returning from Sidney, Nebraska, where he performed a surgical operation. According to historian Ellen Stafford, Johnston "performed many a lifesaving operation on a kitchen table, with someone holding a kerosene lamp for light." He is credited with performing the first appendectomy and the first abdominal section in Wyoming.

In addition to maintaining his own practice, Johnston was also active in public health issues. Bernstein says that he "started a campaign for uniform state medical laws." In 1897, Wyoming's Fourth Legislature considered a "Board of Health Bill." The bill was introduced by Dr. George G. Verbryck, a Republican from Cambria, Weston County. The Board of Health was to "regulate the practice of medicine, surgery and obstetrics in the state" as well as supervise local health boards, according to a report in the *Cheyenne Daily Leader*. The Senate voted unanimously for the bill, but it met some opposition in the House. Some physicians opposed the creation of a board; others felt that the expense of creating a board was wasteful. But those in favor claimed that many people had died at the hands of incompetent physicians; others pointed out that nearly all the states had created boards of health to regulate sanitary conditions. Yet Wyoming did not officially create the Board of Health until 1901.

For his work in supporting the board of health bill, Johnston was presented with Wyoming's first medical license by the Wyoming Board of Medicine in 1899. Before that time, doctors planning to practice in Wyoming had only to register their diploma with the county clerk in the county where they practiced.

Johnston has also been credited with bringing the first registered nurse, Sarah Jane MacKenzie, to Wyoming in 1900. She first worked as assistant head nurse at the State Hospital in Rock Springs, then was hired as Matron and Superintendent of Saint John's Hospital in Cheyenne in April 1901. MacKenzie earned kudos from doctors as an excellent surgical nurse and later became quite active in the Wyoming Nurses' Association. Another woman with medical training, Dr. Letitia Wiseman of Cheyenne, assisted Johnston with medical procedures. She earned her license to practice medicine in 1900.

The year 1900 marked an important turning point for the health of Cheyenne citizens. Diseases such as whooping cough, diphtheria, and smallpox were commonly reported. In March, according to newspaper reports, a disease suspected as smallpox had broken out, and local physicians were vaccinating many people. Patients were quarantined to help curtail the spread of the contagious disease. Some were taken to the "pest house" for recovery. Fear of smallpox was high, although in early April the newspaper stated that a rumor of the disease in the town had been exaggerated.

A disease sweeping the Union Pacific grading camps between Cheyenne and Ogden at that time was also causing concern, especially since local physicians disagreed about what it was. Only one death was thought to have been caused by the ailment. Dr. William Crook of Cheyenne told the newspaper that he thought it was "a cutaneous disease" and believed it had been brought from the West Indies to the lower Mississippi Valley, creating an epidemic. Southern Wyoming was affected, as were the Missouri and Mississippi valleys, and other sections of the southern United States. He dubbed it "papulous erythema." Later articles in the paper highlighted the disagreement between physicians. Some still believed the disease to be smallpox.

The sanitation inspector of the Union Pacific, who believed the illness to be smallpox, thought that the disease was under control by the end of May. At the same time, though, the *Leader* ran an article explaining that many people in Cheyenne who had been vaccinated against smallpox were now ill. Dr. H. H. Mayo of Salt Lake City contacted Cheyenne physician Crook with his belief that the disease was not smallpox but an unfamiliar ailment. Another expert, Dr. Allen Fowler, a physician with much experience in smallpox cases, believed the disease to be smallpox.

During the summer of 1900, Dr. Johnston spent several weeks on an eastern trip, according to the *Leader*. He left on July 17 and returned in mid-August from a visit to Ohio. The day after his departure, the newspaper reported that smallpox was epidemic along the railroad near Rawlins. This marked the second wave of the epidemic. Cheyenne physicians feared that this second outbreak would be worse than the first.

Dr. George P. Johnston received the first medical license issued in the state of Wyoming and enjoyed a lengthy career as a beloved country doctor. (Courtesy Wyoming State Archives)

October proved one of the worst months of all. On October 2, the *Leader* reported a case of typhoid fever. The next day, eight were listed as ill with fever, and three hundred cases of catarrhal fever were reported. Again, physicians disagreed about what the disease was. The *Leader* reported, "All Cheyenne physicians agree that there has not been so much sickness in Cheyenne for years and that the prevailing disease is spreading, but there is a difference of opinion as to what the disease is." Some called it catarrhal fever, some said mountain fever, some thought hay fever. According to the newspaper, "cases are not all alike and no doubt there are some cases of all the fevers mentioned." Some patients experienced similar symptoms, including "a high fever with more or less stomach trouble." Those who thought it was typhoid fever were eventually proven correct.

The paper commended local doctors, saying, "It testifies to the faithfulness and ability of our physicians that with the hundreds of patients that have been under their care, there have been no deaths." And the newspaper argued that very few patients had "the real typhoid…proverbially a serious disease [that] cannot be cured in two or three days." Throughout the week, though, cases increased with between three and eight persons listed as ill in news items each day. On October 6, the Laramie County Hospital (later renamed Saint John's) was full.

On October 8, 1900, the *Leader* carried the ominous headline, "It Is Typhoid." Dr. Amos Barber, another Cheyenne physician (and later governor) believed that the water supply was not infected and suggested instead that a possible source of infection was milk. He advised residents to boil both water and milk. Some people argued that boiling the water made it "unpalatable," so Barber suggested blowing air into the water after it had cooled with a bellows or an atomizer to aerate the water, which supposedly made it taste better.

The doctors' confusion over the disease led to frustration on the part of Cheyenne residents. On October 12, the *Leader* reported, "Many citizens are inquiring why, in view of all the sickness and difference of opinion among the physicians, the board of health [apparently the local group] does not institute an investigation and bring an expert here to make an analysis."

The Wyoming Medical Society (WMS), with Johnston as its president, held its annual convention at the courthouse in Cheyenne on October 11, 1900. Johnston "presided at the sessions of the society and was ably assisted in his work by Doctors Bennett, Barber, Conway, and Maynard" of Cheyenne. The physicians enjoyed an elegant banquet at the Cheyenne Club. Also in attendance at the meeting were several women doctors, including Dr. Lillian Heath of Rawlins, Wyoming's first female physician. Dr. Charlotte Hawk of Green River was elected third vice president of the group. Dr. Heath was enrolled in the group at the meeting as was Cheyenne's

Dr. Letitia Wiseman. Dr. A. W. Barber of Cheyenne also became a member, in addition to several others from throughout the state. "Although in its infancy the association has already accomplished great results," the *Leader* proclaimed. "The enactment of a law prohibiting quack doctors, faikers [*sic*] and frauds from imposing on the community has been largely the work of the association...." Convention attendance was smaller than usual due to the epidemic raging throughout the city. Physicians at the conference admitted to having patients all over the state ill with fevers, but there was "no unanimity of opinion" as to the nature of the epidemic.

In covering the convention, the *Leader* pushed for the creation of a state Board of Health, drawing attention to the recent smallpox epidemic along the railroad, and suggesting that the WMS could be influential in passing such legislation. One recommendation made at the WMS meeting was to create a medical department.

On October 13, the newspaper reported the first death of the epidemic. Berry Land, a tinsmith, died at the county hospital in Cheyenne the day before. He had struggled with the disease for ten days. Several others were reported as "near death's door." The physicians and Cheyenne's acting mayor warned citizens to take proper precautions to help protect them from the disease, by now so rampant that nuns from a Denver hospital came to nurse individuals in their homes. Acting Mayor N. R. Davis took the helm for Mayor W. R. Schnitger, who had fallen ill. Dr. William Mitchell, an expert from Denver, had conducted tests on samples of milk and water from the city. Davis advised residents to boil milk and water until further notice and ordered the police to inspect all sewers, cesspools, grease traps, and vaults in the city. Owners who refused necessary cleaning would be fined. A tongue-in-cheek item printed a few days later in the paper asked whether the epidemic might have been caused by beer but explained no one had suggested boiling that beverage.

A few days after the WMS convention, Johnston's wedding announcement appeared on the front page of the *Leader*. He married Dorothy Lois Miller at Elmcrest, Dexter, Iowa, on October 15, 1900. The report called Johnston "our very esteemed physician, who is very highly respected by all who know him." The newlyweds planned to live at 2119 House Street.

In October, Acting Mayor Davis investigated the county hospital. Conditions at the hospital had deteriorated over the years, making matters even worse as residents fought typhoid. One *Leader* report stated the hospital had just three employees—a steward, a cook, and "an unskilled nurse."

By October 24, the number of new cases of typhoid was decreasing, and the *Leader* stated, "The streets and alleys have all been cleaned and disinfectants have been used freely." In early November, the crisis at the county hospital had passed, with most patients recovering well. The city council, this time with Mayor Schnitger presiding, attended to its business and reconvened as a board of health to adopt rules and regulations for the city and decided to appoint a sanitation inspector. Persons selling milk in Cheyenne were required to register and also to keep boiling water on hand constantly to sterilize milk cans. The illness was noted as rapidly decreasing. By mid-November, the Union Pacific grading camps west of the city were declared free of both smallpox and typhoid.

On December 1, the *Leader* carried a huge article detailing Dr. Mitchell's report. Much of the article was printed in capital letters. Together with Drs. Bennett, Barber, and Conway, Mitchell had performed autopsies on several persons who died of typhoid and declared the lesions found on the spleens and intestinal tracts "as absolutely typical of typhoid fever as it was possible for them to be."

Although a local dairy had been suspected of selling contaminated milk because many fever cases originated with those who consumed the milk, the dairy was found only to have been in "extremely unsanitary condition." No bacteria was discovered in the milk or the water there. Instead, Mitchell's report explained that Cheyenne's water supply was the true culprit. Cheyenne received its water from Crow Creek, six miles northeast of the city. In emergencies, Lake Mahapaluta was also used, but water had not been drawn from the lake for city use for two years. Mitchell found sewage bacteria in the waters of Lake Mahapaluta, which had been used for ice. Mitchell stated the lake water should be condemned as drinking water. Because freezing did not kill the bacteria but instead preserved them, he recommended that ice be used for cold storage only. He also suggested protecting the outflow of the sewer system to keep cattle from wading through it. Though the livestock would not be harmed by drinking the water, milk cows' udders could become contaminated by wading through contaminated water and that in turn could affect their milk.

According to the *Leader*, water on the Union Pacific passenger trains was not contaminated by Cheyenne's epidemic. The company used water from a Granite Canyon spring, which it had purchased many years before. The spring water was used in Pullman and passenger cars in water coolers. The company was especially careful about ice used in drinking water and had shipped ice for the previous two years from the Laramie River.

The epidemic had been severe. Undertakers in Cheyenne reported twenty-three deaths from typhoid that fall. By the end of the year, the disease had been almost conquered.

In November 1901, Cheyenne doctors petitioned the Laramie County commissioners to provide alternate housing for the county's indigent citizens and to use the county hospital exclusively for the treatment of the sick. Dr. Johnston's signature appeared first on the document. Others signers were L. Pierre Desmond, J.H. Conway, H.J. Maynard, Letitia Wiseman, H.M. Bennett, W.A. Wyman, W.W. Crook, and Nelson R. Wetlaufer. Dr. Johnston continued to campaign for better health conditions in the city.

The state, too, continued to try to improve health conditions for its residents. The Sixth Legislature created the Board of Health in 1901. The board consisted of three persons appointed by the governor for four-year terms. Appointees had to be approved by the Senate. One was required to be a physician and served as the secretary and executive officer to the board. According to the *Wyoming Blue Book*, the board's duty was "to take cognizance of interests of health and life among the people of the state; to make sanitary investigations of causes of disease and epidemics, and of sources of mortality and other circumstances bearing upon public health."

In 1901, the Laramie County Hospital benefitted through many improvements instigated through the pleas of the physicians and with the assistance of the county commissioners. The commissioners helped by partially renovating the building, equipping the hospital with steam heat instead of stoves, and including new sanitary plumbing. An experienced matron and trained nursing staff along with a few nicely furnished rooms rounded out the improvements, funded through "a few generous hearted women" and private donors, and the hospital was renamed Saint John's Hospital. On October 28, 1901, two unidentified physicians agreed to devote two or three months each year to visiting the indigent at the hospital free of charge.

The Ladies Hospital Aid, of which Dorothy Johnston was an active member, purchased a rubber-tired, Studebaker ambulance for the hospital at a cost of $530. Private patients paid two dollars for its use, and the county hospital paid one dollar per trip to defray expenses of the vehicle's operation. The ambulance was equipped with "…a fire department hitch, rotary gong, lights for night service, basket stretcher, pneumatic mattresses and pillows, a medicine chest under the driver's seat, plate glass windows in front and on the sides, and a swinging bed." The bed was a modern convenience invented to protect patients from feeling the jolts on rough roads.

On February 25, Dr. Johnston performed another news making and tricky surgical procedure. He removed an abscess from the brain of young Rose Ryan of Fort Laramie. Ryan had been unconscious for several hours before the surgery was performed. After the operation, she regained consciousness and was expected to recover completely.

Two weeks later, the Johnstons moved into their "new mansion" on the corner of Ferguson and Twentieth Street. The cost of the home was an estimated seven thousand dollars. The architect was William Dubois of Cheyenne and the contractor was Harding F. Allen, who had built Cheyenne's Carnegie Library. Dorothy was active in social circles and enjoyed entertaining. In addition to her work with the hospital auxiliary, she was elected as a delegate to the General Federation of Women's Clubs in Los Angeles along with Mrs. N. R. Davis and Mrs. George E. Abbott. Dorothy also was a member of the Shakespeare Club. When she hosted the group in May 1902, she cleverly used quotations as note cards. The quotations "aptly suggested certain virtues or mental attributes of her guestes [*sic*]," according to a society item in the *Leader*. She was also on the program committee for the musical club. The Johnstons had been among the many couples attending Cheyenne's first charity ball held in 1901 to raise the five hundred dollars needed to furnish the hospital's second-floor operating room. In addition to his medical work, Dr. Johnston was a 32nd degree Mason and was active in that fraternal organization. He enjoyed golfing and fishing.

Johnston continued to make news with his medical skills. On August 27, 1902, Drs. Johnston and Conway operated on a five-year-old boy whose skull had been crushed when he was kicked by a horse. The *Leader* reported that the child's skull had been "crushed and shattered over an area two and a half inches long by one and a half inches wkide [*sic*]. About half of this surface was removed by the physicians." Over a square inch of bone was removed from his head. The boy, Francis Fisher, was discharged from the county hospital about a week later.

In September 1902, two medical societies converged on the city. The Wyoming Medical Association, along with the Rocky Mountain Inter-State Medical Association, with members from Colorado, Utah, Wyoming, Montana, Arizona, and New Mexico, held a joint convention. Governor Richards addressed the more than one hundred physicians who attended the conference. Physicians presented technical papers during the convention, "uninteresting to the public at large," according to the *Leader*. Dr. Johnston's presentation was entitled "Some Observations on the Practice of Obstetrics." C.H. Solier, Superintendent of the Wyoming Hospital for the Insane in Evanston, was elected president of the regional association, and Johnston was elected first vice president. Johnston and Cheyenne's H.M. Bennett were the only Cheyenne residents who were previously members of the group, but Drs. A.W. Barber, J.H. Conway, and W.A. Wyman joined during the convention.

On a more somber note, Johnston was called to testify in October 1902 at the trial of Tom Horn. Johnston had performed the postmortem examination on murder victim Willie Nickell, with Drs. Barber and Conway assisting. At that time, Johnston stated he had been practicing medicine and surgery for twelve years. During the trial, Johnston described Nickell's wounds by using attorney Burke to illustrate. Both wounds were three-eighths of an inch in diameter and could have been larger but no smaller, according to the doctor. Johnston also believed Nickell's wounds to have been caused by leaded bullets. He testified that he thought the wounds might have been made by a .38 caliber gun and possibly a larger one but probably not a .30-.30 caliber weapon. He admitted, however, that he couldn't state for certain what size bullet created the wounds. He could only approximate. Because the victim's wounds were round, Johnston deduced that the bullets struck at right angles, explaining that a "wound is never larger than the size of a bullet if the impact is direct." The jury determined that Horn was guilty of the murder, and he was hanged the next year.

When cowboy Frank Irwin was injured "trying to ride a condemned cavalry horse" in 1903, Dr. Johnston treated his broken arm. Irwin had been hoping to ride in the upcoming wild west show to be held in honor of President Theodore Roosevelt's visit to Cheyenne, but the fracture dashed his plans.

Dr. Johnston did not limit his practice to humans but was said to have treated an occasional sick cow or horse as well. His animal practice extended to his own personal pets. On February 25, 1907, Dr. Johnston's thoroughbred bull pup was poisoned when a dog poisoner plagued Cheyenne, harming one or more dogs daily. The *Leader* reported "…prompt action by the physician saved the canine's life." In March, the dog poisoner was still on the loose.

Johnston's fascination with surgery continued throughout his life. He studied surgery and "allied subjects" at the University of Vienna in 1912 and 1913. In 1912, Johnston married Fanny Phelps. (What became of the first Mrs. Johnston is unknown.) Together he and Fannie had two sons, George P., Jr. and Phelps Johnston. George Jr. was at one time the editor of the *Wyoming Eagle* in Cheyenne, while Phelps headed an advertising agency based in Chicago.

Johnston's medical practice spanned nearly sixty years, leading Bernstein to call him "America's oldest country doctor," whose "length of service is believed to be the longest any one doctor has served any single community in the United States."

Dr. Johnston died on September 18, 1956, at the age of ninety-three. Honorary pallbearers included former governor of Wyoming Leslie A. Miller, U.S. Senator Joseph C. O'Mahoney, Judge T. Blake Kennedy, and T. Joe Cahill, along with numerous doctors and others including Cheyenne's mayor. Johnston's obituary called him "A 'country doctor' in the truest sense of the word," stating, "[H]e was known and respected throughout the region by the thousands of persons whom he attended." At the time of his death, the doctor was the oldest member in service to the house of delegates of the American Medical Association (AMA). He had represented Wyoming in the AMA for thirty years.

Charles B. Irwin

Some men stand out in memory by virtue of big personalities, while others remain memorable because of their physical size. One man in Cheyenne's history continues to be remembered for both attributes. Charles B. Irwin was a man of large girth and big reputation who had a way with people and horses. From a young age, Charles Irwin demonstrated his skill with horses. His adventures as a rodeo stock raiser and a Wild West entrepreneur were the inspiration for Anna Lee Waldo's epic novel *Prairie*. In many ways, Charlie Irwin (also known as "C.B.") was a big man—big physically and big in spirit and exuberance.

Charles Burton Irwin was born in Chillicothe, Missouri, in 1875. His father was a blacksmith, and the son learned his father's trade. As a youngster, Charles learned all he could about horses by riding them. Soon he could ride any horse set before him. In *Persimmon Hill*, writer George Williams states that the boy was "a tremendous sprinter but was best known for his gregarious personality...." Irwin's athletic skills would serve him well in life.

On January 1, 1894, Irwin married Etta May McGuckin (spelled in some sources Eta) in Goodland, Kansas. The next year, son Floyd was born. The growing little family joined Irwin's folks in Colorado Springs, Colorado, where they established a blacksmith shop on the site of the Antlers Hotel. Daughters Joella and Pauline were born there.

In 1899, the Irwins moved to Wyoming after a train accident destroyed their business. In Cheyenne, Irwin worked first for C.J. Hysham and Company of Omaha, which had a government contract to supply beef to Indians at the Standing Rock Agency at Fort Yates, North Dakota. In 1900, he went to work as a blacksmith for the Warren Livestock Company. While there, he made friends with Governor Francis E. Warren. Then he worked for John Coble on the Two Bar Ranch. A man named Tom Horn worked on the Two Bar breaking horses, and soon he and Irwin were friends. Irwin admired Horn's ability at steer roping.

Irwin soon became active in the fledgling Cheyenne Frontier Days celebrations. He provided bucking stock but also became an integral part of the entertainment. Irwin "wielded a huge megaphone and treated the audience with renditions of his theme song, 'Alfalfa Hay,'" writes historian Shirley Flynn. "He also shouted out announcements to keep the crowd amused and informed."

Irwin took a string of bucking horses to the Festival of Mountain and Plain in Denver in 1901 while he worked for Coble. Among the bronco group was a black colt named Steamboat. "For the rest of Steamboat's life and the entire rodeo arena career of the famous bucker," writes historian Candy Moulton, "C. B. Irwin was involved in [Steamboat's] history."

In 1902, Irwin again took bucking horses to the Festival of Mountain and Plain in Denver. In October, the *Cheyenne Daily Leader* reported on a controversial event there. As the chapter of George D. Rainsford describes, Thad Sowder, the world champion rough rider, was accused of "pulling leather," or touching the saddle while his horse bucked, which would have disqualified him from the competition. The judges argued heatedly about awarding Sowder the championship title, and the crowd felt the award was given fraudulently to him.

The real winner in the Sowder incident appeared to be Irwin, who was credited with having supervised the roping of the horses and, in general, managed the stock unofficially. He backed Sowder in the controversy, explaining to the judges that as Sowder's manager he felt the cowboy should get a square deal and not be made to take a re-ride under the circumstances, but Sowder was made to re-ride against another cowboy, Thomas Minor. The Cheyenne paper gave a tip of its editorial hat to the livestock handler, saying, "Charley Irwin, who has no equal in pulling off a bucking contest, returned

Charles B. Irwin, a big man with an exuberant personality, was a skilled live-stock handler who provided stock for the Cheyenne Frontier Days rodeos in addition to traveling with his family's own Irwin Brothers Wild West Show. (Courtesy Wyoming State Archives)

from Denver last night, where he had rendered invaluable services to the Denver show people.… Irwin is a whole host on such occasions, and helped to make the occasion pleasant for Wyoming visitors." Public disenchantment with the event caused speculation that the festival would cease to be held in the future, but the annual activities continued until 1912.

In 1903, Coble's ranch was sold, according to Moulton, and Coble, as a joke, gave Steamboat to the Cheyenne Elks Lodge, whose members sold the horse to Irwin. (Steamboat is supposedly the inspiration for the bucking bronc appearing on Wyoming's license plates. A photograph of cowboy Guy Holt atop the bucker is thought to have been artist Allen True's inspiration for the design.)

By 1903, Irwin was the foreman of the Bosler ranch. He had also just been offered a position as the Wyoming representative for an eastern commission house and was slated to manage the livestock used for the wild west show to entertain President Roosevelt on his visit in Cheyenne.

When President Theodore Roosevelt visited Cheyenne in June 1903, he was treated to a special version of the Frontier Days events on June 1. The show included a wild horse race, a stake race, a bronc riding contest, a steeplechase, and a ladies' cow pony race. During a lull in the show, Irwin ran a footrace against a man on horseback. "The first time Irwin fell and in the second trial was beaten by a few feet by the horse," according to an account in the *Cheyenne Daily Leader*. Irwin also earned the best time in the steer roping, clocked at one minute seventeen and one-half seconds. He rode a horse named Buffalo Bill without saddle or bridle and "broke the animal in fine style," the *Leader* reported. Mrs. W. H. Irwin won the ladies' cow pony race. Sowder rode Steamboat for the president, gaining much better press coverage from this rodeo appearance than the one in Denver. Roosevelt complimented Irwin in his thank-you address, saying, "I wish to say especially to Mr. Irwin that the whole business has been managed in such a way which ought to make him well satisfied how it has come out." Irwin later named one of his finest bucking horses Teddy Roosevelt.

If the president's visit was the high point in Irwin's year, one of the lowest occurred in November. Tom Horn's fate didn't allow a long-term friendship. Stock detective Horn was convicted of murdering young

Willie Nickell and hanged for the crime in 1903. Before his death, Horn gave Irwin a cherished rifle. At Horn's request, Charlie and his brother Frank sang "Life's Railway to Heaven" just before the execution.

In 1905, the Irwins moved to Cheyenne to live in town. They remained active in Frontier Days. All four of the children became rodeo performers. Irwin often competed in the steer roping and racing contests. In 1906, he earned championship steer roping honors with an average time of thirty-eight and one-fifth seconds for tying down two steers. He held the record for six years until the steer's one-hundred-foot lead was shortened to sixty feet.

Early in 1907, Irwin was appointed as Stock Yards Inspector. He was already working for the Union Pacific Railroad as a livestock agent. The additional duties included inspecting the stockyards and making suggestions for improvements. Irwin's job for the Union Pacific, according to Williams, allowed him "a specially rigged express car, ready to load a posse and fast grain-fed horses, should the wire tap out word of a train robbery." He rode with posses frequently. Irwin's weight began to rise dramatically about this time as well. A thyroid disorder caused his weight to increase to 350 pounds. Despite his weight gain, Irwin managed to maintain his high energy.

In 1908, Irwin built his own barn, corrals, and cook house at Frontier Park in Cheyenne. Though he had built the cook house to feed his own employees, no one was turned away from a meal there. He was elected to the Wyoming Fair Board and represented Cheyenne Frontier Days at the National Convention of Fair Boards. This connection led to his creation of the Irwin Brothers Wild West Show. Steamboat, the world-famous bucking bronc, was the headliner, and the Irwins worked fairs throughout the nation. They grew famous for providing livestock to well-known rodeos such as the Pendleton Roundup and the Calgary Stampede. The Irwins also provided stock for New York City's first rodeo in 1916.

His billing of his outfit as the Irwin Brothers Cheyenne Frontier Days Wild West Show landed Irwin in a dispute with the Cheyenne Frontier Days committee. The committee filed an injunction prohibiting Irwin from using the term Cheyenne Frontier Days in conjunction with his show in 1913. Irwin is said to have kept the term in his letterhead after the dispute was settled.

Performers for the Irwin Brothers Wild West show included Irwin's son, Floyd, and all three daughters—Joella, Pauline, and Frances. Champion bronc rider Clayton Danks also worked with the Irwins. Sioux Indians from the Pine Ridge Reservation in South Dakota, some of whom Irwin had befriended years earlier when he worked for C. J. Hysham and Company, participated in the show and were considered part of the family.

Working with livestock presented its share of dangers. In late August 1910, Irwin was trampled under horses while working the show for Teddy Roosevelt and Mrs. Frederic Remington's visit to Cheyenne. Irwin's arm was badly injured. A true trouper, he insisted that the show go on.

Steamboat was known as a powerful horse and a strong twister, while Teddy Roosevelt was more adept at spinning, according to Moulton. Irwin advertised a twenty-five dollar prize to anyone in the crowd who could ride either of the horses. Usually, no one came forward and one of the show performers rode the horses, although one man did appear from the crowd once who managed to ride Teddy Roosevelt. Steamboat gained the title of "Worst Bucking Horse of the Year" at Cheyenne's Frontier Days during the years 1907 and 1908. The coveted title allowed Irwin a unique opportunity. As the horse's owner, he knew that people would attend the Frontier Days events expecting to see the bucking bronc, but he could also bill Steamboat as a main attraction of his Wild West Show and gain attendance there as well.

Irwin is credited with organizing Wyoming's first motion picture production company, the Cheyenne Feature Film Company in 1912. Other organizers included Frank J. Carrol of Boston, A. E. Weller of Denver, Otis T. Thayer of Chicago, and T. Blake Kennedy of Cheyenne. According to historian William R. Huey, the company planned to make "specialty movies of 'Cheyenne Frontier Days' and realistic Wild West productions on the plains and mountains in the southern Wyoming, northern Colorado region." The studios were to be in Cheyenne. Although the company raised one hundred thousand dollars capital, only one film was made—about Judge Benjamin Barr Lindsey's juvenile court of Denver.

Nevertheless, Irwin maintained his connections to the movie world. Huey writes that the cast and crew of "The Duke of Chimney

Butte" came to Wyoming on the Union Pacific train in July 1919. Irwin met the train and took the movie makers to Fort D. A. Russell where they stayed during Frontier Days. They visited Frontier Park and Irwin's Y6 Ranch at Meriden to scout locations. The star of the movie, Fred Stone, participated in several of the rodeo events and rode in the parade. In August, the group traveled to Pine Bluffs to film local scenery and also blew up a saloon for a scene in the film. Another movie, "The Pony Express," completed in 1925, was filmed on the Irwin Ranch. The town of Julesburg, Colorado, was recreated at the ranch to give the flavor of the 1860s. About seventy-five percent of the total film was shot on location.

In 1913, Irwin lost the stock contract for Cheyenne Frontier Days. Steamboat, who had appeared there for eleven years, did not appear. In 1914, the horse was badly cut in Salt Lake City during the Irwin Brothers Wild West performance when penned horses grew frightened during a lightning storm, and Steamboat was cut on wire. The horse developed blood poisoning. Irwin, probably coincidentally, grabbed the rifle Tom Horn had given him and put the horse out of his misery. A new bucker filled the void.

By 1916, Irwin was working as a railroad detective for the Union Pacific, according to Bill Carlisle's recollections. Carlisle, the "gentleman bandit," robbed a train near Green River, Wyoming, then jumped from the train and hid behind a snowbank until the train departed. After eight hours of moving around to leave false trails in the snow and to survive the cold, Carlisle walked into town and got a shave and a meal. Upon learning that Irwin was in town, Carlisle put his gun behind his belt buckle and hid this beneath his buttoned coat. At the train station, the bandit found Irwin talking with the ticket agent. Carlisle boldly purchased a one-way ticket to Laramie, recalling that he turned and looked Irwin straight in the eyes. As the agent made change, Carlisle walked away with the ticket. He recalls, "Instantly I felt Irwin's hand on my shoulder. As he whirled me around, my hand slid beneath my coat and we faced each other. But he smiled and said, 'You forgot your change.' I pulled my hand out empty, picked up the money, and said, 'Thanks.'"

In 1917, Irwin's son, Floyd, was killed accidentally while practicing for Frontier Days. He roped a steer, but thinking he had missed, turned his horse. The horse fell when the steer tightened the rope in trying to get away. Floyd suffered a fractured skull and died the next day. After this tragedy, Irwin disbanded the Wild West Show although he continued to provide stock for rodeos.

Irwin's next passion became Thoroughbreds. In 1923, he was considered the nation's leading trainer, with a record of 147 wins at the race track. He raced horses that spring, then produced rodeos during the summer and fall. He spent the winter in Tijuana, Mexico, at the Agua Caliente Track.

His fortunes were estimated to be large, but Irwin was known as a "frontier type," willing to risk money and take a chance on losing it. In 1926, one source states he was bankrupt and owed lenders more than two hundred thousand dollars. Irwin's money woes were well known to Cheyenne attorney T. Blake Kennedy. Irwin had been a client of his and, according to Kennedy, "was the source of much grief to me for years." He had first come to Kennedy when he was leaving the Iron Mountain Ranch Company operated by John Coble. At that time, he began to acquire real estate and livestock for his ranch in Meriden and had begun the Wild West show. "In his show operations Charlie had acquired a considerable number of condemned railroad cars consisting of freight cars, box cars and old passenger cars with a pullman or two and apparently he had got hold of a number of the Union Pacific's cars which he had not purchased. His claim was, and I think correctly, that Mr. Moehler, president of the Union Pacific and a friend of Charlie, had given him the use of them."

The Interstate Commerce Commission believed differently, however, and sued Irwin. "I had the most difficult problem of my life in trying to convince Charlie, in the face of his claim which he could substantiate, that Mr. Moehler had given him the use of these cars, that he should be sued to recover the value of their use," Kennedy writes. The Union Pacific, under Interstate Commerce Law, could not allow free use of their equipment by an individual, so Moehler's action legally had no effect. Irwin finally decided to decrease the number of cars he used so the judgment sought was greatly reduced when entered against him.

The attorney also acted on Irwin's behalf as he financed his ranch and livestock ventures, but Irwin ignored the bills Kennedy sent, while still requiring his services. Kennedy explains, "When he would be in the office and I would appeal to him that I needed money he would laugh at me but finally pull out a roll of bills that would choke the proverbial elephant and peel off a twenty dollar bill and hand it to me saying, 'This will tide you over for the time being.'" Kennedy also recalled Irwin as a demanding client, one who sought advice often when office hours were over. When Kennedy later served as a judge, both Charles Irwin and his wife appeared in his court for bankruptcies. Though frustrated by Irwin's financial actions, Kennedy recalled him with some fondness, saying, "[H]e probably knew more people throughout the Nation than any resident of the State, and everybody liked him with the possible exception of those who had business dealings with him."

In the 1930s, Irwin was considering a run for the governor's seat of Wyoming. He planned to use the slogan suggested by his friend, Will Rogers: "Popular government at popular prices." But this big idea was not to be. Irwin died in a one-car rollover accident north of Cheyenne on March 24, 1934. Daughter Pauline's husband, Claude Sawyer, was his driver and survived the crash. Irwin had a specially made Buick with an extra-large back seat so he could fit. By this time, Irwin's weight was estimated at 450 to 500 pounds. (Irwin was also said to have had a special chair made for him. Mike Fox, curator of collections at the Wyoming State Museum, says the museum has a large chair in its collection said to have been Irwin's, but there is no evidence to document the fact. The pine chair, painted white with a red seat, is large enough to have fit Irwin, measuring more than forty-nine inches high with a seat that is two and one-half feet wide.)

Cheyenne mourners gave the big man a big goodbye. His funeral was held at Cheyenne's McCormick Junior High School, the only building large enough to hold nearly twelve hundred mourners. Sawyer had recuperated enough to attend but had to be carried to and from the auditorium. Pallbearers were a group of cowboys, including Clayton Danks. The final hymn, sung as the casket was carried to the hearse, was "The Last Roundup." Boy Scouts, Cheyenne policemen, and members of the Elks Lodge formed an honor guard for the casket to pass through. A "mile-long cortege followed the remains to the grave in Lakeview Cemetery…," the newspaper reported. Irwin was buried beside his son, Floyd.

Friend Will Rogers had written of Irwin in his syndicated column, "He was a real cowpuncher in his day, and the greatest spirit and best company that ever lived." He depicted Irwin as riding to the gates of heaven and hollering to Saint Peter that "there is a real cowboy coming into the old home ranch." Charles B. Irwin was elected to the National Rodeo Hall of Fame in 1975.

M. P. Keefe

The name M. P. Keefe is mentioned most often in connection with the building of Wyoming's state capitol, but the Cheyenne contractor also was awarded numerous federal government contracts during the latter part of the nineteenth century. Keefe was also active in city politics and served the city council in various capacities throughout the years. His 1903 campaign to clean up the city led to controversy. Photographs of the time show Keefe as a man with a square face, straight nose, apple cheeks, and a thick mustache.

Born September 25, 1853, in Mitchell Town, Ireland, the sixth child of Michael and Margaret (Quinn) Keefe, Moses Patrick Keefe was educated in his home country. According to Bartlett's *History of Wyoming*, building fascinated him in his youth. He left school at age thirteen. In 1870 at the age of seventeen, he moved to Decatur, Illinois, having made the trip abroad alone, and was working in Chicago in 1871 at the time of the great fire. The young man served as foreman for Gould and Company and, later, Call and Kraft while in Chicago. In 1873, he visited Cheyenne for the first time, then returned to Chicago for another three years. But Keefe's interest in the Battle of the Little Bighorn and George Armstrong Custer led him west again. He wintered in 1876 and 1877 in Deadwood, South Dakota, then stayed at Fort McKinney and Fort Laramie until June 1877, working as a construction laborer. In October 1877, Keefe married Eliza Gaynor Kewley of Chicago. After a brief stint in Leadville, Colorado, during the gold boom in 1879, Keefe located in Cheyenne and opened a contracting business.

Perhaps one of his most important construction contracts was the building of Cheyenne's water system on Crow Creek during the years 1884–1885, when Joseph M. Carey served as mayor. Keefe's familiarity with the water system served him well in securing subsequent political positions. In 1886, Keefe, a Republican, served as a representative in the Ninth Territorial Legislative Assembly, which authorized construction of a capitol building in Cheyenne. In July 1886, Congress approved Wyoming Territory's request to build a capitol, and David W. Gibbs & Company of Toledo, Ohio, was selected as the architect. In August, another Toledo firm, A. Feick & Brothers, earned the contracting job with the low bid of $131,275. The ground was broken for the capitol on September 9, 1886, and the cornerstone laid on May 18, 1887. In January 1888, the Tenth Legislative Assembly became the first legislative body to convene in the new capitol; it appropriated $125,000 to build east and west wings onto the building. Governor Thomas Moonlight vetoed the bill as too costly, but lawmakers overrode his objection. Architect Gibbs was retained on the project. Contractor H. W. Newell submitted the low bid of $58,454 to build the east wing, while Keefe bid $59,050 for the west wing and earned the job. Newell asked to transfer his contract on the east wing to Keefe after a few days, and in July 1888, Keefe was officially awarded the contract for both wings. The price was $117,504, not including lighting, plumbing, and heating. The Capitol Building Commission pronounced the work acceptable on April 4, 1890. (Additional wings were built in 1915 under the guidance of Cheyenne architect William R. Dubois and contractor John W. Howard.)

The capitol was not Keefe's only tie to politics. He was elected to the city council and served as chairman of the street and alley committee during his first term in 1886. The next year he served as the chairman of the city park committee. In 1900, the *Cheyenne Daily Leader* praised Keefe's work on that committee. After the council appropriated only enough funds for construction of a drive around the park with gateways on each side, Keefe "continued the good work in a systematic way for three years with a result that was marvelous." In 1890, he was elected Laramie County commissioner.

Although he kept active in community politics, Keefe's true passion, it appears, was construction. An advertisement in the *Cheyenne*

M. P. Keefe, a respected Cheyenne contractor who built a portion of the state capitol, served as an early day mayor who promised to eliminate vice from the city. (Courtesy Wyoming State Archives)

Daily Sun on July 29, 1889, listed Keefe as "General Contractor and Builder," with "all kinds of Carpenter and Jobbing Work Promptly Attended to." He was also "Agent for Fairbank's and Co.'s Scales, Eclipse Windmills, Tanks, etc," along with "Mast, Foos & Co.'s Wrought Iron Fences for Residences and Cemetery Grounds." Keefe stood behind his work as the ad also promised that all work and material furnished were guaranteed. In December 1889, he planned to build two cottages near his own residence at the corner of Evans and Twenty-first Streets.

He built many of the fabulous homes on Cheyenne's cattlemen's row as well as offices, stores, and schools. Among his projects were the Hi Kelly and Eli Whitcomb houses, the South Side and West Side schools, the Majestic Building, a high school, Methodist and Episcopal churches, the Catholic Cathedral, and the Wyoming Trust and Savings building. He is also credited with constructing a large portion of the buildings at Fort D. A. Russell (now F. E. Warren Air Force Base). His other federal government work included a million-dollar contract for the construction of Fort Crook as well as buildings at Fort Omaha and Fort Robinson in Nebraska, and on government posts in Spokane, Washington.

By 1891, Keefe's business was booming. The *Sun* reported that a railroad spur would soon connect Keefe's red sandstone quarries forty-six miles north of the city to the Cheyenne and Northern Railroad main line. The stone had been used in the Methodist church, the Alert Hose house, the new high school, and the H. P. Hynds block.

That same year, however, Keefe suffered losses due to fire. In late July, his ranch house was destroyed. An employee of Keefe's discovered just the remains of the house when delivering lumber to the ranch the morning after the conflagration. The ranch, also called the Valley Ranch, "was the pride of Mr. Keefe, who looks forward to the time when he may retire there and be an old fashioned country gentleman. He has a system of water works there, several acres under cultivation and some fine stock." The property was estimated to be worth three thousand dollars, while Keefe held only nineteen hundred dollars insurance, according to the *Sun*.

About two weeks later, Keefe's stoneyard, located in Cheyenne's west end, also suffered a fire, causing one thousand dollars worth of damage to a house that had been moved there from old Camp Carlin. The occupant of the house, Peter Hamma, who was sleeping there to protect the premises, was apparently unharmed.

Great sadness came into Keefe's life just two years later. Eliza Keefe died in March 1895, after the birth of daughter Lillian, their seventh child. Keefe was working on Fort Omaha at the time.

In January 1900, Keefe went to Cuba and Puerto Rico. He had been sent to Cuba to supervise the rebuilding of the presidential palace in Havana under the direction of the U.S. government. Although some sources state it took eighteen months to complete the project, the *Sun-Leader* reported that Keefe returned from Cuba three months after his departure; the contract was completed by mid-June of 1900. Keefe traveled to Ireland to visit his mother shortly after completing this job.

Although Keefe had spent nearly three years away from Cheyenne while working on government contracts in Spokane, Omaha, and Cuba, the *Cheyenne Daily Leader* ran an editorial in November 1900 supporting him for mayor. His property included "some of our prettiest residences, Keefe hall and other real estate." Henry Altman, the man who succeeded Keefe on the park committee, "speaks in the highest terms of [Keefe's] efficiency and public spirit." George Hoyt, formerly the chairman of the board of Laramie County Commissioners, had also served with Keefe and "says he always found in [Keefe] an earnest, conscientious worker and a man of excellent ideas about public improvements."

The *Leader* felt that Keefe's previous experience with Cheyenne's water system would be increasingly important as the city was expected to grow in population during the next few years. Health was foremost on many Cheyenne residents' minds at that time as well. The city was in the midst of a typhoid fever epidemic, brought about by bacteria in its water system. The newspaper explained that the water and sewage systems would need improvements to protect against future illness. Because Keefe had experience with the water system, he was "the right man in the right place." In spite of this enthusiastic support, Keefe didn't want to run for office. He had taken government contracts, including the building of officers' quarters at Fort Russell and buildings at Fort Crook near Omaha. He also planned to build six brick residences on Sixteenth Street north of Merrill & Company's lumberyard. Keefe explained that these commitments would prevent him from attending properly to the city's business.

The year 1901 apparently was a busy one for building in Cheyenne. The newspaper carried items concerning Keefe's work, mentioning Keefe Hall, a three-story public building used as storerooms and offices, and the second story of the Masonic temple. Keefe also hired a number of carpenters to work on the new buildings at Fort Russell. "Masons in the city are receiving $5 and $6 a day," the newspaper noted, "and the amount of work to be done seems simply unlimited." But Keefe did make time in his busy schedule for romance. On October 16, 1901, he married Elizabeth (Bessie) Tilton of Kansas. The couple was ready to begin receiving visitors on October 27, in their apartment over the annex to Keefe Hall.

On November 1, 1901, the *Leader* again supported Keefe for a political office, this time as a councilman. With a councilman's salary of just fifty dollars per year, competent men who sought the position only did so "on account of the interest they have in the progress of the city, and at the urgent solicitation of others who are also large taxpayers." M. P. Keefe, Max Idelman, and Andrew T. Clark "reluctantly consented" to run for the council. The *Leader* again complimented Keefe, stating, "His name is synonymous with the construction of almost every big building in the city and in all of his dealings he has shown himself to be a man possessing great business acumen, executive ability and all those qualities which go to make a successful businessman and an efficient officer of the city." On November 6, Keefe was elected by a majority of 108 votes over Frank Muler. Clark and Idelman also won seats on the council. Keefe was sworn in as a city councilman in early February. He was appointed to the printing and contingent expenses, public health and cemetery, and water and sewer committees.

In early December, Keefe made news again just by keeping busy with his construction business. The roof of the forty-thousand-dollar Masonic Hall neared completion, three and one-half months ahead of schedule. Keefe expected the building to be completed in time for the Wyoming Consistory reunion scheduled for late February. It was dedicated on February 27. Then a controversy over the stone to be used in the Fort Russell buildings erupted. Keefe had traveled to Chicago "to purchase mantels, hardware and other materials" for the fifty-thousand-dollar Fort Russell project which was scheduled for completion after the first of the year. He planned to use Iron Mountain stone in the project, which was inspected by the government and approved for use in the buildings. But other public building contractors had engaged in what Keefe called "a ruse." They wanted to use Bedford stone from Indiana instead of the Iron Mountain stone. According to Keefe, the contractors would profit twenty thousand dollars from the use of the softer Bedford stone, but they prevailed on the supervising architect to authorize another inspection of the Iron Mountain stone in early January.

On February 14, 1902, Keefe completed a forty-thousand-dollar contract at Fort Robinson. Also that winter he abandoned his idea to create a roof garden on Keefe Hall. He decided to use wooden trusses instead of steel to cover the dancing hall in the rear of the building, according to the *Leader*, and decided that the roof garden was not economically feasible.

In early February, the people of Cheyenne had voted in a seventy-thousand-dollar bond issue to extend the water system as well as fifteen thousand dollars in bonds to improve the sewer. The water bonds were advertised as $100,000 thirty-year bonds.

On May 3, Keefe corrected a rumor that had apparently been circulating. "The report that I am to move away from Cheyenne is incorrect, as I intend to make this my permanent home in the future, as it has been in the past. I will leave soon to be absent a year or more to attend to business affairs in other places, but will return," he explained. "I am disposing of my outside property interests in the city to concentrate my interests in the business portion of the town." He was also considering enlarging Keefe Hall. The report of the May 7 council meeting did not say anything about Keefe leaving town. City business on that evening involved an ordinance to protect property owners from damages due to cattle herds being driven through town. Herd owners were to post a bond that they would pay damages done to property while trailing cattle through the town.

Whatever business Keefe expected to pull him from town apparently didn't materialize, although the newspaper noted that he traveled to Denver in June 1902 on Fort Russell business. By August, he was preparing to work on the fort. In mid-August the paper reported that he bought lots from the Union Pacific on Sixteenth Street between Maxwell and Van Lennen Streets for $1,050, "where the old lawn tennis courts are located."

In October 1902, the newspaper praised Keefe in high terms. "While he has made for himself untold thousands of dollars he has invariably invested his money in the construction of cottages, fine residences and business blocks" and was currently working on the new Keefe Hall. The estimated cost of this new building was forty thousand dollars. The report called Keefe "a generous hearted, liberal man in all of his dealings," saying, "many a time heretofore he has virtually thrown open the doors of the old Keefe hall" to organizations for fairs, festivals, and other celebrations. The newspaper said it didn't have space enough to specifically mention "many heavy contracts Mr. Keefe has taken within the past few years, nor those he has had since becoming a member of the firm of Keefe & Bradley, but they have been many in all parts of the west."

Although the report stated that Keefe "has not cared to mingle in politics to any great extent," the details show that he did "mingle" somewhat. He served two terms as a Laramie County commissioner but declined to run for a third. Keefe was nominated for territorial council in 1888 but did not run. In 1899, he was unanimously nominated for sheriff but declined to run. The reluctant candidate was helping the town in other ways, however. He was said to have paid a quarter of a million dollars to his Cheyenne employees in the previous twelve to fourteen years.

In 1902, Keefe was nominated by the Republican convention to run for mayor of Cheyenne against Democrat J.L. Murray. Keefe "would have been chosen at once but for the uncertainty which prevailed in the minds of many as to whether or not Mr. Keefe would accept the nomination." He was out of town at the time of the convention, and other names were presented. Keefe's friends insisted that he promised to run if he was chosen, and he was nominated unanimously.

But Keefe remained controversial. Two days after the convention, the paper ran an article entitled "M.P. Keefe's Resignation." The Republicans assembled to discuss the fact that he would not run for mayor, but he hadn't submitted a resignation and needed to do so by the next day. Several Republicans were mentioned to replace Keefe, but all declined. The committee discussed leaving a vacancy on the ticket out of courtesy to the incumbent, Mayor Murray, because of his work to reconstruct the water and sewer systems. The next day, the paper reversed itself when Keefe decided to make the run after all.

In November, Keefe was elected mayor. Two months later, work was begun on six new artillery buildings at Fort Russell in addition to two already under construction, according to the *Leader*. Keefe expected to employ 150 men for the project. They would live in the bunkhouses at the fort during the construction. At this time, the fort was located out of the city. Keefe decided to live at Fort Russell while supervising the work and maintaining an office in the city as mayor. On February 4, the *Leader* reported that Keefe was sworn in; his first item of business was to resign as councilman. S. A. Bristol was nominated for the vacancy. This was done instead of calling a special election for the third ward, which would have cost seventy-five dollars.

Keefe wasted no time in announcing his agenda. In a letter read to the council at its February 17, 1903, meeting, he said, "In accepting the nomination for mayor of your city from the Republican Party I did not obligate myself to any faction, corporation or any organized bodies, nor did any individual ask me for a pledge. I have no relatives to put into office. I will simply do what is best for the honor of my Party and the best interests of the taxpayers generally."

Keefe then outlined his plan to "drive vice from the city," explaining that "[g]ambling is honorable when conducted by honorable men." He continued, "I gamble in my every day life. You do. Every business man does." While he believed that selling liquor was as honorable as any other business when "conducted by sober, upright men," he advocated licenses to wipe out the dives and dens of iniquity in the city "in the way of wine rooms where young men and women meet and fall into sin and shame." The new mayor said that he knew of people who left town "because of these damnable back wine rooms and assignation rooms in some of our blocks and so-called private cottages on the outside where married men and women visited, thereby bringing disunion and divorce to their own thresholds and the scattering of once happy families." While some of the west-end houses of ill fame were conducted in a businesslike manner, Keefe said that those persons selling liquor without a license must be stopped through either hefty fines or imprisonment. "I don't wish to put myself up as a most modest or moral man and disturb the peace of the town," he continued, "but with a police force who will work with me and carry out my orders, we will rid the town of many disreputable people. Let us protect the good; the devil will take care of his own." He realized that his plans would not be popular but vowed to "do my duty. I will not ask this council to confirm any policeman until I find the men that will carry out my orders." He also vowed to work on the sanitary condition of the city by consulting city doctors for advice.

On February 19, Cheyenne's entire police force resigned, except for City Marshal Robert Ingalls and Night Patrolman Otto Ahrens whom Keefe asked to stay. The *Leader* explained that in asking for the resignations, "Mayor Keefe does not wish it understood that he lacks confidence in the present force, but simply desires to have men under him of his own choosing." Keefe planned to appoint special patrolmen in addition to the day force and night force to keep the city under constant surveillance. He also planned to employ a "corps of special detectives whose identity will be kept a profound secret." On March 2, the *Leader* listed the new policemen as M. C. Stone, a Union Pacific machinist; W. C. Rath, a freight conductor; and F. W. Bray, a long-time Cheyenne resident. Keefe hired two new city policemen in early April, and soon after, he hired six secret service men "to be invested with police powers, but [who] will wear civilian dress and operate in a secret manner," according to the *Leader*. Their identities were not revealed.

By the beginning of April, Keefe, recognized for "fighting filth," drove around Cheyenne with the city marshal and members of the city council to see the problem spots. While on their rounds, they "discovered many places where the carcasses of dead cats and dogs were lying in the alleys and places where the filth was of such a nature as to endanger the lives of those residing in the city." Keefe planned to appoint a sanitation inspector at the next council meeting. On April 7, the council approved the new position of sanitation inspector, whose duties included "seeking out places where filth and refuse is inclined to accumulate and to compel all residents to live up to the strict sanitary rules, resulting in more healthy conditions, and an improved appearance."

Newspaper reports of the time indicate that Keefe's goal to keep the city clean proved popular. Keefe worked to extend water mains north of Cheyenne near the north end of Ferguson Street to provide water for the trees planted there. For this, the *Leader* said, he "deserves great credit for the extraordinary efforts he has made to give the city a neat and attractive appearance."

Keefe managed to keep the town running while continuing to operate his construction business, and business was good for the Irishman and other contractors in the city. In fact, the *Leader* noted a building boom in Cheyenne, estimating 2.5 million dollars worth of improvements in those buildings already under construction and those proposed, including a public building costing four hundred thousand dollars, the Masonic hall at forty thousand dollars, the Elks Home at thirty-five thousand dollars, Thomas Heaney's block for six thousand dollars, and the *Leader's* new office at six thousand dollars. In addition, 24.6 miles of double railroad track extending west of Cheyenne were being constructed at an estimated cost of 1.5 million dollars. More than half a million dollars in construction was scheduled for Fort Russell, and the Silver Crown storage reservoir and an extension to the sewage system were planned at a cost of one hundred thousand dollars. Proposed construction also included the Joseph Carey office building, a governor's mansion, doctors' offices, and a family hotel. The *Leader* reported that many houses were being built and business blocks in town were being renovated. Labor played a big role in the building boom as well, and unions appeared to be active at the time in the city. Keefe introduced S. J. Kent, the national organizer of the Brotherhood of Carpenters and Joiners of America, before his address at Turner Hall in late April.

One of Keefe's sadder moments as mayor occurred when Governor Richards passed away on April 28, 1903. The next day, Keefe issued a proclamation that all businesses in the city would close from three to five the afternoon of April 30 in respect for the deceased governor.

A month later, President Theodore Roosevelt was scheduled to visit Cheyenne. As mayor, Keefe telegraphed Senator Francis E. Warren with "the people's cordial invitation" to the president. Warren's response advised Keefe that only one troop of cavalry and a battery of field artillery would be present at Fort Russell for the president's visit, and that infantry to replace the others usually on hand was not expected until June. Warren said a "full parade or review of the regulars" in addition to military demonstrations would be an appropriate way to welcome Roosevelt and expressed approval of Keefe's suggestion of a wild west show, including bronc riding, steer roping, and calf roping.

During Roosevelt's visit, Keefe rode in the parade in car number one. The president at the last moment decided to ride horseback in the parade, undoubtedly causing some concern for the city policemen and the secret service men assigned to protect him. Later during his visit, when Roosevelt expressed the wish to visit his old friend Bishop Keane, Keefe personally escorted him to Frontier Park to see the priest.

After the president's visit, Keefe did not decrease the police force as might have been expected. Instead in late June, the *Leader* reported that Cheyenne's police force had expanded to nine policemen, and more would be added. During his time as mayor, Keefe was also credited with building a massive rock dam on Middle Crow Creek, supervising the work himself. In 1910, he established the National Lumber & Mill Company, which Bartlett called "the largest plant in Wyoming." The lumber mill covered nearly two city blocks.

Keefe died in March 1929. He had fallen ill in 1924, suffering occasional heart attacks, frequently preceded by rheumatism. He had begun wintering in California that same year. He had not traveled to California in 1929 because he had felt better and opted to stay in Cheyenne instead. Keefe's obituary states, "In Cheyenne's long and impressive list of pioneers, few if any have been more widely and favorably known; and few if any have played a more conspicuous and helpful part in the building and development of this great western empire." Keefe was "recognized everywhere and admired by all for his sterling qualities of character." The newspaper also called Keefe "[a] man of the very highest integrity, [who] built for himself the unqualified respect of everyone who knew him."

Keefe had been active in many community organizations. He earned the prestigious 32nd degree of Scottish Rite Masons and was also active in the Knights of Pythias, Odd Fellows, and Cheyenne Rotary Club. Earlier, he had been a member of the Volunteer Durant Hose and Fire Company. Masonic services preceded his burial at Lakeview Cemetery in Cheyenne. His wife, Bessie, survived him for forty-three years. She died in 1967 at the age of ninety and was buried beside her husband.

Henry Hay

BUSINESSMEN SOUGHT OPPORTUNITIES for profit when the town of Cheyenne made its magical appearance upon the windswept western plains. As the railroad brought more settlers and more goods, business ventures abounded. And the plains were always a draw for anyone considering earning his keep through cattle ranching. All those business interests were good enough on their own, but astute businessmen captured another market segment—banking. Everybody needed a banker, and a banker had a unique opportunity to participate in the growing economy. Henry Hay found his niche in managing money for others and eventually twice served as Wyoming state treasurer.

Henry Gurley Hay was born in Indianapolis on October 31, 1847. His mother died when he was just two years old. His father moved to Vincennes, Indiana, and left his young son in the care of an aunt. At age nineteen Hay moved to Reedsville, Missouri, working first as a bookkeeper and then as a surface boss at the lead mines. When he arrived in Wyoming Territory, he found work as a surveyor under Silas Reed who was surveyor general of the Territory of Wyoming. He also worked with John B. Thomas with whom he struck up a good friendship. Together, they became deputy surveyors under Reed, surveying the southeastern portion of the territory. Hay's field notes for 1870 record the "survey of the boundary lines of the city of Cheyenne, Wyoming Territory," listing James Stough and Millard W. Whitehead as chain carriers and George R. Thomas, flagman. The notes reveal just how integral the railroad was to the town's growth: "Beginning at stone mound South of Crow Creek from

Henry Hay, a prominent Cheyenne banker, served two terms as Wyoming state treasurer and later worked as assistant treasurer for the U.S. Steel Corporation in New York. (Courtesy Wyoming State Archives)

which: the center of the South Face of the Eastern abutment of the Union Pacific Rail Road when it intersects Crow Creek...." Hay surveyed the Fort D.A. Russell "military reservation" on July 20, 1870. Thomas and Hay set the first survey marker, according to a story in the *Cheyenne Daily Leader* in 1902.

According to John Thomas, Hay was a very determined man and was at his best under pressure. "[I]n critical emergencies," Thomas recalls in the *Breeder's Gazette,* "Henry Hay showed his sterling qualities, always cool and resourceful, never complaining, however arduous the task. He inspired all about him to do their level best, and gave a feeling of confidence that he would 'pull through' under any conditions." In October 1872, Hay and Thomas were working in the Medicine Bow Mountains. Thomas was to wait for

Hay's to come out at Rock Creek. An unexpected snowstorm covered the area with six inches of snow. When the storm broke, Hay, who knew only the general direction of the camp, headed toward it with other members of the crew. They found the camp, but Hay and one of his men froze their feet. Thomas recalls that he had "a good fire going in the Sibley stove, their feet in buckets of cracked ice and water," and sent a courier to the railroad to telegraph the doctor the next day. The messenger returned with supplies and a lengthy letter from the doctor. After two weeks spent recuperating, Hay insisted he could work. Most of the project was finished except the line through the mountains, which was completed the next summer

Hay and Thomas also partnered in sheep ranching in 1870 or 1871. They built the Valley Ranch on Lone Tree Creek, which eventually passed into the ownership of the Warren Livestock Company. They trailed sheep near Natural Fort on Lone Tree Creek about twelve miles from Cheyenne. The sheep market proved profitable for the men as they sold to butchers and the military post. They also claimed to be the first to practice winter feeding of sheep by building sheds for the stock's protection and letting the sheep graze in the area and return to the corral at night.

In 1874, Hay met Ella Bullock at the home of Francis E. and Helen Warren. A romance ensued, and the couple was married November 18, 1874. They began their married life in a cottage located where the Elks Building and the *Wyoming Tribune* eventually stood. Two children were born while they lived here, Henry G. Hay, Jr., and Mildred. The Hays later purchased the home located at Twenty-first and Carey (then Ferguson) from the Carey family.

Henry Hay soon found additional business ventures. He partnered with I. C. Whipple in 1875 in the wholesale and retail grocery business. Whipple and Hay proved profitable, and soon they expanded into the cattle business. He associated with other well-known cattlemen of the time, including Thomas Sturgis, Joseph Carey, R. S. Van Tassell, and Alexander Swan. Writer John Clay describes Hay as "cautious, conservative, reliable," and these qualities undoubtedly helped him in every business venture he undertook. Hay used the funds he earned through these ventures to buy the brands of John "Portugee" Phillips and J. S. Collins.

In 1878, a bad winter caused heavy losses for sheepmen, although Hay was said to have lost fewer head than many ranchers. His stock was a coarse-wool Mexican breed mixed with purebred Merinos and seemed to survive the harsh weather better than other breeds. Hay continued in the sheep business for thirteen years.

In the early 1880s, Hay tried his hand at banking. This field so satisfied him that he remained in it for twelve years. His connections with cattlemen and politicians proved useful. In December 1881, he met with many of the Cheyenne leaders of the time to discuss the possibility of opening another bank in Cheyenne. The Stock Growers' National Bank opened for business on April 19, 1882, with J. M. Carey serving as president, Thomas Sturgis as vice president, and Henry Hay as cashier and running day-to-day operations. While working for the bank, Hay continued to raise cattle. Seeing that the Scottish company that had purchased the Swan holdings at Chugwater appeared to be quite prosperous, Hay borrowed money for his own outfit. Clay writes, "The loan became a load, and the company staggered under it till 1893," when an economic depression hit. "Every cent that they personally made in other ways went into this seemingly bottomless pit. After some negotiations, rather unpleasant, they turned over their property to their creditors and faced the world again." Hay, like many others, suffered deep financial losses.

The bank, at least, prospered until 1887. In 1886, deposits totaled $583,000. By the next year, the deposits dropped to $334,000. The decline likely had been caused by the tremendous livestock losses that occurred in the harsh winter of 1887. As cashier during this period, Hay was "many a time hard-pressed," according to Clay. "He was charging off many of his losses, but if he saw a chance to help a worthy borrower he took a chance, generally with success." By April 1889, Andrew Gilchrist was the bank president, with Hay still serving as cashier. The bank's capital amounted to $400,000 with surplus and undivided profits of $95,000.

Hay served as president of the Cheyenne Board of Trade in 1889 and 1890. The board of trade was formed during the decline in the cattle industry in the area, in an effort to encourage other businesses. Hay was proud of the work accomplished by the issue of the board of trade. Its report in 1888, according to the *Cheyenne*

Daily Sun, "was distributed throughout the country, showed the removal of the old feeling of antagonism between the city and the railroads and their present friendly relations, the location of the great machine shops, the movement in this territory for Statehood, which had its local application in our cities' prosperity, all of the enterprises being aided and carried forward largely by an organized body of non-partisan business men, such as this board of trade represents." At the time, plans were being made for the completion of the Cheyenne & Northern Railroad to Douglas, with a spur to be built from the Hartville iron mines to the main track, and for several new manufacturing businesses in Cheyenne. Along with Sturgis, Warren, Erasmus Nagel, W. W. Corlett, and Phillip Dater, Hay was one of the incorporators of the Cheyenne & Northern Railroad.

By the fall of 1892, the cattle market was again prospering and so was the bank. Hay apparently had a personality well suited for the banking business. He inspired faith in his customers and, Clay says, became "a sort of guardian to many of them." His one fault was that he "carried the whole business in his head." His excellent memory helped him serve his customers on a one-to-one basis.

Hay was also active in the community. He served as a member of the state Constitutional Convention, helped build the Cheyenne Opera House and the Carnegie Library, was one of the organizers of the Cactus Club (predecessor to the prestigious Cheyenne Club), and served as a member of the World's Fair Commission in 1892–1893. In that capacity, Hay often traveled to Chicago, where he networked with many other people throughout the country. Hay also was a 32nd degree Mason and served as chairman of the Laramie County Republican Committee. He became active in the Wyoming Stock Growers Association, serving as treasurer for a number of years beginning in 1890. As manager of the Laramie River Cattle Company, he was instrumental in approving the WSGA as an advocate of brand inspections at various markets.

During this time, Hay did not loan out his extra balances locally, but purchased "choice paper in the east," according to Clay. What may have been a controversial investment strategy paid off for Hay when a financial depression struck in 1893. The local private banking house, T. A. Kent, caused a run on both the Stock Growers' National

Bank and the First National Bank, but "the bank under Hay's guidance stood firm as a rock. While somewhat reckless of his own money, he was ultraconservative of other people's." The eastern investments also helped, for Hay's bank was thus able to meet the demands of his depositors during that rough period. So successful was he at managing his bank's funds that the voters of the state elected Hay as Wyoming state treasurer in 1894. He served for four years in this position, most of them as a widower. Ella Hay died on November 6, 1895.

During 1901, Hay spent two weeks in Washington, D.C., visiting the entire Wyoming delegation, including Senators Francis E. Warren and Clarence Clark and Congressman Frank Mondell as well as W.A. Richards, Estelle Reel, Willis Van Devanter, Elwood Mead, and others. "Never before in his experience had he seen such evidences of prosperity as are apparent at this time," reported the *Cheyenne Daily Leader*. "Everybody is employed and no man who desires work needs to be idle. This condition Mr. Hay attributes to the material increase in foreign trade more than anything else as we are exporting…much more than we are importing, the commercial invasion of the continent by America being a strong reality."

Building on his background in financial management and his networking skills, Hay ran again for Wyoming state treasurer in 1902. The *Leader* reported that the Laramie County Republicans selected him as their candidate in early July. In seeking the support of Republicans voters before the primary, Hay described his opponent, W.R. Schnitger, as supported by gambling advocate and saloon keeper Harry Hynds. Hay pleaded, "I am making this fight alone, unaided by any organization, machine or combination. I need your help and if you keep in mind the main issue and do not allow minor considerations or intimidation to influence you I am sure to receive your support and win the fight."

The *Leader* supported Hay's candidacy, calling him "an exceedingly strong candidate…. He has hosts of old acquaintances throughout the state, and he is an excellent off hand speaker. He will deny this last assertion, but it is nevertheless true. He has a faculty of saying the right thing at the right time and it don't take over ten minutes to make his talk." His ability to surmount obstacles and meet responsibilities and his honesty "won him the confidence and respect of the people," according to the newspaper. About a week later, Hay, obviously still networking, attended a luncheon with Warren and Chief Hydrographer F.H. Newell of the U.S. Geological Survey and distinguished guests from the Colorado and Southern Railroad at the InterOcean Hotel. T.B. Hicks of the First National Bank also attended, as did newspapermen E.A. Slack and W.C. Deming. On the discussion agenda was irrigation, an important topic of the day. In November, the Republicans won sweeping victories across the state. Hay again became Wyoming's state treasurer.

Residents of the state were startled by the news in June 1903 that Hay planned to resign as treasurer. The report, carried first by the *Denver Times*, explained that he intended to relocate to New York. On June 12, 1903, the *Leader* carried Hay's letter to editor E.A. Slack, which explained that Hay planned to remarry but the date had not yet been set. He was "considering a very tempting business proposition" as well. Hay expected to live in New York permanently but would not decide for certain until September. He had not yet resigned from the post of state treasurer nor from his responsibilities at the Stock Growers' National Bank. He tried to put customers at ease, explaining, "Some transfers of the stock of the bank have recently occurred between non-resident stockholders, but the purchasers are my best friends and there is no reason for my leaving on that account."

Hay married Mary S. Seabolt in Denver on July 1, 1903, sold his holdings in the Stock Growers' National Bank, and moved to New York. The exciting business opportunity he had looked forward to was likely his new position with the U.S. Steel Corporation. Hay became assistant treasurer of that company, a job that he held for the rest of his life. Sadly, he would find himself alone for many of those years as Mary Seabolt Hay died June 10, 1907, of heart failure.

In a letter to his son Harry in 1908 Hay shares the frustrations he was experiencing in his job. "I am growing very tired of some [?] of my situation. The work is very exacting—the hours are too long and the foolish little details I am called upon to attend to make it very irksome to a man of my age—who has always been at the head of things and has been used to being treated with respect by his associates. I cannot explain it to you in a letter, but some things in my position have always been very galling and humiliating to me—while Mary was alive I did not mind it so much—as she always made light of it and taught me not to mind it as I was being well paid and by the time I had been with them 5 years I could take my leave—but now that I am alone and have plenty of time to brood over it it gets on my nerves and I often ask myself why I stand it and give up the few remaining years I have to this…lonely life."

Part of Hay's frustration stemmed from the fact that his son was not being treated well by his company either. He writes, "I told [Richard] Trimble [at U.S. Steel Corporation] today that the only object I had in being on the earth now was to get you started in something that would have a future for you—and that if [the new bank in] Gary did not offer it I must go some where…and make an opening—and that I would come back from this trip prepared to make up my mind and to act (?) He does not want me to leave, and he will find it very hard to get a man in my place who has the experience and judgment to run things as I have, who will consent to be made as much of a subordinate as I have." Even feeling as awful about his job as he did, he admits, "I am not going to burn any bridges behind me until I can see a clear road a head but I am going to do a lot of thinking and try to get something more out of it for both you and me in some way.…" Hay told his son, "[W]e may have to stand things as we find them until about the end of 1908 but at that time there must be some kind of a change.…"

Henry Hay died August 18, 1919, in Gary, Indiana. He had lived at the Union League Club in New York City after Mary's death and later moved to Gary to be close to his son who followed in his father's financial footsteps as he served as the first president of the Gary State Bank in Gary, Indiana, and became treasurer of the Gary public schools, the city comptroller, and the town's mayor in 1929.

Daze Bristol

Some people are memory makers. They make life a celebration and, by doing so, bring joy into the lives of others. Cheyenne's Daze Bristol was such a person. Her exuberant personality and winning ways continue to be cherished by those who were fortunate enough to have known her and by those who wish they could have known her. But everyone continues to have an opportunity to know Daze for she has been dubbed "The First Lady of Frontier Days," and the floats she inspired still add fun to the annual Cheyenne Frontier Days parades.

Born Daisy (later spelled Daze and Dazee) McCabe in Moberly, Missouri, in 1878, her bright personality mirrored her name. Her parents were John and Katherine Willett McCabe. She had two brothers, Jack and Robert. Jack, like young Daze, was interested in acting and performance and eventually became an actor on Broadway. The McCabes moved to Cheyenne in 1892.

Before moving to Cheyenne, Daze attended a convent school in North Platte, Nebraska, then graduated from Cheyenne's Central High School in 1897. She may have attended Normal School in Lincoln, Nebraska, before taking a teaching job at Archer, the first railroad stop east of Cheyenne. Her salary was forty dollars a month, with ten dollars subtracted for room and board. She had ten students in ten grades at the school. She started her duties with a tough challenge for someone told her that the previous instructor was fired for teaching students that the world was round. She taught two terms—winter and summer—because the students had fallen behind in their studies.

During those years, women teachers could not marry and retain their jobs. Daze quit her job to marry handsome Lieutenant Charles Bristol, a veteran of the Spanish American War who had been assigned to Fort D.A. Russell. Her mother disapproved because she did not want Daze to give up such a good job. She must have acquiesced, however, as the couple were wed in 1900 in Daze's parents' home. The dramatic flair so often associated with Daze's life came into play at the wedding. As the newlyweds prepared to board the train to their honeymoon destination, soldiers from the fort threw a caisson of old shoes at the couple instead of the customary rice. One of the shoes struck Daze in the eye. When the newlyweds arrived at Denver's Brown Palace, the desk clerk exhibited concern about allowing a bride with a black eye to spend the night in the honeymoon suite with her groom.

Daze was active in the community, appearing in several of the shows presented at Cheyenne's elegant Opera House. She played Little Golden Hair in "Golden Hair and the Three Bears" and a maid in "The Mikado." Her disappointment must have been great when the building was destroyed by fire on December 7, 1902.

In 1903, President Theodore Roosevelt made his second visit to Cheyenne. He had first come to the city when he had been running as William McKinley's vice presidential candidate, but now he had achieved the presidency himself. Among the activities prepared by Cheyennites for Teddy's visit were a wild west show similar to the events held at Frontier Days, a large parade, and a barbecue supper at U.S. Senator Francis E. Warren's Terry Ranch, located several miles south of the city. Guests were asked to ride horseback to the ranch as the president himself did upon his new mount, called Wyoming, presented to him earlier in the day.

Daze and Charles did not own a horse and did not have enough money to rent a carriage to travel to the ranch. So they rented a tandem bicycle and pedaled all the way out to the Terry Ranch. The trip was a tough one, and, tired and hungry, the Bristols arrived at about the same time that the rest of the 150 guests were leaving. They apparently did meet the president but missed dinner. So, still tired and hungry, they pedaled the long miles back to Cheyenne.

In that same year, a childhood schoolmate of Daze's, T. Joe Cahill, participated in the most sensational of Cheyenne events—

the hanging of Tom Horn. Cahill was one of the men who lifted Horn onto the platform of the gallows. Daze was one of the spectators at the execution.

Joy bubbled from Daze, and she and Charles enjoyed the social scene in Cheyenne. Daze was known as an excellent dancer and a gracious hostess, two attributes that would remain throughout her life. The Bristols financial situation soon improved. In 1904, they built a new home at 720 East Twentieth Street. Charles eventually became vice president of the S.A. Bristol Printing & Bindery Company (later Pioneer Printing) owned by his father. Not much information exists about the Bristols during the ensuing years until 1918. That year, Daze got her first taste of organizing a parade when she assisted Mrs. Charles Carey and Mrs. Harry P. Hynds in creating a parade to encourage people to cut down on food consumption and other consumer items to further the war effort during World War I.

In 1926, Daze was featured in a full-page photograph in *Redbook* magazine. She was also featured in a sepia-toned photograph that won a prize at the Saint Louis World's Fair. She had an excellent figure, described as a "perfect 36." That same year, the Cheyenne Frontier Days Committee and the Chamber of Commerce decided that a parade should become part of the annual festivities. Daze's creative imagination soared. She selected and trained square dancers especially for a float she called *Hiram's Dance Hall*. Local fiddler Hiram Davidson played tunes while she accompanied him on a miniature organ and four couples danced. Olive Maxon Jones, a Cheyenne resident of those days, recalls, "Daze was resplendent in sparkling gown and extra large hat covered with ostrich plumes. The dancing continued throughout the whole long parade." Daze also created *Hell's Half Acre*, depicting an early day Cheyenne saloon, complete with handlebar-mustachioed bartender and gamblers playing cards and dancing with daring girls. Other floats included *Silver Crown Mining, Placer Mining, The Blacksmith,* and *The Vigilantes*.

The next year, 1927, tested Daze's mettle. Her mother died, and Charles committed suicide in October, apparently despondent over a serious health condition. He had contracted malaria while stationed in the Phillippines, a disease that continued to plague him throughout his life. Daze had gone out for a car ride with a friend. She had

Daze Bristol always loved acting and created numerous floats for the Cheyenne Frontier Days parades, some of which still delight the crowds. (Courtesy Wyoming State Archives)

encouraged her husband to ride along, but he opted to stay at home. He shot himself while she was away, leaving her a widow at 50. Charles's funeral was conducted by the Cheyenne Elks and the Cheyenne Post of the Spanish War Veterans, who performed the military rites. He was buried in Lakeview Cemetery.

Though the double loss might have sunk many into despair, Daze rallied. A lifelong Catholic, her faith undoubtedly strengthened her during such tragic times. William C. Deming of the *Wyoming Tribune* encouraged Daze to take a writing and advertising class at the University of Denver. Anxious to make a fresh start, Daze did so. One of her first writing efforts was an article about Cheyenne's bus service. She earned a free ride to California for that piece. She soon began working for Deming. Her column "Touring the Shops with Dazee" first appeared on May 3, 1928. The column contained forty-three personal advertisements and covered three-quarters of a page. She asked readers to write to her if they couldn't find an advertised item, and she'd either purchase it or send information. This is probably about the time she began using alternate spellings of her name. (Sometimes her nickname is spelled "Daze" and sometimes "Dazee." The newspaper may have added the extra "e" to reflect the pronunciation of her name.) She visited her customers weekly to compile the information for her columns.

Daze remained active in the community. She helped organize several of Cheyenne's service clubs and other organizations, including Altrusa Club, Cheyenne Women's Club, American Legion Auxiliary, Historical Society, and the B.P.O. Does. She was also a member of the Spanish American War Auxiliary, Saint Mary's Guild, and the DePaul Hospital Guild and a charter member of Wyoming Press Women.

In 1930, Daze was said to have been among the guests at a card party hosted by Agnes O'Mahoney, the wife of Joseph O'Mahoney (who would later become a U.S. senator), where the possibility of beginning a theatrical troupe in Cheyenne was discussed. In early February, a formal proposal was presented to twenty-five people at the Carnegie Library. Soon twelve managers were appointed and the Cheyenne Little Theatre Players was formed. According to Jean Bastian, the twelve managers represented service clubs from the city who had indicated an interest in the project. Daze represented the Altrusa

Club. Other clubs who joined in this venture were the Women's Club, Rotary Club, Elks Club, American Legion Luncheon Club, Lions Club, Music Study Club, Business and Professional Women's Club, Cheyenne Teachers Association, YWCA, Kiwanis, and Fort Warren Study Club. The group scrambled to prepare their first production—three one-act plays directed by William DeVere, presented at the Wyoming Consistory Auditorium on May 7, 1930.

Daze continued her work with the Cheyenne Frontier Days floats. "A Frontier Days legend," writer Phil Riske explained, "Daze Bristol at the organ on her musical float, was a main feature of the 1942 parade." Her specially trained square dancers soon gained a national reputation as they were featured on Arthur Godfrey's television show and later were the first square dancers to appear at Red Rocks, near Denver, Colorado. The dancers performed at the Plains Hotel and the Frontier Hotel during Frontier Days events and often also performed for patients in local hospitals.

Daze continued to be known as an excellent hostess, gaining a reputation for her two annual parties. One was a garden party held during Frontier Days. She hosted as many as 125 people at this party. The other was a holiday celebration at which she served eggnog.

Daze continued writing, too, adding the job of women's editor for the *Wyoming Stockman Farmer* to her journalistic experience. Her page in that publication was entitled "Household Corner." In 1948, on the twentieth anniversary of her "Touring the Shops with Dazee" column, the *Tribune* gave her accolades: "Those not personally acquainted with 'Dazee'...do not have a thorough knowledge of Cheyenne; those who do know her personally enjoy an enviable privilege." Dazee, at age 70, had become a Cheyenne institution. Her column, boasted the *Tribune*, "is the oldest...in point of continuous publication by one editor, and largest in the United States." Even though she enjoyed the writing, Daze told the newspaper that Frontier Days was her "whole life." She'd not been well during that year, suffering a bad fall that required leg surgery; yet, she maintained a cheerful attitude and quipped that she had probably broken everything in her body by now.

Soon her personal shopping guide was included with her column. She had managed to build up a good reputation with her customers by visiting them in person every week and eventually switched to using the telephone to complete her duties. The *Eagle* explained, "During her career, she has collected thousands of cuts which she features with her ads. She can sort through the drawer and come up with the right picture in a matter of minutes." Even so, Daze announced she'd retire. But she kept writing and "floating" into the 1960s. Daze's association with the newspaper lasted for more than thirty years. Her work with the parade floats continued even longer.

And the honors rolled in for her. She earned many national awards for her writing. She was dubbed "Wyoming's pioneer news reporter, columnist and lady," when she earned the National Woman of Achievement title from the Wyoming Press Women in 1963 at age 85. In March 1965, Daze was honored by the local chapter of Business and Professional Women. She was not a member of the organization, but the members felt that she had done such an outstanding job of promoting career women that she deserved recognition. The *Wyoming Eagle* reported, "It is expected that business people know and hold Dazee in high regard, but the astounding thing is to see the hundreds of kids along the Frontier Days parade route jumping up and down and waving at their friend, Dazee." This surely must have pleased her, for Daze did not have children of her own.

On May 12, 1967, a celebration honoring Daze for her forty-one years of participation in the Cheyenne Frontier Days parades was held at the Plains Hotel with local broadcaster Larry Birleffi as the emcee. The event was dubbed "Daze Bristol Day." According to the report in the *Wyoming State Tribune*, three hundred friends attended the program, which featured performances by Daze's square dancers. The Frontier Days committee presented Daze with an oil portrait of her bedecked in her famous dance-hall costume, painted by artist Bill Murray. The Altrusa Club gave her a sixteen-inch doll created in Daze's likeness by Ruth Fox and similarly costumed.

Daze was honored on her hundredth birthday on May 9, 1978, at Cheyenne's Hitching Post. Governor Ed Herschler formally declared the day "Daze Bristol Day," and the Wyoming Press Women again honored Daze. This time, the award came for being the oldest working press woman in the nation. They presented Daze with a plaque commemorating the achievement, and Daze gave it to Mrs. Herschler to hang in the governor's mansion near the library established by the Wyoming Press Women. The afternoon reception, attended by more than six hundred people, was sponsored by the *Wyoming State Tribune & Wyoming Eagle* and the *Wyoming Stockman Farmer,* along with the numerous community groups Daze had helped throughout the years.

Daze continued to live in the house that she and her husband had built near the turn of the century, but ill health forced her to move to the Cheyenne Health Care Center in 1983. She died in early October of that year, at the age of 105. She was survived by only one niece, but practically every resident of the city of Cheyenne claimed her as one of their own. In reporting on the celebration for her centennial birthday, the *Tribune-Eagle* called her "truly an institution in Cheyenne and Wyoming." Daze's ebullience lives on for *Dazee's Dance Hall* and some of her other floats continue to delight parade-goers at the Cheyenne Frontier Days celebrations.

Prairie Rose Henderson

INFORMATION ON THE life of Prairie Rose Henderson is somewhat sketchy. Most of the cowgirl's life is depicted in postcards created by Doubleday, showing her decked out in her rodeo duds. The life she chose contained glamorous moments but also had its share of rough spots. Mystery still surrounds this cowgirl.

Prairie Rose Henderson was born Ann Robbins in the 1870s, the daughter of a Wyoming ranching couple. The young girl's dream was to become a cowgirl; she broke horses at her parents' ranch as well as for local ranchers. According to historian Shirley Flynn, Henderson won the first Cheyenne Frontier Days race for women on August 23, 1899, earning a forty-five-dollar saddle for the half-mile race. "From 1899, except for a few years," wrote Flynn, "rodeo women raced for money at Cheyenne; they became the first professional women athletes in the world." Mary Lou LeCompte, writing in *Cowgirls of the Rodeo*, believed that the first cowgirls "talked their way into the Cheyenne bronc riding competition against the men." Probably the first contest that women entered at Cheyenne was the cow pony race, introduced in 1899. By 1906, cowgirl bronc riding and relay racing were included as part of the Cheyenne Frontier Days events.

Sources disagree about Henderson's career. Debra Munn reported that Henderson left home to join the Irwin Brothers Wild West Show. She rode relay races with the Irwin girls and traveled with the Irwins for several years. The files of the National Cowgirl Museum and Hall of Fame, however, suggest that Henderson began riding in rodeos—though not necessarily sanctioned rodeos—in 1906, then joined the Irwins in 1911. Primarily a bronc rider, Henderson also

Prairie Rose Henderson, an early day bronc rider, clad in her famous bloomers and boots costume known as "Turkish Trousers," died under mysterious circumstances. (From the collection of the Cheyenne Frontier Days Old West Museum.)

excelled at relay races, flat racing, and roping. Flynn reports that Henderson performed in the Cheyenne Frontier Days trick-riding events in 1911 and earned the championship. Henderson appeared in the Los Angeles Rodeo in March 1912, competing in bronc riding. In 1913, in the second Los Angeles Rodeo, Henderson won the bronc riding against fourteen cowgirl competitors. At that time, the number of opportunities for women in rodeo was increasing, with more than one hundred cowgirls competing by 1916. In 1917, for winning the Ladies' Bronc Riding Championship in Cheyenne, Henderson earned a silver buckle from the Union Pacific Railroad. She earned second place that same year in the San Antonio Roundup.

The Queen of England watched her perform at the Tex Austin Rodeo in 1924. At the 1924 Pendleton Roundup, Munn wrote, "Mabel Strickland, Fox Hastings, Lorena Trickey, and Rose Henderson had requested permission to compete in the same contests as cowboys, and thereby vie for the all-around cowboy prize." But the women's request was denied, "show[ing] quite a contrast to the earlier years when women like Bertha Blancett had regularly challenged the men and given them a run for the all-around title."

Prairie Rose also became famous for her riding clothes, called "Turkish Trousers," which she wore when she competed against other well-known cowgirls of the day, Goldie Saint Clair and Jean Bernoudi. Costumes could increase the women's incomes by sparking their popularity. LeCompte explained that Henderson and another bronc rider, Lulu Belle Parr, were both known for designing their own "outrageous" costumes. Henderson's often-photographed outfit was knee-length bloomers beneath a skirt trimmed in ostrich feathers, which she wore with silk stockings and cowboy boots. Parr favored a divided skirt and spotted fur cape. One description pictures Henderson wearing a broad-brimmed hat with "a blouse trimmed in chiffon and sequins, and a wide band of marabou feathers hanging over bloomers, stockings and cowboy boots." Munn wrote, "the rodeo circuit meant everything to 'Prairie Rose Henderson,' whose daring stunts of horsemanship, combined with her exuberance and winning smile, never failed to make her an instant crowd-pleaser."

Perhaps her personal life felt rougher than the broncs she rode. Henderson took the name of her first husband. Whether she divorced him or he died is unknown. The cowgirl then married Johnny Judd, a trick roper, probably in 1925. But that union didn't last either. Henderson's schedule may have had something to do with her broken love affairs. In the late 1920s, Henderson and Judd moved to Tucson, Arizona, to make silent western films. But apparently she didn't like Arizona and returned to Wyoming, "still competing in every major rodeo in the world, including those in Boston and in New York's Madison Square Garden," according to Munn.

In 1929, Henderson met her third husband, Charles Coleman, who had homesteaded eleven miles from Split Rock about fifty miles north of Rawlins. According to reports in the *Rawlins Republican* in 1926, Coleman was a man with a past. As a thirty-four-year-old bachelor, he had fought with a man named Jack A. Allen who suffered a broken neck and died. Coleman was arrested on the charge of involuntary manslaughter and held on five hundred dollars bond. In November, he pled not guilty to the charges, and the case was dismissed because of insufficient evidence.

Henderson, now Mrs. Charles Coleman, retired from the rodeo circuit to live on the Hadsell ranch near Rawlins with her husband. In 1932, he was in jail in Rawlins on charges of cattle rustling while Henderson remained on the ranch. When Coleman was released and returned home, his wife was missing. The *Rawlins Republican Bulletin* reported that "Mr. Coleman was in Rawlins at the time of the disappearance and callers at the homestead first discovered the fact. They found the dogs locked up in the shed as if [his wife] had been expecting to be back soon. It was thought that she had become lost in the timber and snow and a search was made of the entire section."

In July 1939, six and a half years after her disappearance, Henderson's body was found by a sheepherder named Martinez. The coroner and undersheriff agreed that the woman had probably lost her way in a severe snowstorm. There was no evidence of foul play. The skeleton was discovered about fifty-four miles north and west of Rawlins, about one hundred fifty feet from a mountain road on a side hill, at the foot of a pine tree in a section "partially grown over by sagebrush, in the southern part of Fremont County." Ironically, the skeleton was found in an area threatened by a fire. Firefighters parried with the flames just a quarter of a mile from the skeleton.

Had the fire continued out of control, Henderson's body—and any clues as to what happened—would have been lost forever. The newspaper explained, "It was in this small area, rather than in the thousands and thousands of acres of land where she could have been lost, that her remains were found.… Mr. Coleman, who had been among the firefighters yesterday morning and had watched the fire alone from 1 to 5 A.M. not far from the skeleton, could not be located last night to be told of the discovery."

The skeleton was taken to Rawlins. Henderson's brother as well as her husband identified her by her ring, a bridle, her grain bucket, and articles of clothing. A length of rope found near the body tied in a square knot was identified by Coleman as one he'd made for catching horses to saddle and ride. Coleman theorized that his wife had gone out to rope a horse and then became disoriented by the snow. "Evidence that he was correct," surmised the newspaper, "is borne out by the fact that although she was familiar with the area, she had wandered to the opposite side of the mountain, two and a half miles from her own cabin."

Munn believes that Henderson still wanders, looking for her horse. She explained, "According to western writer and former rodeo performer Don Bell, quite a few people have heard Prairie Rose calling for help on stormy nights." Bell said that two or three cowboys and sheepherders had remarked to him about it through the years, as late as the 1960s.

Prairie Rose Henderson was a friend of Princess Blue Water, who came to Frontier Days from South Dakota from the 1920s through the 1960s to perform with the Indians. Current Cheyenne resident Marirose Morris is the granddaughter of Princess Blue Water. When Marirose's mother became Miss American Indian, the forerunner to the title of Miss Indian America, she sometimes traveled with Prairie Rose and Princess Blue Water to rodeos and parades, and the three women became close friends. Later when Marirose was born, her mother planned to name the baby girl after a good friend, but the priest insisted the child should have a Christian first name, so the baby became Marirose instead. Marirose says she is unsure of the origin of her name, but because of the similarity of the sounds of the names, family folklore has it that she nearly became the namesake of the cowgirl Prairie Rose.

Henderson's life in many ways remains mysterious, but her love of riding broncs and her rodeo achievements continue to inspire others. Her enthusiasm shows in the old time photograph depicting her with arms outstretched and wide-brimmed hat raised to the sky. The smiling woman, wearing her famous "Turkish Trousers" and cowboy boots, stands in an arena where she likely spent some of her happiest hours as she welcomes others to come join her and the other cowboys and rodeo riders for some rough-and-tumble fun in Old Cheyenne.

Notes on the Sources

The first citation of a source is given in full. Subsequent citations, including those in later profiles, are abbreviated.

Abbreviations

AHC   American Heritage Center, University of Wyoming, Laramie, Wyoming

WSA   Wyoming State Archives, Cheyenne, Wyoming

WBB   Wyoming Blue Book

Nathan Baker

For information on the railroad's coming to Cheyenne and the city's early days, consult *Wyoming Frontier State* by Velma Linford (Denver: Old West Publishing Company, 1947). *Historical Encyclopedia of Wyoming* (Cheyenne: Wyoming Historical Institute, 1970) lists information on the state's counties. *Wyoming Blue Book*, Vol. 1 (Cheyenne: Wyoming State Archives and Historical Department, 1974) offers a wealth of information and statistics on territorial days. County statistics and information are included in volume two, and equality is featured in volume three. Information about surveys of Cheyenne came from *Cheyenne, Cheyenne: Our Blue Collar Heritage* (Cheyenne: G.P. Jones, 1983).

Early Cheyenne Homes, 1880–1890 (Cheyenne: Laramie County Historical Society, 1962) gives a thumbnail description of Baker's newspaper career in Cheyenne and Wyoming Territory. Elizabeth Keen's "The Frontier Press" in *Studies in Literature of the West* (Laramie: University of Wyoming Graduate School, 1956) offers a good look at the historical period. I relied upon Keen's tracing of Baker's early-day *Leader* articles and of the advancement of the railroad. Coutant Notes, "Wyoming Newspaper—*Cheyenne Leader*" (*Annals of Wyoming* 5, no.1[1927]:36–38) gives good details on the early history of Baker's newspaper. (The Coutant Notes are materials drawn from C.G. Coutant's notes for the second and third volumes of his *History of*

Wyoming, which were never published. The Notes were published in a series of pieces in *Annals of Wyoming.*) T. A. Larson's *History of Wyoming* (Lincoln: University of Nebraska Press, 1978) provides in-depth information about the political folderol occurring during Baker's time. Pat Hall's "Newspapers in Early-Day Cheyenne," in *History of Cheyenne* (Dallas: Curtis Media Corporation, 1989), provides good background for the history of several newspapers, including Baker's *Leader,* and ties the older newspapers in with the new ones. See also *Wyoming Newspapers, A Centennial History* (Cheyenne: Wyoming Press Association, 1990).

Lola Homsher's edited version of James Chisolm's journal, *South Pass 1868: James Chisolm's Journal of the Wyoming Gold Rush* (Lincoln: University of Nebraska Press, 1965), provides excellent background on that city and the gold rush that created it. Wilbur Fiske Stone's *History of Colorado* (Chicago: S. J. Clarke Publishing Company, 1918) gives a good sketch of Baker and his achievements in that state. "McGrath's Pioneers," in *Collections of the Colorado Historical Society* (Denver, n.d.), also contains a brief biography of Baker. Lyle W. Dorsett's *The Queen City: A History of Denver* (Boulder: Pruett Publishing Company, 1977) gives good background into that city's history.

Newspapers consulted for this piece were *Rocky Mountain News,* 28 May 1934, 5 February 1956, 28 October 1962; *Wyoming State Tribune,* 17 June 1932; *Wyoming State Tribune* and *Cheyenne State Leader,* 20 July 1929. For readers interested in perusing the actual newspaper Baker published, copies of his *Leader* are housed at the University of Wyoming's Coe Library in Laramie. The library holds issues from 1867 to 1872 and beyond, although some years are incomplete.

Hiram "Hi" Kelly

In addition to telling of Kelly's experiences at Independence Rock, C. G. Coutant's *History of Wyoming from the Earliest Known Discoveries,* Vol. 1 (Laramie: Chaplin, Spafford & Mathison, Printers, 1899) contains information about the difficulties of travel on the plains in the middle 1800s. Apparently the in-depth personal interview Coutant conducted with Kelly was slated for inclusion in a later volume of the book, which was never published. Daze Bristol and William R. Dubois III's typewritten manuscript, "Hi Kelly Digs His Heels Into Wyoming" (WSA), contains a good biographical sketch of Kelly and of his wife, Elizabeth, and their children. It also provides in-depth information on the Indian troubles Kelly experienced as a freighter, his haying exploits, and his other adventures. Charles A. Guernsey in *Wyoming Cowboy Days* (New York: G. P. Putnam's Sons, 1936) compliments Kelly's skill with a hay scythe. Larson's *History of Wyoming* describes the early history of Wyoming's cattle industry and the fencing conflicts that erupted in disputes about ownership of open range. Hi Kelly's letter appeared in a lengthy piece in the *Wyoming State Tribune* and *Eagle,* 29 July

1923. Other newspapers consulted include the *Wyoming Eagle*, 3 May 1979; *Fort Collins Express Courier*, 3 (or 8?) June 1924.

The story of Raw Hide Buttes appears in Agnes Wright Spring's *Cheyenne-Black Hills Stage Routes* (Glendale, Calif.: Arthur H. Clark Company, 1949) and also in Candy Moulton's *Roadside History of Wyoming* (Missoula: Mountain Press Publishing Company, 1995). Spring's *Cow Country Legacies* (Kansas City: Lowell Press, 1976) recounts the lilac legend and the Virginia Dale information, and gives details on Kelly's sale of his Chugwater ranch and a description of the buildings there. *Early Cheyenne Homes* gives the details of the Kelly mansion in Cheyenne.

Barney L. Ford

Frances Melrose's column "Rocky Mountain Memories" (*Rocky Mountain News*, 18 November 1984) and Frank Hall's *History of the State of Colorado* (Chicago: The Blakely Printing Company, 1895) provide good biographical sketches of Ford. William G. Haas's typewritten manuscript of a speech presented to the Rotary Club in 1959, "The Story of the Inter-Ocean Hotel" (WSA), gives insight into the history of the hotel, mostly after Ford's ownership of it. Consult Dorsett's *The Queen City* for more background on Denver's black history as well as William Katz's *Black People Who Made the Old West* (New York: Crowell Press, 1977) and Larson's *History of Wyoming* for information about blacks in Wyoming's history.

Forbes Parkhill's article "Colorado's Negro 'President Maker'" (*Empire Magazine*, 15 September 1963) examines the politics of the day and the ruckus involved in Colorado's statehood struggle. Parkhill also wrote *Mister Barney Ford: A Portrait in Bistre* (Denver: Sage Books, 1963) which gives more in-depth information on Ford's life and delves into his "law of positivities" algebraic equation. Al White's family biography in *History of Cheyenne* gives information about working in Ford's hotel. Spring's *Cheyenne-Black Hills Stage Routes* recounts the opulence of earlier Cheyenne hotels. I also found articles about Ford in the *Rocky Mountain News*, 22 September 1875, 29 October 1873, and 20 May 1956.

Nathaniel Robertson

In compiling this piece, I interviewed several people knowledgeable about carriages and carriage-makers, including John Gavin, curator, and Richard Davis, carriage collection volunteer, at Cheyenne's Old West Museum, and Susan Green, librarian at the Carriage Museum of America, Bird-in-Hand, Pennsylvania. In addition, I toured the carriage display at the Old West Museum. Don H. Berkebile's *Carriage Terminology: An Historical Dictionary* (Washington D.C.: Smithsonian Institution Press and Liberty Cap Books, 1978) provides a wealth of information about carriage-making and different types of carriages. The *Cheyenne City Directory* for 1884–1885 and the *Denver City Directory* for 1866, 1885, and 1886 helped me place Robertson. I also consulted *Encyclopedia Americana*, Vol. 5 (New York: Americana Corporation, 1961) for background on carriages.

For information about the Cheyenne Carriage Company, see *F.E. Warren Papers, 1868–1974* (Accession Number 13, Series VI, Cheyenne Carriage Company 1882–1900, AHC). Hall's *History of the State of Colorado* and Larson's *History of Wyoming* also proved useful here. The Smithsonian Institution web site (www.smithsonian.org) offers carriage drawings for those who'd like to study further how carriages were made. To obtain carriage drawings, contact Carriage Drawings, National Museum of American History, Smithsonian Institution, Washington, DC 20560.

William Jefferson Hardin

For information on Hardin's legislative work, see *Session Laws of Wyoming Territory, Passed by the Sixth Legislative Assembly, Convened at Cheyenne, November 4, 1879* (Cheyenne: Leader Steam Book & Job Printing, 1879), and *House Journal 1879* (typescript copy, WSA). See also WBB, Vol. 1, for more information on the territorial legislature.

Several articles were helpful in providing background on Hardin's life and career. Eugene H. Berwanger, in "William J. Hardin: Colorado Spokesman for Racial Justice, 1863–1873" (*Colorado Magazine* 52, no. 1 [1975]), sheds light on Hardin's years in Colorado, and Roger D. Hardaway, in "William Jefferson Hardin: Wyoming's Nineteenth Century Black Legislator" (*Annals of Wyoming* 63, no. 1 [1991]: 2–13), details Hardin's two terms of service in the Wyoming territorial legislature. See also Forbes Parkhill's, *Mister Barney Ford*, Larson's *History*, and Lyle Dorsett's *The Queen City* for more information about black history in Wyoming and Colorado during Hardin's time. Larson's book also contains the details about the rivalry between editors Glafcke and Slack.

According to a Wyoming Public Television rebroadcast of its 1991 Martin Luther King/Equality Day program on January 14, 2001, Elizabeth Byrd of Cheyenne became Wyoming's first black state legislator.

Newspapers tell some of the story of Hardin's legislative career and his life. Those consulted for this piece were *Cheyenne Daily Sun*, 19 March 1878, 22 August 1879, 30 August 1879, 31 August 1879, 2 September 1879, 5 November 1879, 9 November 1879, 23 December 1879, 15 September 1889; and *Cheyenne Daily Leader*, 19 August 1879, 21 August 1879, 1 September 1879, 4 December 1879.

R.S. Van Tassell

Shirley Flynn's "Renesselaer Schuyler Van Tassell" (*Annals of Wyoming* 71, no. 3 [1999]: 2–7) is a good biographical sketch of Van Tassell. Other sources of interest are George L. Lemmon's "Stories" in the WPA Collection (WSA), and the F. E. Warren papers at the AHC.

Authors consulted include John Rolfe Burroughs, *Guardian of the Grasslands* (Cheyenne: Pioneer Printing & Stationery Company, 1971); Charles A. Guernsey, *Wyoming Cowboy Days* (New York: G. P. Putnam's Sons, 1936); and Gladys Powelson Jones, *The First Hundred Years 1886–1986: The Van Tassell Carriage Barn, National Register of Historical Places* (Cheyenne: Cheyenne Artists Guild, 1986). William C. Deming's *Roosevelt in the Bunk House* (Laramie: The Laramie Printing Company, 1927) contains William W. "Bill" Daley's "The Famous Ride from Laramie to Cheyenne." Spring's *Cow Country Legacies* tells of Van Tassell's marriage to Moore's widow and other financial details.

See also Jim Newsome's "Van Tassell: Pop. 10" (*Wyoming Horizons,* n.d.) for information on the town. Helena Huntington Smith, in *The War on Powder River* (New York: McGraw-Hill, 1966), delves into the Johnson County War.

Newspapers consulted for this piece were *Cheyenne Daily Sun,* 10 April 1889–21 September 1889, 9 January 1890, 13 February 1891–2 September 1891, 5 May 1892–23 December 1892, 24 February 1893, and 5 March 1893; *Cheyenne Daily Leader,* 10 December 1886; *Cheyenne Tribune,* 29 August 1910; and *Lusk Herald,* 16 April 1931, 23 November 1950.

C.D. Kirkland

Reese Jenkins's *Images and Enterprises* (Baltimore: Johns Hopkins University Press, 1987) and Elizabeth Brayer's *George Eastman: A Biography* (Baltimore: Johns Hopkins University Press, 1996) contain information about Eastman and the history of photography. Kathleen Connor, curator of the George Eastman House in Rochester, New York, provided copies of the George Eastman correspondence and helpful guidance.

For more about J. E. Stimson, see Michael Amundson's *Wyoming Time and Again* (Boulder: Pruett Publishing Company, 1991) and Mark Junge's *J. E. Stimson, Photographer of the West* (Lincoln: University of Nebraska Press, 1985). Historian Dan Davis, formerly of the AHC, graciously shared some of his research on Kirkland with me. See also Spring's *The Cheyenne and Black Hills Stage.*

Stone's *History of Colorado* also tells more about Kirkland, as does Frank Hall's *History of the State of Colorado.* Terry William Mangan's *Colorado on Glass* (Denver: Sundance Limited, 1975) contains a directory of early Colorado photographers. See also the *Colorado State Business Directory and Annual Register,* 1875, 1876, 1895, 1902, and 1910.

Much of the information about Kirkland exists in the Cheyenne newspapers. Those consulted for this piece were *Cheyenne Daily Sun,* 4 May 1889–24 December 1889, and the years 1891, 1892, 1893; *Cheyenne Daily Leader,* 1902; and *Wyoming State Tribune* and *Cheyenne State Leader,* 23 August 1926.

Harry P. Hynds

Two articles by William Howard Moore—"Pietism and Progress: James H. Hayford and the Wyoming Anti-Gambling Tradition, 1869–1893" (*Annals of Wyoming* 55, no. 2 [1983]: 2–8) and "Progressivism and the Social Gospel in Wyoming: The Antigambling Act of 1901 as a Test Case" (*Western Historical Quarterly* 15, no. 3 [1984]: 299–316)—provide excellent historical background on the anti-gambling movement in Wyoming. State ex rel. Hynds v. Cahill, County Clerk, et al. (*Pacific Reporter*, 433) gives the full opinion of the Wyoming Supreme Court.

T. Blake Kennedy's typewritten memoir (Kennedy Papers No. 405, Box 1, Folder 16, AHC) contains some of the judge's thoughts about Hynds and information about some of his business dealings. See also Shirley E. Flynn, "Cheyenne's Harry P. Hynds: Blacksmith, Saloon Keeper, Promoter, Philanthropist" (*Annals of Wyoming* 73, no. 3 [2001]: 2–11). Additional information was gleaned from entries by Lee Bowker, Roy Page, Oscar McIntyre, George Rabou, Mary Ellen Smith, and Evelyn Okamoto in *History of Cheyenne*. Eileen Starr, in *Architecture in the Cowboy State* (Glendo, Wyo: High Plains Press, 1992), gives more details about prominent buildings in the state's history as well as some information about architect William Dubois. Larson's *History* chronicles the early days of saloons and gambling houses and the legislature's early rules, beginning with the 1869 rule on Sunday closing of saloons. Dan Allen, Superintendent of Curt Gowdy State Park, gave the author details about the Hynds Lodge in the park. Mae Urbanek's *Wyoming Place Names* (Missoula: Mountain Press Publishing Company, 1988) helped me decipher the name of Hynds' businesses.

Newspapers consulted were *Cheyenne Daily Sun*, May-June 1889, January 1891–1893, 1895, 23 October 1901–November 1901; *Cheyenne Daily Sun Leader*, 1900; *Cheyenne Daily Leader* 1902, February 1903; *Salt Lake City Herald*, 3 March 1896; *Wyoming Eagle*, 17 March 1933, 22 May 1956; *Wyoming Tribune*, 16 March 1933; and *Wyoming State Tribune*, 22 May 1956.

George D. Rainsford

Herbert Gottfried, in an e-mail interview with the author on April 9, 2001, and Sheila Bricher-Wade on April 6, 2001, provided helpful information for this piece. See also *New York Times*, 28 December 1935, and *Daytona Beach News-Journal*, 27 December 1935. William C. Deming, in *Collected Writings*, Vol. 4 (Glendale, Calif.: Arthur H. Clark Company, 1947), gave additional background as did James N. Vaughn to John W. Cornelison, 6 August 1970. All of these were found in the George D. Rainsford biographical file, AHC. Also consulted was the National Register of Historic Places nomination form for the Rainsford District (State Historic Preservation Office, Cheyenne).

For more background on Rainsford and his architecture in Wyoming, see *Early Cheyenne Homes; Wyoming Platte County Heritage* (Wheatland: Platte

County Extension Homemakers Council, 1981); Starr's *Architecture in the Cowboy State*; Spring's, *Cow Country Legacies*; "Reminisce with Leora Peters," *Platte County Record-Times*, 24 December 1965; and *Chugwater: A Centennial History* (Chugwater, Wyo.: privately published, 1986).

The National Museum of the Morgan Horse, in a telephone interview with the author on February 27, 2001, and Anheuser-Busch Company, in an e-mail interview with the author on March 9, 2001, provided information on Rainsford's horses.

Newspapers consulted were *Cheyenne Daily Sun*, 31 May 1889–September 1889, 1891, 1892; *Cheyenne Daily Leader*, 28 December 1901, 13 October 1902; *Chugwater News*, 13 February 1936; and *Wyoming State Tribune-Cheyenne State Leader*, 13 January 1936.

Elwood Mead

James R. Kluger's *Turning on Water with a Shovel: The Career of Elwood Mead* (Albuquerque: University of New Mexico Press, 1992) is an excellent resource for those interested in learning more about Mead and irrigation practices. Mead's "Letter to Irrigation Committee of the Constitutional Convention" is housed at the Wyoming State Archives in Cheyenne, Wyoming. See also Larson's *History* and Guernsey's, *Wyoming Cowboy Days*.

Excerpts from Mead's books appear in Anne MacKinnon and John Shields's *Selected Writings of Elwood Mead on Water Administration in Wyoming and the West* (Cheyenne: Wyoming State Engineer's Office and the Wyoming Water Association, 2000.) The AHC has a large collection of Mead's papers, including his "Recollections of Irrigation Legislation in Wyoming." At the AHC, I also consulted the Elwood Mead Biographical File and Elwood Mead Papers, 1882–1958 (Accession No. 5258, Box 1, Folders 10–12). The collection also contains much correspondence between Mead and his son Tom. Letters used for this piece were in Box 1, Folders 2, 3, and 5. Also see the Biennial Report of the State Engineer of Wyoming for 1894.

Newspapers consulted were *Cheyenne Daily Sun*, 29 July 1889, 25 October 1889, 26 February 1891, 19 May 1891, 23 July 1892, 27 July 1892, 26 October 1892, 30 October 1892, 2 November 1892, 3 November 1892; *Cheyenne Daily Sun-Leader*, 8 January 1900; *Cheyenne Daily Leader*, 17 February 1903, 9 March 1903. See also *New York Times*, 27 May 1934; *Park County Enterprise*, 27 November 1915; *Casper Tribune Herald*, 27 January 1936; *Guernsey Gazette*, 31 January 1936; *Wyoming Eagle*, 28 January 1936; *The Reclamation Era*, February 1936; and *Capitol Times*, 10 April 1983.

Joseph M. Carey

Robert C. Morris, in *Collections of the Wyoming Historical Society, Illustrated*, Vol. 1 (Cheyenne: The Wyoming Historical Society, 1897), gives a biographical sketch of Carey. Cora Beach, in *Women of Wyoming* (Casper: S. E. Boyer & Company, 1927), gives background on Louisa Carey.

Larson's *History* provides extensive coverage of Wyoming's political history and good background and political information on all three of Wyoming's Grand Old Men—Carey, Warren, and Kendrick—as well as a lengthy section on Carey's gubernatorial term. See also *Governor's Message, House Journal of the Eleventh State Legislature of Wyoming, Cheyenne, Wyoming, 1911* (Laramie: Laramie Republican Printers & Binders, 1911) and *Governor's Message, House Journal of the Twelfth State Legislature of Wyoming, Cheyenne, Wyoming, 1913* (Laramie: Laramie Republican Printers & Binders, 1913). T. Blake Kennedy's typewritten memoirs (AHC) shed light on Carey's personality and also are a good source of background for Wyoming history.

George W. Paulson's master's thesis, "The Congressional Career of Joseph Maull Carey" (University of Wyoming, 1962), gives an in-depth look at Carey's service in Congress. See also *Congressional Record*, Forty-Ninth Congress, Fifty-First Congress, and 1888.

Lewis L. Gould, in "Joseph M. Carey and Wyoming Statehood" (*Annals of Wyoming* 37, no. 2 [1965]: 157–169), uses the correspondence between Carey and Van Devanter to illustrate the difficulties Carey encountered as territorial delegate. Linford's *Wyoming Frontier State* contains an informative section about Wyoming statehood and Carey's involvement in the push to gain that status. *WBB*, Vol. 1, contains Carey's speech to the House about statehood. David's *Malcolm Campbell, Sheriff*, gives some background on Carey's ranching pursuits. Burroughs's *Guardian of the Grasslands* provides the centennial history of the Wyoming Stock Growers Association and contains much information about Carey's involvement in that organization.

Early Cheyenne Homes tells of the Carey mansion in Cheyenne. Spring's *Cow Country Legacies* gives information on Carey's work with the Opera House and other details of Carey's life. "Recollections of the Great Rough Rider," by Honorable Robert D. Carey, Joseph's son, appears in William C. Deming's *Roosevelt in the Bunk House*.

History of Cheyenne contains several articles about Carey. See Pat Hall's "Newspapers in Early-Day Cheyenne"; John Brewster's "Joseph M. Carey, His Political Career" and "Joseph M. Carey: Joseph M. and Louisa"; and Jean Bastian's "Cheyenne's Opera House."

Newspapers consulted were *Cheyenne Daily Sun*, April 1889–December 1889, January 1891–April 1893, January 1895; and *Wyoming State Tribune* and *Cheyenne State Leader*, February 6, 1924.

Asa Shinn Mercer

Much of the information on Mercer came from the Dorothy Weintz Papers in the University Archives at the University of Washington, Seattle

(Accession No. 2697–001). In particular, see Mrs. L.A. Webb, "A Prophetic Speech: An Address Delivered by A.S. Mercer in the Year 1866, Now Rapidly Proving Its Claim to Prophecy," Buffalo, Wyoming, 5 March 1912; Ben Holladay to A.S. Mercer, 17 October 1865; Receipt for the trip from New York to San Francisco, 3 January 1866; John B. Kendrick to A.S. Mercer, 10 August 1917; Thomas W. Prosch, "Beginnings of the University"; I.S. Bartlett, "The Unique Story of Col. Mercer's Cargo of Girls." "The Family Lineage of the Mercer Family" letter from Mercer to Tillotson is also included in the Weintz Papers. See also Linnie Marsh, "Presidents of the University" (*The Washington Alumnus* 4, no. 13 [December 17, 1910]). Avril Madison, assistant university archivist, was especially helpful to me.

See also Thelma C. Nason, "Brides for the West" (*Empire Magazine*, n.d.); Lewis Gould, "A.S. Mercer and the Johnson County War: A Reappraisal" (*Arizona and the West* 7, no. 1 [1965]); Flora A.P. Engle, "The Story of the Mercer Expeditions" (*Washington Historical Quarterly* 6, no. 4 [1915]); N. Orwin Rush, "Asa Mercer's Little Black Book" (*Persimmon Hill* 9, no. 4 [1980]); Charles W. Smith, "Asa Shinn Mercer, Pioneer in Western Publicity" (*Pacific Northwest Quarterly* 27, no. 4 [1936]); and Mrs. Noel Morgan, "Ralph Mercer, Memories of a War" (*The Billings Gazette*, 6 January 1963).

Additional helpful information can be found in Smith's *The War on Powder River* and I.S. Bartlett's *History of Wyoming* (Chicago: The S.J. Clarke Printing Company, 1918). Larson's *History* tells more about the Johnson County War.

Newspapers consulted were *Portland Oregonian*, 13 August 1869, 23 October 1869; *Cheyenne Democratic Leader*, 3 August 1884, 14 July 1894; *Cheyenne Daily Leader*, 6 November 1883, 23 July 1884, 23 August 1892, 18 October 1892, 19 October 1892; *Cheyenne Daily Sun*, 18 October 1892, 27 October 1892, 1 November 1892, 8 November 1892; *Laramie Boomerang*, 31 August 1889; *Big Horn County Rustler*, 15 September 1911, 17 August 1917; and *Wyoming Tribune*, 15 August 1917.

Estelle Reel

Primary sources for this piece came from several archival collections at the WSA. They include the following four scrapbooks from the Estelle Reel Meyer Collection (#H60-110, Box 83, Scrapbooks and Printed Matter, WSA):

NEA scrapbook, 1895, unidentified newspaper clippings: "Teachers in Session," August 28; "Two First Woman State School Superintendents," n.d.; "The State Teachers," n.d.; "Teachers in Session," n.d.

Indian Affairs and Institutes scrapbook: "Higher Education," *Denver Times*, 26 July 1898; unidentified newspaper clipping, 20 July 1898, regarding Colorado Springs Indian School Institute; "Indian Institute Closes," *Colorado Springs Evening Telegraph*, 5 August 1898; "National Institute of Indian

Teachers at Colorado Springs," *Denver News*, 18 July 1898; "Miss Estelle Reel," *Rock Springs Miner*, 31 October 1894; "Miss Reel's Report," *Cheyenne Sun Leader*, 8 January 1897; and "Miss Reel Begins Her Duties," *Cheyenne Sun Leader*, 12 July 1898.

Personal Political and Miscellaneous from 1890–1898 scrapbook: *Black Diamond*, 27 September (probably 1894); *Cheyenne Leader*, n.d., article supporting Reel for state superintendent; "An Insult to the State," *Cheyenne Sun*, 2 November (probably 1894); *Journal of Education*, Boston, Massachusetts, 14 July 1898.

Information from Estelle Reel's scrapbook at the Toppenish Museum, Toppenish, Washington, includes "Was Taught in Chicago," *New York Sun*, 10 March 1896; "Cort Meyer Dies At Age of Ninety," n.d., n.n.; "The Protest of Superintendent Reel," *New York Sun*, 11 March 1896. Marian Ross of the Toppenish Museum in Toppenish, Washington, gave additional helpful direction and information in several conversations by telephone and in correspondence in 1998.

Other sources consulted include *Fifty-Ninth Annual Report of the Commissioner of Indian Affairs to the Secretary of the Interior, 1890*; *House Documents, Volume 27, Number 5, Reports of Department of Interior, 1900*. Indian Affairs Commissioner, 56th Congress, Second Session, 1900–1901; House Documents, Volume 18, Number 5, Reports of Department of Interior, 1899. Indian Affairs, Part I. 56th Congress, First Session, 1899–1900; also Report of Superintendent of Indian Schools, October 20, 1899.

Also the Seventh Annual Report of the Board of Charities and Reform, Wyoming 1897.

See also Records of the County Superintendent of Schools, Laramie County, Wyoming Territory from 1868 to 1903; Enrollment Register, Laramie County School District #1, RG1126 1876–1889; Reel, Estelle. "Wyoming: Educational Advantages." Typed manuscript, WPA 1557, Wyoming General (MA1065, April 7, 1899); all WSA.

Additional sources include Cora Beach's *Women of Wyoming*, WBB Volume II, and Edgar B. Wesley, *NEA: The First Hundred Years: The Building of the Teaching Profession* (New York: Harper Brothers Publishers, 1957).

I appreciate also the information provided by the Denver Public Library, Western History Department, and the North Dakota State Archives Research Library.

Willis Van Devanter

Cases referred to for this article were *Black v. Territory*, Pac Rep 22, 1090 (1890); *Boburg v. Prahl et al.* Pac Rep 23, 70 (1890); *Link v. Union Pacific Railway Company*, Pac Rep 29, 88 (1892); *Perkins v. McDowell*, Pac Rep 23, 71 (1890); *Redman v. Union Pacific Railway Company*, Pac Rep 29, 88 (1892);

Ward v. Race Horse, 163 US 504 (1896); *White v. Hinton*, Pac Rep 30, 953 (1892); and *Wolcott v. Bachman*, Pac Rep 23, 72 (1890).

In the *Papers of Willis Van Devanter, 1884–1941*, Archival Manuscript Material Collection, Library of Congress, Washington, D.C., see Willis Van Devanter to Joseph M. Carey, 18 October 1892; to Francis E. Warren, 19 October 1892; Willis Van Devanter Papers, 1884–1941; and F.E. Warren to Van Devanter, 19 March 1892, 3 April 1897. In the F.E. Warren Papers, 1868–1974 (AHC), see Warren to Willis Van Devanter, 19 March 1892, 20 April 1896, 2 May 1896, 11–12 March 1897.

See Christobelle Van Deventer, *The Van Deventer Family* (Columbia, Mo.: E.W. Stephens Company, 1943), for family background. Daniel Nelson, in "The Supreme Court Appointment of Willis Van Devanter," (*Annals of Wyoming* 53, no. 2 [1981]: 2–11), and David Burner, in "Willis Van Devanter" (*The Justices of the United States Supreme Court 1789–1969: Their Lives and Major Opinions* (New York: Chelsea House Publishers, 1969), give information on Van Devanter's legal career. See also *Early Cheyenne Homes*; Lewis Gould's "Joseph M. Carey and Statehood"; and M. Paul Holsinger's "Willis Van Devanter: Wyoming Leader 1884–1897" (*Annals of Wyoming* 37, no. 2 [1965]: 157–169) for more information. Nancy Jennings at the Johnson County Library assisted me with research regarding Van Devanter's time as Republican State Chairman of Wyoming; Larson's *History* contains more information on Van Devanter, the politics of the 1892 campaign, and the Johnson County War. Smith's *The War on Powder River* also is a good source on the Johnson County War, including information about Van Devanter and his role in events. See also David's *Malcolm Campbell, Sheriff*; (www.spartacus.schoolnet.co.uk/USAdevanter.htm); and WBB, Vol. 2. See also Kluger's, *Turning on Water with a Shovel* for Van Devanter's role in territorial legalities.

Newspapers consulted include *Cheyenne Daily Sun*, 1889, 1890, 1891–1895, 1897; *Cheyenne Daily Leader*, 1900–1903; and *Rocky Mountain News*, 9 February 1941.

C.G. Coutant

C.G. Coutant's *The History of Wyoming From Earliest Known Discoveries* contains much early-day Wyoming history. Sandy Adams, of Adams & Adams antiquarian bookstore, informed me of the rarity of Coutant's book. Biographical data and a copy of the death certificate for Charles Griffin Coutant were located in the biographical file, WSA. For more about the history of the state library, see WBB, Vol. 2.

Additional information was gleaned from Larson's *History*; "Wyoming's Fiftieth Anniversary Year Marks Hundredth Anniversary of C.G. Coutant" (*Annals of Wyoming* 12, no. 1[1940]: 33–34); John C. Thompson, "In Old Wyoming," *Wyoming State Tribune*, 23 September 1941, 13 January 1942, and 19 June 1942; Pat Hall's "Between the Lines," *Sunday Magazine*, 19 and 26 September 1971; and Alfred J. Mokler's *History of Natrona County, Wyoming 1888– 1922* (Casper: K. Hemry, 1989).

Newspapers consulted were *Cheyenne Daily Sun*, 21 August 1891; 15 October 1889, 1892; *Cheyenne Daily Sun-Leader*, 1900; *Cheyenne Daily Leader*, 1901–1903; and *Rogue River* (Oregon) *Courier*, 19 January 1913.

Dr. George P. Johnston

Tim Wilson, Director of the Board of Public Utilities, Cheyenne, helped me understand more about Round Top, a water facility that the city still uses. Records of the State Board of Medicine verify Johnston's license as the first issued in the state in 1899. WBB, Vol. 2, provides information about the organization and duties of the State Board of Health. Larry Birleffi, a friend of the Johnston family, gave some of his insights.

Other sources include "G.P. Johnston, Pioneer Doctor, Dies at 93," in biographical files, WSA; *Early Cheyenne Homes*; Ellen Stafford, "History of Memorial Hospital of Laramie County, Wyoming," in *History of Cheyenne*; and Beach's *Women of Wyoming*, which tells of pioneer nurse Sarah Jane McKenzie. See also Cal Bernstein, "The Oldest 'Country Doctor,'" *Denver Post Empire Magazine*, 4 March 1956.

Newspapers helped clarify the picture of what it was like to be a doctor in Johnston's time in Cheyenne. Those consulted for this piece were *Cheyenne Daily Sun*, 1892; *Cheyenne Daily Sun Leader*, January-May 1900; *Cheyenne Daily Leader*, 1897, 22 May 1900–December 1900, 1901–1903, 1907; *Wyoming State Tribune*, 19 September 1956; *Wyoming Tribune*, 11 September 1958; and *Wyoming Eagle*, 12 September 1958.

Charles B. Irwin

Pat Sneddon, in the *Cheyenne Star* for 2 July 1967, and Mike Fox, curator of collections at the Wyoming State Museum, gave helpful information regarding Irwin's oversized chair. Also helpful with Irwin's background were Mrs. Darrel Abernathy, grounds history committee for Cheyenne Frontier Days, and John Gavin, curator of the Cheyenne Frontier Days Old West Museum.

See also John Francis, "Y6 Feeders, Exemplifying Diversification," (*Wyoming Livestock Roundup* [2001 Winter Cattleman's Edition]); and George Williams's "C.B. Irwin, High Roller" (*Persimmon Hill* 7, no. 2 [1977]). "Ex-Con Found Life in Jail Led Him to Life in Faith" (*Wyoming Catholic Register*, 25 July 1958), details Bill Carlisle's startling encounter with Irwin.

Anna Lee Waldo's *Prairie* (New York: Berkley Publishing Group, 1987) tells the story of Charlie Irwin in epic fiction form. For nonfiction, see Shirley Flynn, *Let's Go, Let's Show, Let's Rodeo!* (Cheyenne: Wigwam Publishing Company, 1996). Candy Moulton and Flossie Moulton's book *Steamboat:*

Legendary Bucking Horse (Glendo, Wyo.: High Plains Press, 1992) tells the story of the famous bucking bronc and includes much information on the people of the time.

Articles on Irwin and the Irwin Brothers Wild West Show appear in *History of Cheyenne*, as does William R. Huey's "Cheyenne Goes 'Hollywood,'" and various articles about movies made in Cheyenne. T. Blake Kennedy's memoirs contain interesting information about the time period as well as about Charlie Irwin.

Newspapers consulted were *Cheyenne Daily Leader*, 8 October 1902, 13 October 1902, and all of 1907; *Torrington Telegram*, 29 March 1934; *SunDay Magazine*, July 24, 1977; and *Casper Star-Tribune*, 19 March 1978. See also Kathryn Gress "Charlie Irwin Comes Alive in New Book," *SunDay Magazine*, n.d., WSA bio file.

M.P. Keefe

Most of the information available on M. P. Keefe exists in the newspapers, but I.S. Bartlett's *History of Wyoming*, Vol. 2, and WBB, Vol. 2, give some good background. See also "Mayors of Cheyenne," Rick Ewig's "Wyoming's Capitol," and Patricia Keefe Taylor's "Keefe Family," in *History of Cheyenne*.

Newspapers consulted were *Cheyenne Daily Sun-Leade*r, 1900; and *Cheyenne Daily Leader*, 1889, 1891, 1893, 1897, 1901, 1902, and 1903.

Henry Hay

Much information for this piece was gathered from Hay Family Papers, 1799–1978 (Accession No. 10031, Box 1, Folder 4; Box 2, Folder 1; Box 4, Folders 1–2; and Scrapbook, AHC). See especially Henry G. Hay to Harry Hay (Henry G. Hay, Jr.), 27 January [1908?]; Henry G. Hay to Helen Hay (Pierrot), 25 December 1916; Henry G. Hay, Jr. to Louise Smith, 9 June 1940; and Henry G. Hay to Republican Voters, 8 July 1902.

I also consulted John Rolfe Burroughs's *Guardian of the Grasslands,* which tells of Hay's association with the Wyoming Stock Growers Association; *Early Cheyenne Homes*; and John Clay, "The Rise of a Western Cattleman" (*The Breeder's Gazette*, 23 December 1920).

Newspaper consulted was *Cheyenne Daily Leader*, 25 September 1902.

Daze Bristol

Sources on Daze Bristol include Sharon Lass Field, "Bristol, Charles and Daze"; Olive Maxon Jones, "Jones-Maxon Family"; Phil Riske's article on Frontier Days; Jean Bastian's article on the Cheyenne Little Theater; and Louise Flynn Underhill, "Cheyenne Press Women," all in *History of Cheyenne*.

Additional information can be found in "Party Will Honor Daze on Her 100th," (*Wyoming Tribune-Eagle*, May 1978); Heidi Anderson's "Daze's Creative

Spirit Rose to Every Cheyenne Occasion" (*Wyoming Tribune-Eagle*, 21 July 1985); "Military Funeral Given Remains of Charles Bristol" (28 October 1927, n.n., WSA). See also *Wyoming State Tribune*, 3 October 1983; *Wyoming Eagle*, 12 March 1965; and *Wyoming State Tribune*, 13 May 1967. William Dubois also provided helpful information for this piece.

Prairie Rose Henderson

Elizabeth Clair Flood, *Cowgirls: Women of the Wild West* (Santa Fe: Zon International Publishing, 2000); Shirley Flynn, *Let's Go, Let's Show, Let's Rodeo!* (Cheyenne: Wigwam Publishing Company, 1996); Candace Savage, *Cowgirls* (Vancouver, B.C.: Greystone Books, 1996); and Mary Lou LeCompte, *Cowgirls of the Rodeo* (Urbana: University of Illinois Press, 1993), give good background information on cowgirls of the time as well as on Prairie Rose. Debra D. Munn, in *Ghosts on the Range* (Boulder: Pruett Publishing Company, 1989), tells about Prairie Rose's possible ghostly appearances.

Jennifer Nielsen at the National Cowgirl Museum and Hall of Fame in Fort Worth, Texas, provided information from that institution for this article. Charles E. Rand, Research Center Director at the National Cowboy and Western Heritage Museum in Oklahoma City, Oklahoma, also provided information, as did Robert Gant at the Cheyenne Frontier Days Old West Museum, and Joyce Kelly at the Carbon County Museum in Rawlins. Marirose Morris also gave information about her grandmother and her name.

See also *State of Wyoming v. Charles W. Coleman*, file no. 1399, 19 November 1926 (Carbon County Clerk of District Court).

Newspaper consulted was *Rawlins Republican-Bulletin*, 29 July 1926, 22 July 1939, and 25–26 July 1939.

Bibliography

Abernathy, Mrs. Darrel. Grounds History Committee for Cheyenne Frontier Days. Telephone interview with author, 10 January 2002.

Adams, Sandy. Adams & Adams antiquarian bookstore. Telephone interview with author, 19 April 2001.

Allen, Dan. Superintendent, Curt Gowdy State Park. Correspondence and telephone interview with author, 26–28 February 1998.

American Legion, Department of Wyoming. Information regarding the American Legion Ferdinand Branstetter Post No. 1 in Van Tassell, Wyoming.

Ammerman, Ada. Cheyenne County (Nebraska) Historical Association Research Team. Correspondence with author, 23 February 2001.

Amundson, Michael. *Wyoming Time and Again.* Boulder, Colo.: Pruett Publishing Company, 1991.

Anheuser-Busch Company. E-mail interview with author, 9 March 2001.

Bartlett, I.S. *History of Wyoming.* Chicago: The S.J. Clarke Publishing Company, 1918.

Beach, Cora, ed. *Women of Wyoming.* Casper, Wyo.: S.E. Boyer & Company, 1927.

Berkebile, Don H. *Carriage Terminology: An Historical Dictionary.* Washington, D.C.: Smithsonian Institution Press and Liberty Cap Books, 1978.

Bernstein, Cal. "The Oldest 'Country Doctor,'" *Denver Post Empire Magazine,* 4 March 1956.

Berwanger, Eugene H. "William J. Hardin: Colorado Spokesman for Racial Justice, 1863–1873," *Colorado Magazine* 52, no. 1 (1975).

Big Horn County Rustler. 15 September 1911, 17 August 1917.

Biographical files. Wyoming State Archives, Cheyenne, Wyoming.

Birleffi, Larry. Telephone interview with author, 5 April 2001.

Black v. Territory, Pac Rep 22, 1090 (1890).

Blair, Neal L. "Saddles and Saddlemakers," *Wyoming Wildlife* 32, no. 5 (1968): 27–34.

Boburg v. Prahl et al., Pac Rep 23, 70 (1890).

Brayer, Elizabeth. *George Eastman: A Biography.* Baltimore: Johns Hopkins University Press, 1996.

Bricher-Wade, Sheila. E-mail interview with author, 6 April 2001.

Brown, Larry K. *The Hog Ranches of Wyoming.* Glendo, Wyo.: High Plains Press, 1995.

——. "Just Ice," *True West* (June 1997).

——. "'Meanie' Made the Best," *Persimmon Hill* 27, no. 3 (Autumn 1999).

——. E-mail interview with author, 6 July 2001.

Burner, David. "Willis Van Devanter," *The Justices of the United States Supreme Court 1789–1969: Their Lives and Major Opinions.* New York: Chelsea House Publishers, 1969.

Burroughs, John Rolfe. *Guardian of the Grasslands: The First Hundred Years of the Wyoming Stock Growers Association.* Cheyenne: Pioneer Printing & Stationery Company, 1971.

Capitol Times. 10 April 1983.

Carlisle, William. *Bill Carlisle, Lone Bandit: An Autobiography.* Pasadena, Calif.: Trail's End Publishing Company, 1946.

Casper Star Tribune. 19 March 1978.

Casper Tribune Herald. 29 January 1936.

Chatterton, Fenimore C. *Yesterday's Wyoming: The Intimate Memoirs of Fenimore C. Chatterton, Territorial Citizen, Governor, Builder.* Denver: Powder River Publishers & Booksellers, 1957.

Cheyenne City Directory, 1884–1885. Cheyenne Frontier Days Old West Museum, Cheyenne, Wyoming.

Cheyenne Daily Leader. Various issues from 1875, 1876, 1879, 1880, 1883, 1884, 1886, 1887, 1892, 1897, 1900, 1901, 1902, 1903, 1907.

Cheyenne Daily Sun. Various issues from 1876, 1878, 1879, 1889–1895, 1897.

Cheyenne Daily Sun Leader. Various issues from January–May 1900.

Cheyenne Democratic Leader. Various issues from 1884, 1889, 1891, 1893, 1894.

Cheyenne Star. 2 July 1967.

Cheyenne Tribune. 29 August 1910.

Chugwater: A Centennial History. Chugwater, Wyo.: privately published, 1986.

Clay, John. "The Rise of a Western Cattleman," *The Breeder's Gazette,* (23 December 1920).

Collections of the Colorado Historical Society. Denver, Colorado, n.d.

Collections of the Wyoming Historical Society, Illustrated, Vol. 1. Cheyenne: Wyoming Historical Society, 1897.

Colorado State Business Directory and Annual Register. 1875, 1876, 1895, 1902, 1910. Colorado Historical Society, Denver, Colorado.

Congressional Record, 49th Congress, 51st Congress, and 1888.

Connor, Kathleen. Curator, George Eastman House, Rochester, New York. Telephone interview with author, e-mail, and other correspondence, 21 February 2001, 2 March 2001, 9 February 2002.

Coutant, C.G. *History of Wyoming from the Earliest Known Discoveries*, Vol. 1. Laramie, Wyo.: Chaplin, Spafford, & Mathison Printers, 1899.

Cuckow, Elizabeth. Manager, Information Services, Laramie County Library, Cheyenne. E-mail interview with author, 20 April 2001.

Davis, Richard. Old West Museum, Cheyenne, Wyoming. Telephone interview with author, 18 September 1997.

Daytona Beach News Journal. 27 December 1935.

Deming, William C. *Roosevelt in the Bunk House*. Laramie: The Laramie Printing Company, 1927.

———. *Collected Writings*, Vol. 1. Glendale, Calif.: Arthur H. Clark Company. 1947.

Denver City Directory, 1866, 1885, 1886, 1890, 1894, 1895, 1900. Colorado Historical Society, Denver, Colorado.

Denver Post. 21 June 1951.

Dorsett, Lyle W. *The Queen City: A History of Denver*. Boulder, Colo.: Pruett Publishing Company, 1977.

Dunn, Nora H., with T.A. Cobry and Mrs. James Garrett. "Frank A. Meanea, Pioneer Saddler," *Annals of Wyoming* 26, no. 1 (1954): 25–32.

Early Cheyenne Homes, 1880–1890. Cheyenne: Laramie County Historical Society, 1962.

Engle, Flora A.P. "The Story of the Mercer Expeditions," *Washington Historical Quarterly* 6, no. 4 (1915).

Enrollment Register, Laramie County School District #1, 1876–1889. Wyoming State Archives, Cheyenne, Wyoming.

"Ex-Con Found Life in Jail Led Him to Life of Faith," *Wyoming Catholic Register*, 25 July 1958.

Field, Sharon Lass, ed. *History of Cheyenne, Wyoming*. Dallas: Curtis Media Corporation, 1989.

Fifty-Ninth Annual Report of the Commissioner of Indian Affairs to the Secretary of the Interior. Washington, D.C.: Government Printing Office, 1890.

Flood, Elizabeth Clair. *Cowgirls: Women of the Wild West*. Santa Fe: Zon International Publishing, 2000.

Flynn, Shirley. *Let's Go, Let's Show, Let's Rodeo!* Cheyenne: Wigwam Publishing Company, 1996.

———. "Renessalaer Schuyler Van Tassell," *Annals of Wyoming* 71, no. 3 (1999): 2–7.

———. "Cheyenne's Harry P. Hynds: Blacksmith, Saloon Keeper, Promoter, Philanthropist," *Annals of Wyoming* 73, no. 3 (2001): 2–11.

Fort Collins (Colorado) *Express Courier*. 3 June 1924.

Fox, Mike. Curator of Collections, Wyoming State Museum. Telephone interview with author, 4 June 2001.

Francis, John. "Y6 Feeders, Exemplifying Diversification," *Wyoming Livestock Roundup*, Winter Cattlemen's Edition (2001).

Gant, Robert. Cheyenne Frontier Days Old West Museum, Cheyenne, Wyoming. Correspondence with author, 25 January 2001.

Gavin, John. Curator of Old West Museum, Cheyenne, Wyoming. Telephone interviews with author, various dates, September 1998 and December 2001.

George Eastman House collections, Rochester, New York.

Gottfried, Herbert. E-mail interview with author, 9 April 2001.

Gould, Lewis L. "A.S. Mercer and the Johnson County War: A Reappraisal," *Arizona and the West* 7, no. 1 (1965).

———. "Joseph M. Carey and Statehood," *Annals of Wyoming* 37, no. 2 (1965): 157–169.

Governor's Message, House Journal of the Eleventh State Legislature of Wyoming, Cheyenne, Wyoming, 1911. Laramie, Wyo.: Laramie Republican Printers & Binders 1911.

Governor's Message, House Journal of the Twelfth State Legislature of Wyoming, Cheyenne, Wyoming, 1913. Laramie, Wyo.: Laramie Republican Printers & Binders 1913.

Green, Susan. Librarian, Carriage Museum of America, Bird-in-Hand, Pennsylvania. Telephone interviews with author, September 1998.

Gress, Kathryn. "Charlie Irwin Comes Alive in New Book," *SunDay Magazine*, n.d.

Guernsey, Charles A. *Wyoming Cowboy Days*. New York: G.P. Putnam's Sons, 1936.

Guernsey Gazette. 31 January 1936.

Haas, William G. "The Story of the Inter-Ocean Hotel." Mss. 794. Wyoming State Archives, Cheyenne. Wyoming.

Hall, Frank. *History of the State of Colorado*. Chicago: Blakely Printing Company, 1895.

Hall, Pat. "Between the Lines," *SunDay Magazine*, 19 and 26 September 1971.

Hardaway, Roger D. "William Jefferson Hardin: Wyoming's Nineteenth Century Black Legislator," *Annals of Wyoming* 63, no. 1 (1991): 2–13.

Hay Family Papers, 1799–1978. American Heritage Center, University of Wyoming, Laramie, Wyoming.

Henry, Will. *I, Tom Horn*. New York: Bantam Books, 1975.

Historical Encyclopedia of Wyoming. Cheyenne: Wyoming Historical Institute, 1970.

Holsinger, M. Paul. "Willis Van Devanter: Wyoming Leader, 1884–1897," *Annals of Wyoming* 37, no. 2 (1965): 170–206.

Homsher, Lola, ed. *South Pass, 1868: James Chisolm's Journal of the Wyoming Gold Rush*. Lincoln: University of Nebraska Press, 1960.

House Documents, Volume 18, Number 5, Reports of Department of Interior, 1899. Indian Affairs, Part I. 56th Congress, First Session, 1899–1900; also Report of Superintendent of Indian Schools, October 20, 1899.

House Documents, Volume 27, Number 5, Reports of Department of Interior, 1900. Indian Affairs Commissioner, 56th Congress, Second Session, 1900–1901.

House Journal, 1879. Typescript. Wyoming State Archives, Cheyenne, Wyoming.

Jenkins, Reese. *Images and Enterprises.* Baltimore: Johns Hopkins University Press, 1987.

Jennings, Nancy L. Johnson County (Wyoming) Library. Correspondence with author, 31 January 2001.

Jones, Gladys Powelson. *Cheyenne, Cheyenne: Our Blue Collar Heritage.* Cheyenne: G.P. Jones, 1983.

——. *The First Hundred Years 1886–1986: The Van Tassell Carriage Barn, National Register of Historical Places.* Cheyenne: Cheyenne Artists Guild, 1986.

Junge, Mark. *J.E. Stimson, Photographer of the West.* Lincoln: University of Nebraska Press, 1985.

Katz, William. *Black People Who Made the Old West.* New York: Crowell Press, 1977.

Keen, Elizabeth. "The Frontier Press," in *Studies in Literature of the West,* ed. Ruth Hudson. Laramie: University of Wyoming Graduate School, 1956.

Kelly, Charles. *The Outlaw Trail.* New York: Devin-Adair Company, 1959.

Kelly, Joyce. Carbon County Museum, Rawlins, Wyoming. Correspondence with author, 13 February 2001.

Kennedy, T. Blake. Kennedy Papers. American Heritage Center, University of Wyoming, Laramie, Wyoming.

Kluger, James. *Turning on Water with a Shovel: The Career of Elwood Mead.* Albuquerque: University of New Mexico Press, 1992.

Krakel, Dean. *The Saga of Tom Horn.* Lincoln: University of Nebraska Press, 1954.

——. "As I Was Saying," *Persimmon Hill* 8, no. 4 (1978).

Kuykendall, William. *Frontier Days: A True Narrative of Striking Events on the Western Frontier.* Denver: J.M. & H.L. Kuykendall, 1917.

Laramie Boomerang. 31 August 1899.

Larson, T.A. *History of Wyoming,* second edition, revised. Lincoln: University of Nebraska, 1978.

LeCompte, Mary Lou. *Cowgirls of the Rodeo.* Urbana: University of Illinois Press, 1993.

Lemmon, George L. "Stories." WPA Project, Wyoming State Archives, Cheyenne, Wyoming.

Lindmier, Tom and Steve Mount. *I See By Your Outfit.* Glendo, Wyo.: High Plains Press, 1996.

Linford, Velma. *Wyoming Frontier State.* Denver: Old West Publishing Company, 1947.

Link v. Union Pacific Railway Company, Pac Rep 29, 88 (1892).

Lusk Herald. 16 April 1931, 23 November 1950.

MacKinnon, Anne and John Shields. *Selected Writings of Elwood Mead on Water Administration in Wyoming and the West.* Casper: Wyoming State Engineer's Office and the Wyoming Water Association, 2000.

Madison, Avril. Assistant University Archivist, University of Washington Libraries. Various e-mails and correspondence with author, 2000.

Mangan, Terry William. *Colorado on Glass.* Denver: Sundance Limited, 1975.

Marsh, Linnie. "Presidents of the University," *The Washington Alumnus* 4, no. 13 (1910).

Mead, Elwood. "Letter to Irrigation Committee of the Constitutional Convention." Wyoming State Archives, Cheyenne, Wyoming.

——. "Biennial Report, State Engineer of Wyoming, 1894." American Heritage Center, University of Wyoming, Laramie, Wyoming.

——. Papers, 1882–1958, Accession No. 5258. American Heritage Center, University of Wyoming, Laramie, Wyoming.

Melrose, Frances. "Rocky Mountain Memories," *Rocky Mountain News*, 18 November 1984.

Mokler, Alfred J. *History of Natrona County, Wyoming 1888–1922.* Casper, Wyo.: K. Hemry, 1989.

Moline (Illinois) *Daily Dispatch.* 13 December 1957.

Monaghan, Jay. *Last of the Bad Men.* Lincoln: University of Nebraska Press, 1997.

Moore, William Howard. "Pietism and Progress: James H. Hayford and the Wyoming Anti-Gambling Tradition, 1869–1893," *Annals of Wyoming* 55, no. 2 (1983): 2–8.

——. "Progressivism and the Social Gospel in Wyoming: The Antigambling Act of 1901 as a Test Case," *Western Historical Quarterly* 15, no. 3 (1984): 299–316.

Morgan, Mrs. Noel. "Ralph Mercer, Memories of a War." *The Billings Gazette*, 6 January 1963.

Morris, Marirose. E-mail and telephone interviews with author, 29 January 2001.

Moulton, Candy. *Roadside History of Wyoming.* Missoula, Mont.: Mountain Press Publishing Company, 1995.

——. *Writer's Guide to Every Day Life in the Wild West, 1840–1900.* Cincinnati: Writer's Digest Books, 1999.

Moulton, Candy and Flossie Moulton. *Steamboat: Legendary Bucking Horse.* Glendo, Wyo.: High Plains Press, 1992.

Nason, Thelma C. "Brides for the West," *Empire Magazine*, n.d.

National Museum of the Morgan Horse. Telephone interview with author, 27 February 2001.

Nelson, Daniel A. "The Supreme Court Appointment of Willis Van Devanter," *Annals of Wyoming* 53, no. 2 (1981): 2–11.

Newsome, Jim. "Van Tassell: Pop. 10," *Wyoming Horizons,* n.d.

New York Morning Telegraph. 21 November 1920.

New York Times. 27 May 1934, 28 December 1935.

Nielsen, Jennifer. National Cowgirl Museum and Hall of Fame, Fort Worth, Texas. Telephone interview with author and correspondence, 2001.

Park County Enterprise. 27 November 1915.

Parkhill, Forbes. "Colorado's Negro 'President Maker,'" *Empire Magazine,* 15 September 1963.

——. *Mister Barney Ford: A Portrait in Bistre.* Denver: Sage Books, 1963.

Paulson, George W. "The Congressional Career of Joseph Maull Carey." Master's thesis, University of Wyoming, 1962.

Perkins v. McDowell, Pac Rep 23, 71 (1890).

Portland Oregonian. 13 August 1869, 23 October 1869.

"Rainsford District Nomination Form to the National Register of Historic Places." State Historic Preservation Office, Cheyenne.

Rand, Charles E. Research Center Director, National Cowboy and Western Heritage Museum, Oklahoma City, Oklahoma. Correspondence with author, 29 January 2001.

Rawlins Daily Times. 24 December 1965.

Rawlins Republican-Bulletin. 29 July 1926, 2 May 1939, 22 July 1939, 25–26 July 1939.

Reclamation Era. February 1936.

Records of the County Superintendent of Schools, Laramie County, Wyoming Territory from 1868 to 1903. Wyoming State Archives, Cheyenne, Wyoming.

Redman v. Union Pacific Railway Company, Pac Rep 29, 88 (1892).

Reel, Estelle. Estelle Reel Meyer Collection, #H60–110. Wyoming State Archives, Cheyenne, Wyoming.

Rocky Mountain News. 28 May 1934, 9 February 1941, 5 February 1956, 28 October 1962.

Rogue River (Oregon) *Courier.* 19 January 1913.

Ross, Marian. Toppenish Museum, Toppenish, Washington. Telephone interviews with author, various dates in 1998.

Rossi, Paul. "Makers of the Forty Dollar Saddle," *Persimmon Hill* 4, no. 2 (1974).

Rush, N. Orwin. "Asa Mercer's Little Black Book," *Persimmon Hill* 9, no. 4 (1980).

Saddles, Bits and Spurs: Cowboy Crafters at Work. Exhibition catalog. Cheyenne: Wyoming State Museum, 1995.

Salt Lake City Herald. 3 March 1896.

Savage, Candace. *Cowgirls.* Vancouver, B.C.: Greystone Books, 1996.

Session Laws of Wyoming Territory, Passed by the Sixth Legislative Assembly, convened at Cheyenne, November 4, 1879. Cheyenne: Leader Steam Book & Job Printing, 1879.

Seventh Annual Report of the Board of Charities and Reform, 1897.

State of Wyoming v. Charles W. Coleman. File no. 1399, November 1926. Carbon County Clerk of District Court, Rawlins, Wyoming.

Smith, Charles W. "Asa Shinn Mercer, Pioneer in Western Publicity," *Pacific Northwest Quarterly* 27, no. 4 (1936).

Smith, Helena Huntington. *The War on Powder River*. New York: McGraw-Hill, 1966.

Spring, Agnes Wright. *The Cheyenne and Black Hills Stage and Express Routes*. Glendale, Calif.: Arthur H. Clark Company, 1949.

———. *Cow Country Legacies*. Kansas City: Lowell Press, 1976.

Starr, Eileen. *Architecture in the Cowboy State, 1849–1940: A Guide*. Glendo, Wyo.: High Plains Press, 1992.

State ex rel. Hynds v. Cahill, County Clerk, et al., Pacific Reporter, 433, 18 February 1904.

Stone, Wilbur Fiske. *History of Colorado*, Vol. 2. Chicago: S.J. Clarke Publishing Company, 1918.

SunDay Magazine. 27 July 1977.

Thompson, John C. "In Old Wyoming," *Wyoming State Tribune*, 23 September 1941, 13 January 1942, 19 June 1942.

Thrapp, Dan L. *Encyclopedia of Frontier Biography*, three volumes. Glendale, Calif.: Arthur H. Clark Company, 1988.

Torrington Telegram. 29 March 1934.

Trenholm, Virginia Cole, ed. *Wyoming Blue Book*, three volumes. Cheyenne: Wyoming State Archives & Historical Department, 1974.

Van Devanter, Willis. Willis Van Devanter Papers, 1884–1941, Archival Manuscript Material Collection. Library of Congress, Washington, D.C.

Van Deventer, Christobelle, comp. *The Van Deventer Family*. Columbia, Mo.: E.W. Stephens Company, 1943.

Van Pelt, Lori. *Dreamers and Schemers, Volume 1*. Glendo, Wyo.: High Plains Press, 1999.

Vertical file. Wyoming State Archives, Cheyenne, Wyoming.

Waldo, Anna Lee. *Prairie: The Legend of Charles Burton Irwin and the Y6 Ranch*. New York: Berkley Publishing Group, 1987.

Ward v. Race Horse, 163 US 504 (1896).

Warren, F.E. F.E. Warren Papers 1868–1974, Accession Number 13. American Heritage Center, University of Wyoming, Laramie, Wyoming.

Weintz, Dorothy. Dorothy Weintz Papers, Accession 2697–001. University Archives, University of Washington Libraries, Seattle, Washington.

Wesley, Edgar B. *NEA: The First Hundred Years: The Building of the Teaching Profession.* New York: Harper Brothers Publishers, 1957.

White v. Hinton, Pac Rep 30, 953 (1892).

Williams, George. "C. B. Irwin, High Roller," *Persimmon Hill* 7, no. 2 (1977).

"Willis Van Dacanter. Spartacus Educational Web Sit, n.d., http:www.spartacus. schoolnet.co.uk/USAdevanter.htm (accessed 23 A pril 2006).

Wilson, Tim. Director, Board of Public Utilities, Cheyenne. E-mail interview with author, 19 April 2001.

Wolcott v. Bachman, Pac Rep 23, 72 (1890).

Wyoming Board of Medicine, Cheyenne, Wyoming.

Wyoming Eagle. Various issues from 1929, 1933, 1936, 1956, 1958, 1965, 1967, 1979.

"Wyoming's Fiftieth Anniversary Year Marks Hundredth Anniversary of C. G. Coutant," *Annals of Wyoming* 12, no. 1 (1940): 33–34.

Wyoming Loan & Trust Co. v. W. H. Holliday Company, Pac Rep 24, 193 (1890).

"Wyoming Newspaper—*Cheyenne Leader*," Coutant Notes, *Annals of Wyoming* 5, no. 1 (1927): 36–38.

Wyoming Newspapers: A Centennial History. Cheyenne: Wyoming Press Association, 1990.

Wyoming Platte County Heritage. Wheatland: Platte County Extension Homemakers Council, 1981.

Wyoming State Journal and Lander Clipper. 28 February 1908.

Wyoming State Tribune. Various issues from 1928, 1932, 1944, 1956, 1967, 1983.

Wyoming State Tribune and Cheyenne State Leader. 23 August 1926, 20 July 1929.

Wyoming State Tribune and Eagle. 29 July 1923.

Wyoming State Tribune and Wyoming Eagle. Frontier Days Edition, 21–24 July 1959.

Wyoming Tribune. 15 August 1917, 16 March 1933, 11 September 1958.

Wyoming Tribune-Eagle. 7 May 1978, 21 July 1985.

Yost, Nellie Snyder, ed. *Boss Cowman: The Recollections of Ed Lemmon, 1857–1946.* Lincoln: University of Nebraska Press, 1969.

Index

Acknowledgments

I DID NOT CARRY the only flashlight in attempting to illuminate this group of "Dreamers and Schemers." Many people helped me in myriad ways. I gratefully acknowledge the help of the following people and others listed in the bibliography:

The staff at the Wyoming State Archives in Cheyenne, Wyoming, especially Ann Nelson, Jean Brainerd, LaVaughn Bresnehan, Cindy Brown, and Carl Hallberg, and the staff at the American Heritage Center, University of Wyoming, Laramie, Wyoming, especially Rick Ewig, Sally Sutherland, Leslie Shores, Carol Bowers, Melanie Francis, Dan Davis, and Monte Kniffen. Mary Henning and Val Vasquez at Coe Library, University of Wyoming; Barbara Dey and Jennifer Bosley at the Colorado Historical Society; Fred Bauman at the Library of Congress, Washington, D.C.; Kathleen Connor, Curator, George Eastman House, Rochester, New York; Avril Madison at the University of Washington Libraries; Debi Person and Tim Kearley at the University of Wyoming Law Library; Mike Fox, Curator of Collections at the Wyoming State Museum, Cheyenne; Bob Gant and the staff at the Old West Museum, Cheyenne; Judy Sargeant at the Wyoming State Capitol; Susan Green at the Carriage Museum of America, Bird-in-Hand, Pennsylvania; Marian Ross, Toppenish Museum, Toppenish, Washington; Ruth Hackett, Saratoga branch librarian, Saratoga, Wyoming; Elizabeth Cuckow, Laramie County Library, Cheyenne; Nancy Jennings, Johnson County Library, Buffalo, Wyoming; and Sharon Lass Field of Cheyenne.

My thanks also to William Dubois, Jerry and Ann Palen, Larry K. Brown, Chip Carlson, Ann Redman, Viola Bixler, Kris Wendtland, and Candy Moulton. Special thanks to Nancy Curtis, Tracy Eller, and Barbara Bogart for their work in publishing and editing the book. My family—Eugene, Cid, and Marilyn and E. W. Walck, Sr.—again gave much time and support to me during this project.

Lori Van Pelt is an award-winning author whose most recent books include a collection of short stories, *Pecker's Revenge and Other Stories from the Frontier's Edge* (University of New Mexico Press, 2005) and a biography, *Amelia Earhart: The Sky's No Limit* (Forge, 2005), one of the premier titles in the American Heroes series.

Lori's story "Pecker's Revenge," the title tale in her short fiction collection, won the 2006 Western Writers of America Spur Award for Best Short Fiction. Her biography of Earhart was named to the New York Public Library's Best Books for the Teen Age 2006.

She is also the author of the nonfiction Wyoming-based *Dreamers & Schemers* series published by High Plains Press. She writes regularly for the Western Writers of America's *Roundup Magazine* and for the *Wyoming Rural Electric News* (WREN). In addition, she serves as a correspondent for the *Casper Star-Tribune* and an essayist for Wyoming Public Radio's "Open Spaces." She lives with her husband Eugene Walck, Jr., on his ranch near Saratoga, Wyoming.

A special limited cloth edition
of 500 copies of this volume
was printed simultaneously with the trade paperback edition.
The special edition is Smythe sewn, bound in juniper Arrestox cloth,
and stamped in copper foil.
It is wrapped in a four-color dust jacket.

The text on both editions is composed in
11.5 point Adobe Garamond.
Display type is Post Antiqua by Adobe
with ornaments from Border Dingbats.
The book is printed on sixty pound Joy White
acid-free, recycled paper
by Thomson-Shore.

High Plains Press is committed to preserving ancient forests and natural resources. We elected to print *Capitol Characters of Old Cheyenne* on 30% post consumer recycled paper, processed chlorine free. As a result, for this printing, we have saved:

12 trees (40' tall and 6-8" diameter)
5,285 gallons of water
2,125 kilowatt hours of electricity
583 pounds of solid waste
1,144 pounds of greenhouse gases

High Plains Press made this paper choice because our printer, Thomson-Shore, Inc., is a member of Green Press Initiative, a nonprofit program dedicated to supporting authors, publishers, and suppliers in their efforts to reduce their use of fiber obtained from endangered forests.

For more information, visit www.greenpressinitiative.org